# Achieving Project Management Success in the Federal Government

# Achieving Project Management Success in the Federal Government

*Jonathan Weinstein, PMP*
*Timothy Jaques, PMP*

**MANAGEMENT**CONCEPTS

**MANAGEMENT**CONCEPTS
8230 Leesburg Pike, Suite 800
Vienna, VA 22182
(703) 790-9595
Fax: (703) 790-1371
www.managementconcepts.com

Copyright © 2010 by Management Concepts, Inc.

All rights reserved. No part of this book may be reproduced or utilized in any form or by any means, electronic or mechanical, including photocopying, recording, or by an information storage and retrieval system, without permission in writing from the publisher, except for brief quotations in review articles.

Printed in the United States of America

Library of Congress Cataloging-in-Publication Data

Weinstein, Jonathan.
Achieving project management success in the federal government / Jonathan Weinstein, Timothy Jaques.
    p. cm.
  ISBN 978-1-56726-275-9
  1. Public administration—United States.  2. Project management—United States.  I. Jaques, Timothy.  II. Title.
  JF1351.W45 2010
  352.3'650973—dc22
                                                                              2009048304

10   9   8   7   6   5   4   3   2   1

# PRAISE FOR
# Achieving Project Management Success in the Federal Government

"The authors have distilled a remarkably complex topic into meaningful, digestible pieces that will contribute to the advancement of project management in the federal government. As a taxpayer, it is refreshing to see that significant and important progress continues to be made."

—NEAL WHITTEN, PMP
PROJECT MANAGEMENT AUTHOR, SPEAKER, CONSULTANT, TRAINER, MENTOR

"This groundbreaking book presents the success stories, the works in progress, the rationale for continued maturation, and the essential components for successful projects in the federal government, the largest single enterprise in the world. Don't start a complex project in the federal space without consulting this book. It is genius!"

—KITTY HASS, PMP
KATHLEEN HASS & ASSOCIATES, INC.

"I highly recommend this book as a valuable resource for current and future government project managers. The authors capture the particular skills required to manage projects in the government and provide important insights."

—GREGORY T. HAUGAN, PHD, PMP

# About the Authors

**Jonathan Weinstein**, PMP, has worked in a variety of roles in the project management and management consulting arena. His project experience spans the private sector, from insurance to IT organizations, and the public sector, including agencies at all levels of government—local, state, and federal, civilian and defense. Jon has been a featured speaker at U.S. and international conferences and seminars, and has co-authored, with Tim Jaques, chapters in two recent books on project management.

**Timothy Jaques**, PMP, focuses on helping clients tackle tough problems by applying the discipline of project management. He has worked in a variety of federal and state government agencies, where he has managed projects, developed project management methodologies and PMOs, and delivered training. Tim is a practitioner and advocate of organizational change management, especially in the project environment. He has also written extensively on various aspects of project management and organizational change.

Jon and Tim are founding partners at Line of Sight (www.line-of-sight.com), which delivers project management, process reengineering, and organizational change management services to government and private sector clients.

*To our amazing families. Your gift was to allow our time and attention to be elsewhere as we toiled away at the office, in libraries, airports, cafes, and various locations around the globe.*

*Margaret, your constant encouragement and extreme patience continue to energize me. Zach and Ben, you guys have inspired me more than you can imagine. Thank you.*

—JW

*To Katarina, everyone should have such a best friend. And to Dylan and Eli, my favorites.*

—TJ

# Contents

Foreword ................................................... xix
Preface ..................................................... xxi
Acknowledgments ........................................... xxv

**CHAPTER 1   The Evolution of Federal Project Management:
            Then and Now** ................................. 1
Projects in the Federal Sector ................................ 3
The Evolution of Project Management in the
   Federal Government ...................................... 6
   Back in the Day .......................................... 6
   Fast Forward to the 20$^{th}$ Century ........................ 8
   Midway through the 20$^{th}$ Century ......................... 9
   By the End of the 20$^{th}$ Century .......................... 12
Project Management in Government Today ..................... 13
Challenges Ahead for Project Management
   in the Federal Government ................................ 16

| PART 1 | Organization and Structure | 19 |

**CHAPTER 2  Fitting Project Management into the
              Organization: Round Peg/Square Hole ..........21**
The Origin of Project Management in an Organization ...........22
Key Organizational Dimensions ...............................23
    Culture ..................................................26
    Systems..................................................31
    Structure................................................34
Degree of Centralization .....................................38

**CHAPTER 3  Regulations and Legislation: The Emerging
              Context for Federal Project Management ........43**
Who's Who in Federal Project Management......................44
    Office of Management and Budget ..........................45
    Government Accountability Office..........................45
    Chief Acquisition Officers Council Project Management
       Working Group .......................................46
    Chief Information Officers Council .........................46
    Federal Acquisition Institute ..............................47
    Project Management Institute .............................47
Laws Influencing Federal Project Management ..................48
    Federal Managers Financial Integrity Act of 1982 ..............49
    Chief Financial Officers Act of 1990 .........................49
    Government Performance and Results Act of 1993 .............51
    Federal Acquisition Streamlining Act of 1994 .................51
    Information Technology Management Reform Act of 1996.......52
    E-Government Act of 2002................................52
Directives and Regulations Affecting Federal
    Project Management ....................................53
    OMB Circular A-109, Major Systems Acquisitions ..............55
    OMB Circular A-11, Part 7, Capital Programming Guide,
       and Exhibit 300.......................................55
    Program Assessment Rating Tool ...........................58

## CHAPTER 4 Building Strong Teams: The Vehicle for Successful Projects .......... 61

Team Types and Structures .......... 62
    Integrated Project Team .......... 64
    Virtual Team .......... 67
    Other Team Types .......... 69
Establishing the Project Team .......... 71
    Set Team Rules .......... 73
    Define Roles and Responsibilities .......... 74
Developing the Project Team .......... 77
Managing the Project Team .......... 79
Working with Contractors .......... 80

## CHAPTER 5 Leveraging Technology for Project Success: New Tools of the Trade .......... 87

Information Technology in the Federal Environment .......... 88
Technologies in the Project Environment .......... 91
    Basic Project Management .......... 92
    Intermediate Project Management .......... 92
    Advanced Project Management .......... 93
Assessing Project Needs .......... 93
    Planning .......... 94
    Executing .......... 95
    Measuring .......... 96
    Reporting .......... 96
Government 2.0 .......... 97
Technology Trends in Project Management .......... 98

## PART 2 People .......... 101

## CHAPTER 6 The Crucial Role of Communication: Telling the Story .......... 103

The Project Manager's Role in Communication .......... 104
Setting the Context .......... 105
Communication Matrix and Plan .......... 107
A Model for Communication (and Change) Management .......... 110
The Role of the Media .......... 114
Information Access and Security .......... 115

**CHAPTER 7 Leadership and the Project Manager:
Bearing the Brunt of the Storm** .................119
Leadership in a Project Context ..................................121
Balancing Leadership and Management. ........................123
    Facilitator .................................................125
    Mentor ..................................................125
    Change Leader. ..........................................126
Characteristics and Traits of Project Leaders. ...................127
    Authority vs. Responsibility ..............................127
    Confidence. ..............................................128
    Recognizing and Facing Reality. ..........................129
The Role of Leadership .........................................129
Leading and Managing Projects in the Federal Government. ......132

**CHAPTER 8 Engaging Stakeholders: Establishing
Effective Project Relationships** .................137
Who Are the Stakeholders in Federal Projects?. ..................138
Stakeholder Management in Action .............................144
Managing Stakeholders in a Complex Environment ..............147
Conducting a Stakeholder Assessment ..........................149
Manage Stakeholders (or Be Managed by Them) .................154

**CHAPTER 9 Project Management Competencies and Skills:
Success through Experience** ....................157
What Are the Critical Skills?. .....................................159
Core Project Management Skills ................................160
    Leadership ..............................................161
    Coordination. ...........................................161
    Supervision .............................................162
    Risk Assessment/Management ...........................162
    Project Analysis and Requirements Definition. ..............163
    Contractor Management. .................................163
    Stakeholder Management .................................164
    Schedule, Scope, and Change Management .................164
    Lessons Learned .........................................165
    Financial Analysis and Budgeting. .........................166

Contents

　　Communication Skills . . . . . . . . . . . . . . . . . . . . . . . . . . . . . . . . . . . . . . . . . . 167
　　　Information Sharing . . . . . . . . . . . . . . . . . . . . . . . . . . . . . . . . . . . . . . 167
　　　Engaging Executives. . . . . . . . . . . . . . . . . . . . . . . . . . . . . . . . . . . . . . 168
　　　Negotiation . . . . . . . . . . . . . . . . . . . . . . . . . . . . . . . . . . . . . . . . . . . . . 168
　　　Communicating with Clarity. . . . . . . . . . . . . . . . . . . . . . . . . . . . . . . 169
　　　Teaching and Mentoring. . . . . . . . . . . . . . . . . . . . . . . . . . . . . . . . . . 169
　　Emerging Project Management Skills. . . . . . . . . . . . . . . . . . . . . . . . . . 170
　　　Framing . . . . . . . . . . . . . . . . . . . . . . . . . . . . . . . . . . . . . . . . . . . . . . . . 170
　　　Messaging and Context. . . . . . . . . . . . . . . . . . . . . . . . . . . . . . . . . . . 170
　　　Integration . . . . . . . . . . . . . . . . . . . . . . . . . . . . . . . . . . . . . . . . . . . . . 171
　　　Workflow Management. . . . . . . . . . . . . . . . . . . . . . . . . . . . . . . . . . . 171
　　　Facilitation . . . . . . . . . . . . . . . . . . . . . . . . . . . . . . . . . . . . . . . . . . . . . 172
　　　Curiosity and Imagination . . . . . . . . . . . . . . . . . . . . . . . . . . . . . . . . 173
　　　Integrity . . . . . . . . . . . . . . . . . . . . . . . . . . . . . . . . . . . . . . . . . . . . . . . 173
　　Subject Matter Expertise . . . . . . . . . . . . . . . . . . . . . . . . . . . . . . . . . . . . . 174

**CHAPTER 10　Project Manager Professional Development:
　　　　　　　　Building the Project Management Corps. . . . . . . 177**
　　Project Management Certification. . . . . . . . . . . . . . . . . . . . . . . . . . . . . 178
　　Organizational Certification . . . . . . . . . . . . . . . . . . . . . . . . . . . . . . . . . 181
　　FAC-P/PM Program . . . . . . . . . . . . . . . . . . . . . . . . . . . . . . . . . . . . . . . . 182
　　Competency Development . . . . . . . . . . . . . . . . . . . . . . . . . . . . . . . . . . 185

**PART 3　Process . . . . . . . . . . . . . . . . . . . . . . . . . . . . . . . . . . . . . . . . . . . . . 189**

**CHAPTER 11　Governance and Project Portfolio
　　　　　　　　Development: Steering the Ship . . . . . . . . . . . . . . . 191**
　　Organizational Governance . . . . . . . . . . . . . . . . . . . . . . . . . . . . . . . . . 193
　　Project Portfolio Management . . . . . . . . . . . . . . . . . . . . . . . . . . . . . . . 199

**CHAPTER 12　Adopting and Applying Methodologies:
　　　　　　　　Choosing the Right Path . . . . . . . . . . . . . . . . . . . . . . 207**
　　Project Management Methodologies. . . . . . . . . . . . . . . . . . . . . . . . . . 209
　　　Waterfall Methodology . . . . . . . . . . . . . . . . . . . . . . . . . . . . . . . . . . . 210
　　　Agile Project Management . . . . . . . . . . . . . . . . . . . . . . . . . . . . . . . . 213
　　　Other Federal Project Management Methodologies . . . . . . . . . . . 215
　　Product Development Lifecycles . . . . . . . . . . . . . . . . . . . . . . . . . . . . . 216

Project Management Enablers ................................. 219
   Organizational Project Management
      Maturity Model (OPM3®)................................. 219
   Capability Maturity Model Integration (CMMI®).............. 220
   Six Sigma ................................................ 220
   National Competence Baseline ............................. 221
   Process and Enterprise Maturity Model (PEMM™)............. 222

**CHAPTER 13**   **Aligning Federal and Project Planning Cycles:
Untangling the Knot........................ 225**
The Federal Project Planning and Reporting Environment ....... 227
GPRA and Project Management ............................... 228
   Strategic Plan............................................. 230
   Performance Plan ......................................... 231
   Performance Budget....................................... 232
   Performance and Accountability Report ..................... 233
Performance Assessment Rating Tool.......................... 234
Linking Projects with Planning Outputs ....................... 234

**CHAPTER 14**   **Implementing Knowledge Management
Practices: Reusing the Wheel ................. 241**
Knowledge Management Defined ............................. 243
Knowledge Management in the Federal Environment ........... 245
The Role of Knowledge Management in
   Project Management ...................................... 246
Challenges of Knowledge Management ........................ 248
   Volume ................................................. 248
   Complexity............................................... 250
   Information Assurance ................................... 251
   Discipline ................................................ 252
Knowledge Management in Action ............................ 253

**CHAPTER 15  Understanding Project Performance
Management: Uncovering Success Early** .......259
Performance Management in the Federal Government ...........261
    Establishing Project Performance Measures...................263
    Managing Project Performance...............................270
    Overseeing Project Performance .............................273
The New Role of Chief Performance Officer .....................274

**CHAPTER 16  The Promise of Project Management
in the Federal Government:
Looking Ahead** ............................277
Perspectives on Key Trends and Lessons Learned ................278
    Organization and Structure .................................278
    People ..................................................280
    Process .................................................283
The More Things Change ......................................285
The Outlook for Project Management in the
Federal Government ........................................287

**Recommended Resources** ....................................289

**Index** ...................................................295

# Foreword

The great challenge for government managers is to take the broad brushstrokes of their agency's or organization's strategy and mission and translate them into actions—actions that are effective and measurable.

The most well-meaning executives, managers, and elected officials can propose great initiatives but without the proper planning, leadership, and tools, their efforts may go nowhere. Effective government is measured by outcomes. Project management offers a disciplined approach that can turn those great initiatives into reality. Through a variety of real-life examples, this book shows how dedicated public managers have used the discipline of project management to achieve results.

The increased emphasis on oversight from Congress, the Office of Management and Budget, and the Government Accountability Office points clearly to the need for a standardized and formal approach. Thus, the discipline of project management, which has been used in the government for many years, is enjoying a resurgence. The spotlight on oversight will only intensify as taxpayers demand more accountability from their government.

The stories of accomplishment achieved through project management in *Achieving Project Management Success in the Federal Government* offer practical guidance on how to accomplish mission-critical tasks. The "lessons learned" in each of the cases present different perspectives, yet they all bring the organization's strategy or mission down to a manageable set of objectives and actions.

By exploring different aspects of a representative group of projects, Jonathan Weinstein and Timothy Jaques share a workable and highly readable look into the state of project management in government today. The authors interviewed the project managers involved with these success stories, who were not hesitant to point out the challenges they encountered.

Project management is a powerful tool for any government manager; this book shows how that tool has been used successfully in a variety of settings to reach different goals. The authors also address the fundamentals of project management, demonstrating how building strong teams, engaging stakeholders, and developing both traditional and emerging skills and competencies are so important to project success.

There is a plethora of media coverage of projects gone wrong, with the resulting cost overruns and disappointing results. The public would be better served if more of the success stories—the hard-won success stories—in this book were more widely shared.

Although the book focuses on federal agencies, anyone in government—whether at the federal, state, or local level—will find important insights and much value in this material.

*—Hon. Thomas M. Davis III, Director, Deloitte Services LP*
*Former Chair, House Committee on Oversight and Government Reform*

# Preface

> *We can't solve problems by using the same kind of thinking we used when we created them.*
>
> —Albert Einstein

Projects pervade our everyday work and life, and governments have dealt in the realm of projects since the beginning of recorded time. The U.S. federal government has employed project management since its earliest days and in recent years has begun the process of formalizing the methods it uses to carry out a wide-ranging spectrum of projects.

Project management varies widely across the federal government. Our goal in this book is not to provide an exhaustive enumeration of project management practices, but rather to offer a realistic cross section of the project management discipline—a "state of the practice" in the largest single enterprise in the world, the U.S. federal government. We hope this book will enlighten and serve to improve project management for federal leaders, project teams, and others who influence the direction of projects.

Describing project management within the federal government—its three branches, 15 departments, and myriad establishments, authorities, commissions, and corporations—is a study in frustration. On one level, project management is a function that has a clear set of objectives. Yet below the surface lies a complex and highly diverse web of organizational cultures, locations, missions, and funding streams. The forces that bind federal agencies together include a common set of laws and a dedication to continuous improvement.

Throughout our interview and research efforts for this book, we met project management practitioners who were open, honest, and eager to share their challenges, lessons, and advice with their colleagues across the government. Their messages are full of insights and actions for others to adopt. Our intent is to encourage success across the project management discipline in the federal government by sharing their experiences.

*Achieving Project Management Success in the Federal Government* presents effective practices from organizations across a vast enterprise. Clearly, the tools and techniques employed by one organization are not necessarily a prescription for success in another. Key factors such as organizational culture, executive support, resource availability, staff capability, and the nature of the organization's services all contribute to the environment in which project management will either thrive or stagnate.

In view of the scale of the federal government and the breadth of project management topics, we chose not to present the information in this book as a technical manual or "how to" guide on topics like earned value or risk analysis. Instead, this book focuses on project management practitioners, senior managers, directors, and executives who recognize the value of project management and are applying the right mix of skills, knowledge, experience, resources, and common sense to improve (in some cases significantly) the success of projects in their organizations.

This book is organized into three parts that define project management from different vantage points. Together, the parts address the entire scope of project management, from organization to methodology, technology to leadership. The chapters in each part address project management topics that share similar characteristics. The topics we focus on grew out of our interviews of government practitioners and our analysis of relevant research.

In *Part 1: Organization and Structure*, we present key elements and practices that contribute to framing or supporting project management in the federal sector. We address common project management structures and environments in organizations (Chapter 2), the guidance, laws, and regulations that create the context for project management in the federal government (Chapter 3), the organization and management of project teams (Chapter 4), and the role of technology in government project management (Chapter 5).

*Part 2: People* describes project management practices that engage government personnel and stakeholders in projects and improve the quality of their participation. This part highlights practices and successes in the areas of communication (Chapter 6), project leadership (Chapter 7), stakeholders (Chapter 8), key competencies and skills (Chapter 9), and project manager professional development (Chapter 10).

*Part 3: Process* addresses the processes that provide the operational context for project management practices. This part describes the emergence and application of project lifecycles, including governance and project portfolio management (Chapter 11), project management methodologies (Chapter 12), the alignment of key "external" planning cycles (Chapter 13), the practice of knowledge management as an integral component of improving project performance (Chapter 14), and efforts to measure project—and project management—performance (Chapter 15).

The book concludes with Chapter 16, providing advice "from the field" along with a discussion of the prospects for and promises of project management across the federal government.

Throughout the book we use case studies and examples, mostly from civilian agencies and a few from the Department of Defense. Clearly, significant differences characterize the execution of project management in these two arenas, particularly with regard to the command-and-control orientation of defense-related endeavors. Nevertheless, we believe that our examples highlight some of the very best practices of project management in the federal government.

We hope we have achieved our goal of accurately representing project management in the federal government today. Our many conversations with project management leaders and practitioners throughout the federal government have convinced us that significant and important progress is being made toward *Achieving Project Management Success in the Federal Government*.

*Jon Weinstein*
*Tim Jaques*
January 2010

# Acknowledgments

A modern-day sales expert cum philosopher, Jeffrey Gitomer, once said that the two most important things another person can give are time and attention. Researching and writing a book that covers the breadth of the U.S. government requires the contribution of time and attention by many individuals. We gratefully acknowledge the wellspring of information, candid discussion, and access to documents provided by so many dedicated federal employees. We thank you for allowing us into your particular world of project management.

Among those who supported us were Allan Roit, Jason Hill, and Shaun Willison, Department of the Treasury; Will Brimberry, Department of the Interior; James Rispoli (retired) and Jack Surash, Department of Energy; Lesley Field, Office of Management and Budget; Karen Pica, former director, Federal Acquisition Institute; Darren Ash, James Corbett, Susan Daniel, and Nancy Chamberlin, Nuclear Regulatory Commission; Jerry Harper, Department of Commerce; Bill McDade, Federal Emergency Management Agency; Mike O'Brochta (retired), Central Intelligence Agency; Ed Hoffman, National Aeronautics and Space Administration;

Arnold Hill, Bill Guerrin, and AnnMarie Sweet-Anshire, General Services Administration; Steve Backhus, Government Accountability Office; and the Honorable Elijah Cummings, U.S. House of Representatives.

We wish to acknowledge Myra Strauss, editor extraordinaire. Thank you for many hours of thoughtful reading and edits, an open door policy, and tough criticism. We also wish to thank several Management Concepts authors, including Greg Haugan and Neal Whitten, for supporting us with critical reviews, advice, and research tips.

We are greatly indebted to the Project Management Institute government relations team, Gary Klein and Valerie Carter, for providing us with excellent advice, numerous contacts, and support throughout the process.

We simply could not have completed this book without our exceptional team manning Line of Sight's offices and customers: Julie Rodgers, JP Hussey, Jana Hussman-Meacham, Charlie Strauss, Reed Ulrich, and Amy Glasser. We thank you for pushing us and covering our backs.

## Chapter 1

# The Evolution of Federal Project Management: Then and Now

> *We need to internalize this idea of excellence.*
> —President Barack Obama

Throughout history mankind has labored to achieve amazing feats that defy our imagination: the great pyramids of Giza, the Taj Mahal, the Great Wall of China, the D-Day invasion. Human beings—and governments—naturally seek to apply resources toward the creation of monuments, public works, and war. Although such efforts have spanned thousands of years, only in the past 60 years has the discipline of project management come to be formally recognized and defined.

The U.S. Government Accountability Office (GAO) describes the federal government as "the world's largest and most complex entity."[1] In terms of scale, the federal government expended about $3 trillion in fiscal year 2008 on operations and myriad projects to develop and provide new products and services—from bridge construction to aircraft development, from AIDS awareness to nuclear material disposal. The expenditure of these funds represents the single largest government marketplace in the world, employing many millions of people directly or indirectly. Federal project dollars are spread across state and local governments, often defining entire industries such as defense.

This is a massive machine, yet no single central, civilian entity has the authority for establishing, promoting, or enforcing standards and guidelines for the project management discipline across the federal government enterprise. The absence of this authority is not the result of a conscious decision to allow different agencies and departments to adopt the system that works best for their particular circumstances. Rather, project management within the federal government has grown and thrived seemingly at random, developing idiosyncratically in the various agencies, laboratories, and field offices where the federal government works and where support for project management is strong.

Project management has evolved into a set of practices that has only recently come into its own across the U.S. federal government. Project management in the federal sector has evolved like the first stars arriving on a summer night—little glowing pockets here and there, lacking order, with the occasional fiery star dominating a corner of the sky. While standards and some requirements exist, no unified field theory, so to speak, of project management within the federal government has yet evolved. Few common templates specific to the project management discipline have been developed to provide suggested or required standards that each agency can adapt to its own needs. Nevertheless, for all the apparent randomness, the evolution of project management within the federal government is a story of great achievement.

## **PROJECTS IN THE FEDERAL SECTOR**

What is a project? The classic definition is a temporary endeavor undertaken to create a unique product, service, or result. The product, service, or result is developed through a specific effort that includes a beginning, a middle, and an end. A project is different from a program, which has two general definitions in the federal government. We define *program* as a group of related projects that are managed in a harmonized way and contribute to the achievement of a common goal. A program often includes elements of ongoing work or work related to specific deliverables. An example is the space shuttle program, which encompasses distinct projects aimed at developing a vehicle, buildings, software, etc. The government also uses *program* to mean a continuing overall operation or grouping of services, such as Medicaid or the Small Business Administration's Loan Guaranty Program.

Projects satisfy a deeply held need in the human psyche to commune and conquer. Projects are designed to create change and are at once logistical, political, physical, and mental. They demand our attention and require us to work toward a common goal. Projects are the manifestation of hope—a wish for things to be better in the future if we work hard enough—combined with the need to carry out a finite activity, to set measurable goals and objectives, and to be able to declare success when the goals are reached and the objectives are met.

When everyday work is ongoing, we invoke the mechanisms of process management. When current work is aimed at achieving a specific goal or objective, then the mechanisms of project management are involved—scoping, scheduling, and measuring—in an effort to increase the likelihood of success and realize our ambitions for some future achievement. Infusing project management within an organization that views all work as process management is as much a cultural reformation as it is a procedural one.

Project management asks us to measure twice and cut once. Philosophically this approach makes sense, but when measuring twice costs millions of dollars and takes many years, the demands on a project intensify. The forces that drive project management are largely contextual, evoked by the mission and structure of the host organization. The dynamics in the federal sector revolve around authority and power, scarcity and abundance (two elements that frequently cohabit in an organization), and change readiness and acceptance. Other factors come into play as well, and for these reasons, no two organizations will follow the same exact style of project management.

Projects in the federal sector differ in many ways from projects in other sectors or industries. The Project Management Institute (PMI)[2] has identified several factors that affect how project management works in the public sector[3] (particularly for large projects but not necessarily for the thousands of small projects that are regularly performed across the federal government):

1. *A wide array of important stakeholders is involved.* Projects may involve input from or output to world leaders, Congress, high-ranking appointees, taxpayers, policy makers, special interest groups, and others. Managing powerful constituencies invokes new dimensions of communication management.

2. *Project outcomes often have great consequences.* Launching space shuttles, consolidating military bases, developing a vaccine to fight

a pandemic, and building billion-dollar bridges all represent potentially significant public consequences. Because public projects are highly visible, a failure can live on for a generation or more.

3. *The revolving political landscape means constant change.* New administrations arrive every four years, much of Congress turns over every two years, and agency leadership often changes even more frequently. With each new political cycle comes a new or revised set of priorities, legislation, and often a new approach to management. Civil servants and appointees must work together to effect change in the context of current political and ongoing organizational priorities.

4. *Public scrutiny magnifies mistakes.* Publicly funded projects must endure—indeed, must embrace—a continuous open window to the public. The public includes individual citizens, special interest groups, nongovernmental organizations (NGOs), and corporate interests. While some federal projects are shielded from continuous external inspection, freedom of information laws and the public sentiment can influence a project manager's approach or the project's execution or outcomes.

5. *Dramatic failures can lead to intense oversight.* Examples of "extreme" failures in federal projects (such as the response to Hurricane Katrina and oversight of the financial industry) often elicit intense reactions from key stakeholders, especially Congress. However, project management is a highly contextual field and Congress has not yet adopted laws specific to project management practices.

Recent legislative attempts have sought to establish trigger points for greater oversight, even project cancellation, if major projects begin to fail, as with Senate Bill 3384, the Information Technology Investment

Oversight Enhancement and Waste Prevention Act of 2008 (2<sup>nd</sup> session of the 110<sup>th</sup> Congress). Even in the absence of legislation, however, it is possible to codify the structural components of project management, and the federal government has been moving steadily toward instituting more formalized processes.

In this context, project management in the federal government is both exciting and challenging. Successful project managers must deal with the realities of fickle priorities, political administrations, tenuous budgets, and the tangled web of regulations, laws, and policies that direct federal activities. Yet the federal government, with all its subordinate agencies, departments, administrations, and commissions, still must take the long road to successful project management, implementing one piece at a time. How did such a complicated environment come into being?

## THE EVOLUTION OF PROJECT MANAGEMENT IN THE FEDERAL GOVERNMENT

The practice of project management in the federal government has evolved over the course of the nation's history. Since the early days of the United States, there have been numerous minor improvements and major innovations in the discipline and practice of project management. The impact of some of the more important milestones is evident in project management in the federal government even today.

### Back in the Day…

The government has used documented planning techniques since the earliest days of the nation. Journals, lists, and diagrams characterized planning documents dating back to the late 1700s. These documents often took the form of correspondence regarding administrative details.

# CHAPTER 1 The Evolution of Federal Project Management

Early American society relied on experiential cues more than information for planning projects. People learned by doing much more than by attending schools or gathering information, and access to independent information sources was limited. Early civil projects depended on the hands-on experience and training of the chief engineer. Thus, projects often represented an individual's interpretation and pursuit of personal or group objectives.

The term *project* did not come into its current usage until the early 20th century. Throughout the nation's early years, *project* meant something akin to an undertaking, an endeavor, or a purpose. Compare that with today's dictionary definition of the word, "a collaborative enterprise, frequently involving research or design, that is carefully planned to achieve a particular aim,"[4] or PMI's more focused definition, "a temporary endeavor undertaken to create a unique product, service or result."[5]

A good example of these early endeavors involves Thaddeus Kosciuszko, the famous military engineer of the Revolutionary War. Kosciuszko[6] was a key figure in the Continental Army's bid to maintain control of the Hudson River and Fort Ticonderoga on the southern end of Lake Champlain. Kosciuszko's topographical skill, expertise, and experience enabled him to establish superior defense works by taking advantage of natural terrain and creating effective fields of fire. His approach to planning and constructing defenses is documented in materiel lists and correspondence. There is no evidence of any schedules linking resources to tasks or budgets to time in any formal way. Kosciuszko managed to defy the attacking British generals through confounding defenses that included earthen mound fortifications, strategically placed dams designed to flood roads, and fortifications positioned on high ground. Kosciuszko likely made his instructions clear and then left it to the soldiers to carry out his orders, with some on-scene supervision and inspections.

## Fast Forward to the 20th Century . . .

Over the next 120 years, the management of projects evolved in engineering, construction, scientific endeavors, and other increasingly knowledge-centric fields. Although there was little apparent emphasis on project management as a discipline, many of the foundational concepts of management were forming at this time. Formalized project management evolved out of the management theory emerging during the industrial revolution, when concepts like standardization, quality control, work planning, and assembly construction were beginning to take hold.

In 1911, Frederick Taylor published the seminal work *Principles of Scientific Management*, in which he defined many of the elements of project management today: task planning and instruction, job specialization, and effective supervision. Taylor's worldview emanated from the factory, and his theories shifted the emphasis from the worker role's of defining and resolving task problems to the manager's role of significantly influencing task problems. The federal government adopted these private sector-based theories and management paradigms, creating multilayered organizations staffed by managers of managers. Where manufacturing organizations were organized around assembly lines, government organizations were organized into self-contained and organized units, some oriented functionally and some operationally.

A colleague of Taylor's, Henry Gantt, worked alongside Taylor literally and figuratively in the development of modern management theory. Gantt's ideas greatly influenced key project management theories in use today. In particular, his ideas on work planning have contributed to modern scheduling practices. Working with production facilities that were developing weaponry and goods for the U.S. government, Gantt understood that production and assembly work was sequenced, segmented, and measurable. He devised a concept called the "balance of work," which presented work as measurable units. Workers were required to fulfill a day's quota of work. This work could be reduced to a plan and laid out on a graphical horizon, which later became known as the Gantt chart.

Gantt applied these insights to his work with the federal government as a contractor. He understood that work was time-based rather than a function of materials. Effective management of production required an understanding of how work occurred over a period of time and the role of the trained worker.

The now-infamous Gantt chart was originally a bar chart depicting work scheduled and actually performed for each person over time. By using a bar to identify the work actually performed, Gantt succinctly captured a revolutionary insight into the nature of work and established a method for measuring performance. This new type of chart was truly remarkable—an early management tool that enabled management to see, graphically and numerically, the progress of the effort. This new view enabled managers to understand which machines or which specific workers were lagging in production and to take corrective action accordingly. Gantt's ideas formed the basis for modern planning and control techniques, whereby managers could use timely information to change the work being performed.

## Midway through the 20th Century...

Project management began to take on its modern form after World War II. The first substantial evidence of government-based project management was the Navy's *Polaris* missile project, initiated in 1956 as part of the fleet ballistic missile program, with Lockheed Missile Systems Division as the prime contractor. The *Polaris* project delivered a truly complex product, the most advanced submarine-based nuclear missile of the day, at a time when the United States was determined to win the nuclear arms race.

The use of multiple major contracts for one product was a new development. There were no tools for integrating the various contracts and understanding the impact on the overall program of schedule changes by contractors. To address the complexity and uncertainty associated with *Polaris,* the Navy's special projects office developed the Project Evaluation and Review Technique (PERT). PERT was a key element in an "integrated planning and control system for the Fleet Ballistic Missile program."[7]

The *Polaris* missile represented the integration of five distinct areas: missile, launcher, navigation, fire control, and ship and command communications.[8] For PERT to be effective, the tasks needed to be organized into product groupings rather than by resource or department. This rearrangement of tasks drastically improved the way the teams could envision and plan their parts in the Polaris project. At the time, this was referred to as "banding" because all the events that related to a particular area were shown graphically in bands on the PERT networks.

Other optimization practices were developed during the 1950s, including the line of balance (LOB) programming model, which preceded PERT, and the management operation system technique (MOST), which improved on PERT estimates. The commonly used work breakdown structure (WBS), a multilevel outline of the work to be performed within a project, was introduced as a concept in concert with the implementation of PERT and came into formal use in the early 1960s.[9] With the develop-

# CHAPTER 1  The Evolution of Federal Project Management

ment of these new planning and reporting tools to assist in the management and integration of major weapons system components, the project management discipline demonstrated that truly complex endeavors could be estimated and organized effectively. It was during this period that the term *project management* was coined.

In a concentrated effort to address the increasing complexity of projects, several other key concepts emerged during these early years. The DuPont Corporation developed critical path methodology (CPM) in 1957 to support the construction and maintenance of chemical plants. DuPont and the Remington Rand corporations jointly developed an algorithmic approach to schedule development using the UNIVAC computer developed by Rand. The idea was to feed activity schedules into a computer, let the computer create the project schedule, and thereby reveal the critical versus noncritical tasks. The network of activities defined which tasks would materially delay the project and which would not. As schedule revisions occurred, CPM could be used to calculate the new set of critical tasks.

In the early 1960s, the Air Force, Army, Navy, and Defense Supply Agency jointly developed the cost and schedule control system criteria (C/SCSC) approach as a way to gain better access into large, contractor-run projects. The *Minuteman* project was plagued with cost and schedule overruns—and a contractor that was reluctant to share project performance data with its customer. In 1967, the Department of Defense (DoD) established a set of 35 criteria, grouped into five major categories, that allowed government contract managers to understand schedule performance and cost performance. C/SCSC resulted in the core elements of what was to be eventually renamed earned value management (EVM).

## By the End of the 20th Century...

The end of the 20th century was an interesting time to be involved in project management. Engineers with interest in management were given responsibility for running projects. Project management was in its early stages as a stand-alone discipline. Throughout the 1960s and 1970s, project management became the focus of increased intellectual endeavors. The number of academic papers, journals, and new ideas exploded, many of which focused on federal government projects. In 1969 PMI was founded on the premise that the practices inherent in managing projects spanned a wide range of disciplines, from aeronautics to bridges to computer design and beyond.

Whereas the federal government led early development in modern project management, private industry and academia led after the 1970s. The construction industry boomed in the 1980s, leading to major advances in estimating and logistics. The emergence of the personal computer enabled individual project managers to automate planning and control activities themselves and not rely solely on project personnel. Of course, on the larger projects, planning and control staffs were still essential.

Throughout the 1970s and 1980s, the government adopted many of these new practices. In 1976, the Office of Management and Budget (OMB) issued Circular A-109, the first federal directive to address program management. This document solidified the role of C/SCSC in federal projects. Circular A-109 and the C/SCSC practices remained in place until 1996, when A-109 underwent a major revision. The development and revision of federal guidance related to project management was a clear sign that practices implemented within various civilian and defense organizations were being codified for government-wide use.

The 1990s saw a big push for governmental accountability and reform. Political winds drove key legislation that introduced strategic planning, the chief information officer role, and technology planning. Large technology projects were prone to delay and failure, requiring increased visibility, management, and justification. In response, OMB introduced a series of requirements dealing with capital and technology expenditures, reporting, and management. In June 2002, OMB issued regulations that applied to major acquisitions and major IT systems or projects that required the implementation of earned value management systems using the American National Standard Institute standards (ANSI/EIA 748-A-1998),[10] officially ending reliance on C/SCSC.

## PROJECT MANAGEMENT IN GOVERNMENT TODAY

This is an exciting time to be a project management practitioner in the federal government. Project management is reaching a new level of maturity and recognition as a critical skill set. The project management career is on the rise. A new breed of manager is emerging—one that was raised on the precepts of project management. Federal project management is evolving from a purely homespun set of practices into a formal discipline. Evidence of this evolution abounds:

- *Organizations are seeking to balance technical expertise with project management competencies,* often having to decide whether to assign technical experts to manage projects or skilled project managers to lead highly technical projects. Achieving this balance raises the question of what is more important in managing a project—expertise in the discipline or in the subject matter of the project.

- *In the past several years, the federal government has begun to promote agencies' development of an internal certification process for project and program managers.* This trend, coupled with the emergence of "new" skills that integrate with "traditional" skills (e.g., negotiation, facilitation, personnel management), is placing demands on federal project managers to adjust and adapt to new project environments. Acquiring and honing these skills will be essential for project managers and projects to achieve success.

- *Legislative and policy efforts have introduced greater oversight into large projects.* This increased oversight has contributed to advancements in project performance measurement, including the development and implementation of EVM practices.

- *Project management technologies have advanced to form a system that supports the full lifecycle of projects,* from concept and planning to implementation, operations, and maintenance.

Despite these achievements in project management, however, challenges that will continue to limit the ability of the federal government to manage projects successfully remain. These challenges include:

- *Project size.* In these trying economic times, there is no shortage of large-scale projects. Both civilian and defense agencies are in the throes of planning and implementing projects that are large in scale, scope, budget, and importance. Many of these projects represent the collaborative efforts of multiple organizations, yet personnel are not familiar with the concepts of project management.

- *Intervention into troubled projects.* With no consistent approach for escalating, intervening, and resolving projects in crisis, agencies often must take steps to fix troubled projects without a clear set of guidance. Timely intervention, as early in the project lifecycle as possible, is a critical success factor for troubled projects, yet often agency leaders do not have sufficient insight into the project or the knowledge and experience to understand the warning signals at an early stage.

- *Managing through the bureaucracy.* Project success often depends on the ability to remain nimble and free of classic bureaucratic constraints. The federal government has yet to define protocols and safeguards that will allow projects to move quickly when needed, eliminating unnecessary or burdensome activities while still adhering to checks and balances to protect project investments.

- *Mission diversity.* The diversity of missions presents a challenge for establishing enterprise project management structures and practices in many large agencies. To operate effectively in the face of this diversity, project management expertise must permeate the organization and be adapted to the "local" environment.

- *Acquisition vs. project management.* OMB has developed policies that promote sound and consistent acquisition policies across the federal government. The introduction and implementation of the federal acquisition certification for program and project managers (FAC-P/PM) is an example of efforts to foster greater linkages between the acquisition and project management specialties. The jury is still out on how effectively project management practices and project execution can be applied to acquisition.

- *Unpredictable funding.* Many government projects can't count 100 percent on their budgets being funded from year to year. Some simply hope for the best and plan that the money will be there, while others spend precious time planning and developing "what-if" scenarios to address possible variations in funding levels.

- *Resource allocation, capacity, and capability.* Increasing project complexity demands increased project management capabilities. The "inventory" of trained or certified project managers does not meet the demand in most federal organizations, so on-the-job training is common. Assigning the right project manager to the right project at the right time remains a challenge for many government organizations.

The federal project management environment is rife with successes, challenges, and opportunities. The first step is to uncover the real drivers and obstacles to successful projects.

## CHALLENGES AHEAD FOR PROJECT MANAGEMENT IN THE FEDERAL GOVERNMENT

At the heart of project management today are questions that have yet to be answered to the satisfaction of project management skeptics. As indicated by recent, in-depth studies by PMI and others, efforts are still being undertaken to determine whether project management delivers value. In the case of the federal government, is value returned to the taxpayer in the form of improved services, more modern infrastructures, or a stronger economy? Answering this fundamental question will enable the dialogue to shift toward considering the answers that will improve the project management discipline—which tools to use, when to use them, and the best way to use them in the federal government environment.

Describing project management within the numerous and diverse agencies, departments, authorities, and commissions of the federal government is daunting. On one level, project management is a function that has a clear set of objectives. Yet below the surface is a complex and highly diverse web of organizational cultures, locations, missions, and funding streams. The forces that bind federal agencies together include a common set of procurement laws and regulations, while another set of forces, the myriad legislative and appropriations requirements, demand that they work separately.

GAO provides a unique and challenging service, performing audits of projects, programs, and organizations at the request of Congress, while seeking to deliver actionable recommendations that will enable the organizations to improve their performance. One well-known GAO activity is the "high-risk list." Updated and published at the start of every new Congress, the list is a catalogue of federal programs, policies, and operations that GAO has identified as being at risk for waste, fraud, abuse, or mismanagement or in need of significant improvements. The list includes projects, programs, or organizations that are experiencing performance issues or are at risk of failing to achieve their goals.

According to Steve Backhus, GAO's Director for Quality and Continuous Improvement, "Four recurring issues [are] uncovered in our studies of government programs that point to the need for improvements in..."[11]

- *Strategic planning*, which should result in doing the right projects, consistent priorities, and alignment of resources, projects, and strategy
- *Performance measurement*, whereby organizations establish and align the right goals and the right measures, and develop the ability to collect or analyze the right data
- *Critical controls* to manage fiscal resources or support effective decision-making (e.g., separation of duties, review of decisions)
- *Access to and availability of good information* with regard to reliability, timeliness, and quality.

The practical experiences of federal project managers, sponsors, and executives speak to these issues and trends. President Obama's suggestion that we need to internalize the idea of excellence not only offers a challenge to the federal workforce but also describes the efforts underway in many government agencies today: making excellence the standard for managing projects.

## NOTES

1. http://www.gao.gov/products/GAO-09-271 (accessed February 20, 2009).
2. PMI, PMBOK, PMP, CAPM, and OPM3 are registered marks and PgMP is a mark of the Project Management Institute, Inc.
3. Adapted from "Project Management in the Public Sector," Project Management Institute, 2008, retrieved from http://www.pmi.org/Pages/ProjectManagementinthePublicSector.aspx (accessed May 11, 2009).
4. *Oxford English Dictionary,* Online Edition, "project," <http://www.askoxford.com/concise_oed/project?view=uk>.
5. Project Management Institute, *A Guide to the Project Management Body of Knowledge (PMBOK® Guide)—Fourth Edition* (Newtown Square, PA: Project Management Institute, 2008), p. 5.
6. James R. Thompson, *The Samaritan Review*: a review of *Thaddeus Kosciuszko: The Purest Son of Liberty*, by James S. Pula (New York: Hippocrene Books, 1999), http://www.ruf.rice.edu/~sarmatia/100/thompson.html (accessed May 11, 2009).
7. Gregory T. Haugan, *Project Planning and Scheduling* (Vienna, VA: Management Concepts, 2002), p. 28.
8. Willard Fazar, "Progress Reporting in the Special Projects Office," *Navy Management Review*, April 1959.
9. Gregory T. Haugan, *The Work Breakdown Structure in Government Contracting* (Vienna, VA: Management Concepts, 2003), pp. 7–9.
10. American National Standards Institute, "Earned Value Management System." ANSI/EIA-748-B, June 2007.
11. Personal interview with Steve Backhus, Director, Office of Quality and Continuous Improvement, U.S. Government Accountability Office, November 28, 2008.

# Part 1
# Organization and Structure

The first of the three pillars of project management in the federal government is organization and structure. In this part, we present the framework in which project management is performed within the federal government. Each of the chapters views project management from a different organizational, regulatory, and structural perspective.

In Chapter 2, *Fitting Project Management into the Organization: Round Peg/Square Hole*, we discuss three main elements found in the federal government environment: culture, systems, and common structures. Culture describes the attitudes, beliefs, and rituals in an organization that influence the formulation of project management practices. The systems reflect those activities, processes, or technologies that enable work to be accomplished. Common organizational structures include the project management office.

Chapter 3, *Regulations and Legislation: The Emerging Context for Federal Project Management*, describes the legal and regulatory framework within which projects are executed. We discuss relevant laws, directives, and regulations, as well as the agencies that enact or enforce them.

Chapter 4, *Building Strong Teams: The Vehicle for Successful Projects*, focuses on the various team types and structures, highlighting their strengths and challenges. The roles of key team members are briefly described, along with techniques for developing effective teams that contribute to project success.

Chapter 5, *Leveraging Technology for Project Success: New Tools of the Trade*, introduces and describes how technology is employed in managing projects in the federal government. Current trends and their implications for the future of project management are discussed as well.

## Chapter 2

# Fitting Project Management into the Organization: Round Peg/Square Hole

> *There are no problems we cannot solve together, and very few that we can solve by ourselves.*
> —PRESIDENT LYNDON BAINES JOHNSON

The town of Parkersburg, West Virginia, sits at the confluence of the Little Kanawha and the Ohio rivers. This small, comfortable city of 35,000 is home to the Parkersburg High Big Reds, the *Sentinel* newspaper, and the Treasury Department's Bureau of the Public Debt. A glass and concrete building houses the bureau's Administrative Resource Center (ARC), which provides administrative support services to other government agencies. ARC is one of those unusual quasi-governmental business units: a franchise department that is allowed to operate as a self-sustaining business. ARC provides its customers—other federal agencies—financial and administrative support services.

By signing up for ARC's services, a federal agency is able to streamline its financial reporting process and ensure that its financial reporting requirements are met. In a typical arrangement with customers, ARC staff converts the data stored in the client's databases to ARC's hosted services. These projects are process- and change management-intensive, causing the customer to standardize its typical business functions. In 2004, recognizing that it needed a more structured path for customers, ARC created a project management office (PMO) to manage customers through the conversion process. For the past five years, the PMO has been quietly at work transforming the way ARC operates.

For the PMO to be successful, it needed to fit itself into the existing organization. ARC leadership considered how to best integrate the services and processes of the PMO into and across the entire organization. The challenges ARC faced in introducing more formalized project management processes and navigating organizational dynamics are shared by many federal agencies.

## **THE ORIGIN OF PROJECT MANAGEMENT IN AN ORGANIZATION**

The initial "spark" for project management practices helps determine the direction the discipline takes in an organization. An "organic" origin implies that the project management discipline evolved from the way the organization does business. For example, project management began in ARC with a couple of project managers and a relatively open agenda. They grew the practice gradually, until it was recognized as a real asset, whereupon a more formal practice was established.

**CHAPTER 2** Fitting Project Management into the Organization

Mission-oriented or project-centric organizations like the National Aeronautics and Space Administration (NASA) and the Department of Energy (DOE) are apt to implement a more structured approach to project management. An "applied" path reflects practices, typically externally developed, that are adopted or engineered to address a project challenge (or failure) or to implement a new capability. For example, NASA now has the capability to create a new PMO, complete with standards, tools, and objectives that are all aimed at addressing a specific mission.

Regardless of the origin, organizations have to start with either an organic or an applied orientation and move toward the other. If grown organically, project management eventually needs to be matured through an applied process to achieve its potential. If developed in an applied fashion, project management will need to evolve organically to fit within the existing culture and organizational context. Figure 2-1 depicts the stages of organic and applied origins for project management in the organization.

## KEY ORGANIZATIONAL DIMENSIONS

Successful project management in federal agencies must address project management across three organizational dimensions: culture, systems, and structure. Culture is the hardest dimension to address because it is the least concrete and can take many years to change. The systems layer deals with how work gets accomplished—from information technology to human resources, core services, budgeting and finance, planning, etc. The structure dimension is often the most accessible dimension to navigate, as it deals with functional reporting and authority.

These three dimensions define the landscape within which project management will operate. Because they are organization-specific, the project management discipline will vary across civilian agencies in the federal government. One organization may follow mature project management practices while another has virtually no formal practices at all. Unlike in DoD, where more overarching guidance has been promulgated, project management in civilian agencies is a discipline that requires a sustained effort and executive support to evolve to an enterprise level.

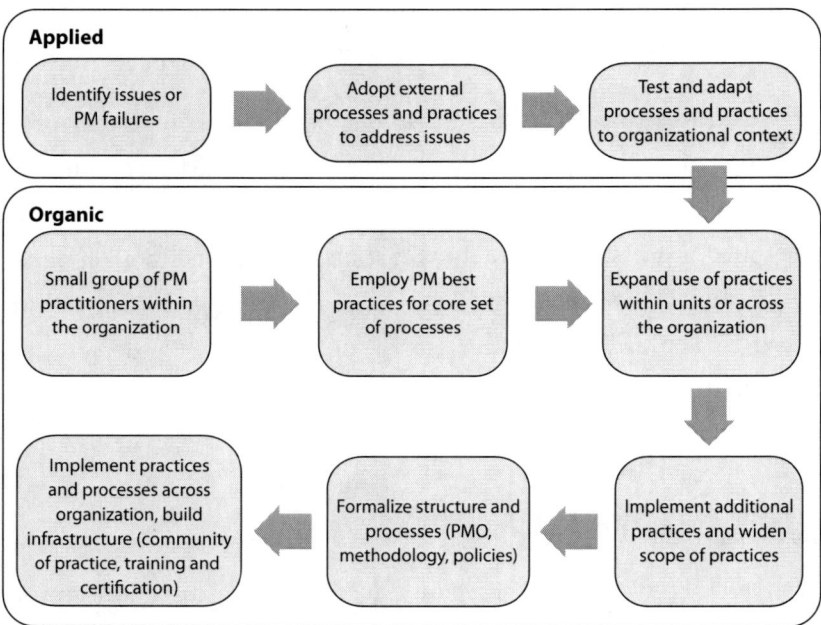

**FIGURE 2-1:** Applied versus Organic Growth of Project Management

Successful project management in federal agencies means that stakeholders must address structure, systems, and culture. These three dimensions play key roles in determining the tenor of the organization's project management practice. At a high level:

- *Culture* refers to the behaviors, attitudes and beliefs, language, and organizational rituals in place within a work setting. Culture describes the human environment, which may enhance or inhibit the success of project management.

- *Systems* connotes a related set of activities, processes, technologies, and supporting materials organized around a specific objective or desired outcome.

- *Structure* refers to the configuration of business units, divisions, directorates, and other constructs that make up an organization.

These three dimensions collectively define the environment within which project management will either thrive or wane.

When one or more of these dimensions is ignored, unintended consequences can result (see Table 2-1). For example, if the organizational structure is not in alignment with the supporting systems, informal processes and "back channels" may be relied on to get work done. When the organizational structure is misaligned with the culture, the environment may favor loud personalities rather than sound thinking. Likewise, a lack of systems may lead to unclear roles and responsibilities across units: The culture may reward heroic individual or team contributions rather than the steady individual or team that is consistently on time and on budget. Finally, if the culture is not properly aligned toward a project management environment, project management may not be recognized as a legitimate function and significant organizational resistance may arise.

| A Lack of... | Can Lead to... | | |
|---|---|---|---|
| | Structure | Systems | Culture |
| Supporting Culture | Project management not recognized as legitimate | Organizational resistance, lack of effective sponsorship | |
| Alignment with Systems | Unclear roles and responsibilities | | Heroic efforts rewarded |
| Aligned Structure | | Shadow systems used; back channels required | Dominant personalities valued |

**TABLE 2-1:** Consequences of Ignoring Key Dimensions of Project Management

The beginning of wisdom is calling things by their right name. So goes an ancient Chinese proverb. To create an environment where project management can thrive, we must first be able to recognize and identify these key facets of culture, systems, and structure. Only then can these areas will be shaped in a way that enables project management to flourish in the organization.

## Culture

Project management is a discipline that naturally reflects the culture of the organization. Projects leverage the people, processes, and systems within the organization, all of which are imbued with facets of the culture. Culture can be defined as the confluence of behaviors, attitudes and beliefs, language, and rituals that form the basis for a "normal" experience in an organization.

How can understanding culture help a project management practice? An effective project management practice must align itself culturally within its environment. This does not mean that it can never impose change or go against the grain; projects are often at the forefront of change. To be successful in the federal environment, a project management orientation must be absorbed into the culture and adopted. It must operate within the normative ranges behaviorally, in its underlying attitude, in its language, and in its adherence to ritual.

Introducing formal project management into an organization will naturally expand the culture, yet culture is organic and difficult to change by any deliberate means because an organization will always seek cultural homeostasis—a return to its neutral state. Therefore, understanding culture and its implications for project management will help reduce resistance to incorporating project management.

It is natural for stakeholders to resist the incursions of a newly formalized project management practice. (When project management is introduced into an organization, it often comes at the expense of removing a responsibility from another part of the organization.) Resistance comes in many forms, including indifference, exclusion, misinformation, denial, criticism, and containment. If left unaddressed, resistance produces a failure to thrive, whereby the formal processes of project management are ignored, denied, and ultimately rejected outright. For example, a PMO that seeks to implement a project management methodology that is extremely rigid within an organization that promotes innovation and flexibility will meet with strong organizational and cultural resistance. The introduction and use of project management practices will need to take cultural differences into account to gain acceptance by the larger organization.

Behaviors, attitudes and beliefs, language, and rituals create a powerful mix of elements that form the culture of an organization. The culture is usually anchored around one of those elements, such as a belief set or even a particular person. Changing the culture of any organization takes time and sufficient critical mass to overcome the forces that represent the current culture.

### Behaviors

Within every organization a set of unwritten behavioral rules forms a baseline of "normal." Behavioral rules are specific to an organization, and they reflect the type of organization. In military organizations, for example, displays of respect for superiors, such as saluting, are formally documented and commonly practiced. Yet saluting would be out of place and awkward at a research laboratory within the Centers for Disease Control.

Behavioral norms can also be manifested through body language, social comportment, use of humor, interpersonal spatial cues, and other more subtle indicators. An off-color joke in one organization, for example, may be entirely acceptable in another. Socially normative behaviors play an important role in an organization, creating safety zones of accepted behavior as well as boundaries defining aberrant behavior, which ultimately creates shared expectations that bind the collective together. Most professional organizations share a set of behaviors that denote proper professional decorum. For federal agencies, behavioral norms are further shaped by the practices and protocols set forth in civil service laws, executive orders, and other regulations.

To be adopted and implemented successfully, project management practices in federal agencies must adhere to behavioral norms. For example, imposing excessive rigidity or lacking sufficient formality can each equally undermine the practice of project management and breed mistrust of the overall project management discipline.

### Attitudes and Beliefs

The people within an organization often share common beliefs, such as "The world is better off because of our work," "We are the last line of defense," or "We preserve the past to ensure the future." These attitudes create a potent, yet often invisible, container around the organization, binding people together within a common belief set. Attitudes and beliefs also shape the pecking order in the organization. For example, medical organizations place doctors at the top of the heap, which means that they are given preference in everything from patient care to office space and parking spots. In part, this stems from a belief set shared across the organization that goes something like "doctors are the most important resource we have because they are in charge of patients."

Attitudes and beliefs also play a key role in defining an organization's project management practice. To be successful, project management leadership must ensure that beliefs and attitudes reflect the mission and priorities of the organization and are not in conflict with the unwritten belief set that pervades the organization.

### Language

Language is an elemental form of interaction. As the basic currency for understanding and meaning, language involves both written and oral communication, making use of words, syntax, punctuation, inflection, emphasis, and nuance. We use thousands of words each day, striving to be heard. The structure, complexity, and types of words used in an organization inform the culture. Language infers a knowledge set that is shared by the members of that community. The understanding of key concepts in an area, even the use of jargon, invites trust.

Embedded in language is the data we wish to impart and the "wrapper" that is the silent message about the culture. That wrapper is the nonverbal cues that provide the bulk of the meaning in any face-to-face communication. Nonverbal cues include postures, facial expressions, eye contact, and proximity to one another, which all provide a wealth of information about our true meaning. Organizations naturally establish and constantly maintain the rules around nonverbal cues. For example, is it appropriate to lay a hand on someone's shoulder in the office? How loud can laughter be in an office setting? These micro-rules can change from office to office, or even by time of day. In organizations that engage in shift work, such as hospitals, for example, once the administrative leaders leave for the day, the evening shift may apply a different set of cultural rules.

Verbal and nonverbal language is especially important in project management. Projects instantiate change, and change arouses conflict. As many industrial psychologists note, there is a continuum of conflict that ranges from healthy to unhealthy. In a healthy environment, conflict arouses vigorous debate and the verbal and nonverbal cues denote a willingness to come to consensus. In unhealthy conflict, the nonverbal cues demonstrate a flight-or-flight response, such as aggressiveness or shutting down. Project managers need to work at improving the way they manage conflict by recognizing both verbal and nonverbal cues and opening a dialogue about how to engage in a different way.

### Rituals

Holiday parties, annual review cycles, a one-on-one with the boss, retirement parties—all are rituals that serve as important tent poles holding up the culture. Rituals serve many functions: to convene groups, to instantiate or recognize something new, to execute rites of passage, to reject something that does not fit, and to conclude a phase. Rituals provide tangible ways to measure the passage of time. They also denote a common set of experiences for all staff. Successful federal project management practices align with and adhere to organizational rituals.

Project teams can leverage rituals to support project management. For example, project teams can develop rituals around phase kickoffs or successful milestone completions. These rituals can serve as a way to recognize performance, reward results, and close out a phase.

## Systems

*Systems* is a broad-based term that connotes a related set of activities, processes, technologies, and supporting materials organized around a specific objective or desired outcome. Examples of systems in an organization include resource management, service delivery, contract management, and communications.

Organizational systems can be documented, formal processes or age-old methods for getting things done. Regardless, projects must be able to access and use the various technical and process-based systems that enable an organization to function. To be successful, project management must access these systems and be able to interact with them in ways that support the organization.

As a relatively new arrival in many agency hierarchies, project management faces the challenge of integrating with long-held anchor systems such as human resources, finance, contracts, and operations. Project managers must be able to leverage human resource processes in hiring staff, assigning project resources, or providing support for necessary training. In the federal sector, there is no best practice for how a project management practice should integrate within these systems. Yet projects must operate across existing systems and silos to retain resources and achieve results (see Figure 2-2).

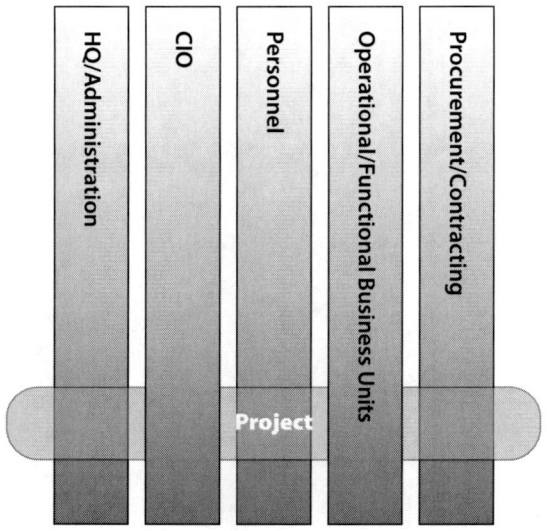

**FIGURE 2-2:** Intersection of Projects and Functions

Organizational units are vertically focused on their functional mission. However, the typical project runs horizontally across the organization to access resources from a number of organizations. For project management to succeed, it must have access to systems within the organizational units. These systems include processes, core operations, and technology—any type of common workflow that results in a standard organizational deliverable or result. Successful agencies in the federal sector have defined clear boundaries and processes for using existing systems. PMO directors have established relationships with their counterparts in human resources, finance, and contracts to ensure that requests are handled properly.

Systems in organizations reflect the intersection of two distinct, elemental drivers—the degree of formality and the configuration of authority—each of which shapes the implementation of the individual systems. Formality and authority are shaped by the culture of the agency, driving the tenor and tone of project management. For example, a highly formal organization with strict authority lines, like the Secret Service, will naturally install a project management method that operates differently from that implemented in an organization with more moderate formality and authority, like the U.S. Census Bureau. Project management is as much a product of the culture of the organization as it is a product of the structures and practices that give it substance.

Degree of formality and configuration of authority shape how project management is manifested in organizations. Successful project management practices in the federal sector recognize and respect the importance of systems.

### *Degree of Formality*

Formality denotes an emphasis on following procedures, fulfilling requirements, and attending to customary practices. Federal government organizations exhibit a range of degrees of formality, which are in turn reflected in their style of project management, from informal to highly structured. In an informal environment, project management practices are inconsistent, nonrepeatable, and usually dependent on a champion or the "heroic" efforts of individual project managers or team members.

Increasingly, federal organizations are moving toward more formal practices for managing projects. For example, since 2005, ARC has migrated from having no defined methodology or roles to an environment that has a PMO, defined project manager roles, and a documented project management methodology with formal review and approval checkpoints. The degree of formality will naturally extend beyond managing single projects to span multiple projects or programs and eventually the organization's entire portfolio of projects.

### Configuration of Authority

Authority refers to the power bases and structures that exist within an agency. The types and uses of authority in an organization influence how project management operates. Authority may be granted via a titular role (based on title and formal authority), charisma (based on force of personality and allegiances), expertise (based on knowledge), or tradition (based on a role that is not formally empowered with authority).

In federal agencies, the organizational culture further determines how that authority is exercised. One obvious example is traditional military organizations, which operate on a premise of command and control. In this environment, orders are given and obeyed. In contrast, in a research laboratory, authority is bestowed upon scientists who have expertise in a field of study. In the military setting, authority will be exercised through direct orders, but in the laboratory setting, authority will be exercised through indirect means such as information and allegiance.

## Structure

Structure represents the most formal connection between project management and the organization (think of an organization chart). The structure of an organization should reflect long-term goals as well as a recognition of services, delivery models, and alignment of staff. While structure is often difficult to establish initially, it may be the easiest organizational dimension to change.

Unlike culture and systems, changing structure is a matter of moving reporting responsibilities, staffing, and physical space to accommodate a new set of priorities. This is no small feat and should not be minimized by suggesting it is simple. Yet, structure is one area where relatively fast changes can be made to accommodate a function like project management.

Project management must be anchored appropriately to the organization. Federal agencies display a wide range of organizational configurations of project management. All project managers are part of some type of reporting structure, although the details will vary from agency to agency and department to department. In some cases, projects report through a chief information officer (CIO). Other organizations have projects reporting up through the administrative function or chief administrative officer (CAO) or across a variety of executive lines. This variation is a natural result of the influences and forces that project management must address in becoming established and growing within an organization, including economics, intra-agency politics, external politics (i.e., dealing with elected officials), physical space, alignment with mission, and the sense of criticality of project management.

Where the project management practice developed naturally in an organization, it often evolves as shadow processes with no clear lines of authority. While a bottom-up approach serves early project management practices well, these practices must eventually become properly linked to the organization or risk being seen as an intrusion and disruption. Once established within the structure of the organization, project management can operate legitimately and projects can be properly sponsored and staffed. Ideally, a way will be found to combine the entrepreneurial spirit with the organizational strength of an established project management system.[1]

The project management office, the program management office, and the outcome management office are the mainstay business structures through which projects are channeled in the federal government. (Keep in mind that the term *program* in federal parlance often represents an ongoing operation that is legislatively mandated, such as Medicare. The traditional project management definition of *program* is a series of projects or related subprojects.)

### Project Management Office

The PMO typically is a permanent organizational unit chartered to coordinate project resources and improve overall project success. Several variants of PMOs currently operate within the federal government:

- *Center of excellence.* This type of organization is typically a support unit, providing information, best practices, mentoring, and coordination services. A center of excellence has no direct authority for projects and does not maintain direct responsibility for the organization's project managers.

- *Functional PMO.* Many PMOs are created within a division or directorate to satisfy that particular area's project needs. In an IT PMO, for example, the information technology organization maintains a PMO to plan and deploy its projects effectively.

- *Controlling PMO.* This type of PMO operates to ensure adherence to organizational standards, policies, and procedures, with an emphasis on compliance and audits.

PMOs perch awkwardly on the organization chart, reporting to the groups that happen to need them. Project managers must learn organizational ballet, gymnastics, or rugby (depending on the culture) to obtain resources for their projects.

### Program Management Office

The program management office (PgMO) is often established to meet a specific program's objectives. For example, in replacing a legacy system over a period of five years, the PgMO is a useful organizational construct that provides a legitimate home for the various projects that fall under this initiative. Once the program objectives are met, the office is disbanded.

For all but a few mission-focused organizations like NASA and parts of DoD, program management practices have not yet been fully integrated. Owing in part to the disparate definitions of the term *program*, there is no standard configuration for a PgMO within the federal government. Each federal department or agency defines its own configuration of program management as a function within the organization.

### Outcome Management Office

The outcome management office (OMO) is a newer organizational concept that represents a new frontier for project management in the federal government (but is being used in the Canadian government and some U.S. state governments, including New York). Designed specifically to monitor the results of large organizations, particularly departments, OMOs work closely with other project- and program-related organizations to measure the outcomes of specific initiatives.

The OMO has evolved in recent years from the need to measure the longer-term business outcomes of projects. Initially, organizations develop forms (e.g., benefits realization forms, outcome management templates) to begin to capture the promises made when the project was first being considered. When projects end, the organization is left with a need to integrate the results of the project into the fabric of day-to-day operations.

Although the project objectives may have been met, the business objectives usually take time to realize. For example, a new claims processing system may take 18 months to realize the full scope of efficiencies that was originally promised. Once the project team is disbanded, the OMO owns those results.

## DEGREE OF CENTRALIZATION

Centralized project management in the federal government is rare at the enterprise level. In PMI parlance, a centralized structure represents a strong matrix that enables the organization to become truly project-based. Resources are assigned by project codes rather than by organizational codes. To accomplish this, organizational accounting needs to be built around a project structure. This is usually feasible only at lower levels of the organizational budget, below the organizational cost codes. Centralized project management tends to have strong processes, standards, roles, and portfolio management. The most common form of a centralized project environment involves programs.

The level of centralization connotes a certain amount of authority. Similarly, the level of formality connotes a certain array of practices. Where authority and practices meet helps shape the impact of project management across all three dimensions: culture, systems, and structure (see Figure 2-3).

Distributed project management is more common across federal agencies. In this realm, agencies maintain loose coordination of project resources while retaining their essential organizational structures. In a distributed organization, standards are generally localized to one directorate. Varying project management practices may be used across the enterprise, with no real need to integrate them. Distributed project management is usually unevenly applied across the organization, with some areas of the agency highly evolved and other areas having little or no expertise.

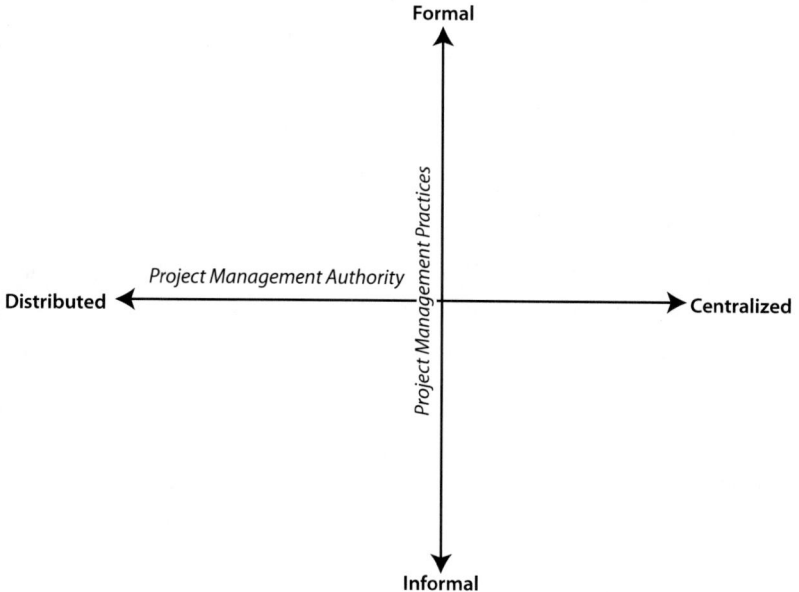

**FIGURE 2-3:** Confluence of Project Management Authority and Practices

One key characteristic of a distributed environment is a general awareness of project management across the organization. The Central Intelligence Agency (CIA) provides an interesting example. The agency relies on a system of internal safeguards to protect the nation's security. The credo at CIA is "need to know." From a project perspective, the organization intentionally engages in compartmentalization of work. Whereas most organizations expend effort trying to collapse project and resource information into a consolidated view, the CIA intentionally prevents this information dispersal. Certain individuals may have a need to know about the portfolio of projects in a given area of the agency, but most do not have those privileges. This purposeful decentralization is somewhat mitigated by the strong mission orientation of CIA personnel.

Decentralized project management is common among federal agencies, particularly in organizations new to project management. In a decentralized environment, the organization exercises very little coordination over resources, standards, or practices. Pockets of expertise exist, but no organizational channels are available for sharing expertise or resources across units or for promoting project management standards. The challenges presented by this model are the development of competing methodologies within an organization and the inefficient use of resources, both of which contribute to duplication of effort and unnecessary expenditures. Increased entrepreneurship within semi-autonomous units can mitigate these effects to some degree.

> Establishing, expanding, or institutionalizing project management within an organization requires an ability to navigate through three key organizational dimensions:
>
> - Adherence to cultural standards and norms
> - Working within organizational systems
> - Effectively anchoring to the organizational structure.
>
> Each of these dimensions represents an opportunity for a project management practice to embed itself deeply within the organization. It is important to note that all three dimensions must be attended to; the project management practice risks becoming imbalanced if one dimension is ignored. Lacking the minimum momentum in one or more of these layers will result in an unclear implementation of project management.
>
> To flourish, project management needs to succeed across the cultural, systems, and structural layers of the organization. Each layer must be implemented to a sufficient degree to gather the necessary momentum to continue to progress on its own. For many federal agencies, such as ARC, project management is taking root and being adopted throughout the organization.

## NOTE

1. See Paul Roberts, *Guide to Project Management* (London: The Economist and Profile Books, 2007), pp. 42–69; and Rick A. Morris, *The Everything Project Management Book* (Avon, MA: Avon Media, 2002), pp. 101–108.

# Chapter 3
# Regulations and Legislation: The Emerging Context for Federal Project Management

> *The Lord's Prayer is 66 words, the Gettysburg Address is 286 words, there are 1,322 words in the Declaration of Independence, but government regulations on the sale of cabbage total 26,911 words.*
>
> —NATIONAL REVIEW[1]

Since the 1970s, the federal government has adopted laws and regulations aimed at improving the accountability, efficiency, and effectiveness of government operations. From presidential orders on management paradigms to long-standing legislative cornerstones, these laws and regulations provide a framework for project and program management.

As projects and programs have grown increasingly large and complex, the Office of Management and Budget (OMB) and other agencies have issued guidance on performance-based management that aligns with the tenets of project management and, in some cases, addresses specific topics like earned value management, certification, and project/program inventory. The federal government appears to be in the process of creating an enterprise structure for centrally governing the scope and scale of projects.

To understand the federal context that supports project management, it is important to understand how the project management discipline has formed from the bottom up, with agencies, groups, and committees variously taking turns to improve the structure and methods associated with the management of projects. These efforts have yielded an environment that is largely unlegislated, unregulated, and loosely coordinated. In contrast, several government-wide institutions have pushed for a more strategic role and the structured execution of project management. For example, OMB has played a central and important role in advancing policies that support good project management. OMB continues to play a leadership role in the development of effective project managers and use of the acquisition lifecycle to ensure project success.

## WHO'S WHO IN FEDERAL PROJECT MANAGEMENT

Numerous organizations are involved in the development of project management-related policies or the promotion of best practices. Some are formal government organizations and others are groups or associations organized around a topic or a particular role.

## Office of Management and Budget

Part of the executive branch, OMB supports the President in developing and implementing the federal budget. OMB also oversees executive branch agencies and ensures the effectiveness of agency programs. As part of this mission, OMB has played an integral role in developing project management guidance at the organizational and individual levels. Working primarily through acquisition rules and regulations, OMB has made significant contributions toward the development of a federal standard for project management.

Within OMB, the Office of Federal Procurement Policy (OFPP) is the primary driver of government-wide project management practices. OFPP was created in 1974 to administer federal procurement policies. Today, the office plays a key role in defining how large projects are reviewed and rated.

## Government Accountability Office

As a result of large wartime expenditures and a public outcry for greater accountability, GAO, originally known as the General Accounting Office, was created under the Budget and Accounting Act of 1921.[2] GAO has long served a critical audit function in the U.S. government. GAO strives to help federal agencies improve performance, ensure accountability, and meet statutory requirements.

GAO has a major impact on projects across the federal government through its audit and review function. GAO audits hundred of projects annually—projects of all sizes and in all areas of expertise. It maintains a high-risk list of large-scale projects that are failing to meet the objectives set down by the planning team. GAO maintains reports on thousands of failed or endangered projects.

## Chief Acquisition Officers Council Project Management Working Group

Established in 2007, the Project Management Working Group (PMWG) (www.CAOC.gov) serves as "an inter-agency focal point for promoting increased awareness of project management responsibilities and competencies, sharing of best practices, and fostering the consistent implementation of capital planning and project management-related policy, regulations, processes and practices across the Federal government."[3]

PMWG is dedicated to advancing a consistent set of capital planning and project management principles and practices for both IT and non-IT projects. This group provides guidance on the best practice applications of performance-based management.

## Chief Information Officers Council

The CIO Council (www.cio.gov) provides a venue for interagency best practice and information sharing on information technology. Originally established in 1996 by Executive Order 13011, the CIO Council was codified into law by Congress in the E-Government Act of 2002. The chair of the CIO Council is OMB's Deputy Director for Management. The CIO Council comprises a number of committees that address all aspects of federal IT, including project management.

The council issues memos and work products that address improving IT project management. It also maintains a list of training resources, survey results, and other information that can assist agencies in advancing project management.

## Federal Acquisition Institute

Established in 1976, the Federal Acquisition Institute (FAI) "facilitates career development and strategic human capital management in support of a professional federal acquisition workforce."[4] FAI has developed a certification program for federal project and program managers. Dubbed the "federal acquisition certification-program and project managers," or FAC-P/PM, this certification establishes a set of baseline competencies and related requirements. The FAC-P/PM certification is relatively new, but it is being adopted by a host of agencies.

## Project Management Institute

The Project Management Institute (PMI) (www.pmi.org) is a non-government, global association of project management practitioners with a membership of more than 265,000 across 170 countries. PMI offers a set of credentials corresponding to different specialties in project management, such as project management, program management, and scheduling. PMI supports a number of programs aimed at the federal government. First and foremost is the Washington, D.C., chapter of PMI. The largest PMI chapter in the world, it offers an active membership a wide array of programs and symposiums.

The PMI government community of practice is a virtual community that brings together elected and civil servant government officials, as well as contractors and others, for the purpose of improving the management of projects in the public sector. The PMI® Roundtable is a government-focused venue for information and practice sharing. The PMI® Forum is an executive-level environment for discussing strategic and leadership issues in project management. PMI also advocates for the profession through its Washington, D.C., office.

## LAWS INFLUENCING FEDERAL PROJECT MANAGEMENT

No federal laws deal directly with project management practices. Instead, the implementation of project management practices depends heavily on the idiosyncrasies of the organizations applying its various practices. Nonetheless, it is possible to codify the structural components of project management, and the federal government has moved steadily toward instituting more formalized processes.

A number of major laws, regulations, and policies influence, constrain, and guide the practice of project management in the federal government. As Figure 3-1 depicts, each layer of oversight produces increasingly detailed guidance as it relates to the management of projects and programs. These key pieces of legislation create opportunities for project management to flourish as a discipline beyond any single agency's walls.

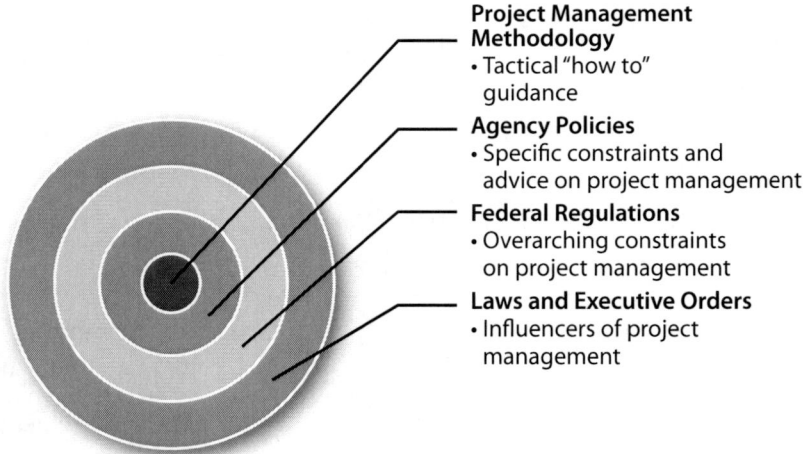

**FIGURE 3-1:** Layers of Oversight in Federal Project Management

## Federal Managers Financial Integrity Act of 1982

This law amended the Budget and Accounting Act of 1921, as well as the Budget and Accounting Procedures Act of 1950, by increasing the level of internal controls and accountability applied by an executive agency. The act requires executive agencies to establish financial controls in accordance with the Comptroller General; it places the onus of responsibility squarely on the agency head by requiring that official's signature and statement on the financial condition of the agency. Agency heads are required to establish controls that will ensure that their agency's revenues and expenditures are properly recorded and that its assets are protected from waste and abuse.

The law also extended OMB's role by requiring it to establish guidelines for agencies to assess their accounting systems' level of compliance with the Comptroller General's standards. This law laid the groundwork for OMB's advances in project management by extending its role into the performance of an agency.

## Chief Financial Officers Act of 1990

The early 1990s were an interesting time for the U.S. federal government and indeed the world. Technology had finally made its way to the desktop, and government employees were stepping into the future of government. But many of the core computerized systems, including financial management and accounting, were antiquated, based on pre-World War II accounting assumptions. The Chief Financial Officers Act (CFO Act) brought about wholesale changes in the way the government performed financial management.

This law represented the most comprehensive overhaul of financial management since the Budget and Accounting Procedures Act of 1950.

Since 1950, agencies had been largely left to their own devices to develop systems and procedures for financial management. Moreover, neither Congress nor the executive branch had the necessary legal framework to maintain control over government spending. Recognizing the shortcomings of the Federal Managers Financial Integrity Act of 1982, especially in view of blossoming technological advances, the CFO Act became an imperative for advancing the government's management paradigm. The nascent information age, with its technologies and organizational constructs, brought with it the promise of a new era of financial controls and instant information. This law created financial leadership and long-term planning structures.

At the agency level, the act created the role of chief financial officer and assigned responsibility for an organization's overall financial health to its CFO. Agencies were required to submit audited financial documents. Perhaps as important, the legislation provided OMB new authority to oversee the modern environment of federal financial management. OMB's Deputy Director for Management was provided the authority to establish government-wide financial policies, monitor financial management systems and agency structures, and manage execution of the federal budget. This law supported a project environment by requiring the development of integrated accounting and financial management systems. Project financials and earned value management systems could be integrated under this new construct. The act also established specific reporting requirements that stipulated the evaluation of individual government programs. The emphasis on program evaluation and increased accountability gave rise to more formalized scope management and project documentation.

## Government Performance and Results Act of 1993

Born out of the Clinton administration's "reinventing government" initiative, the Government Performance and Results Act (GPRA) stipulated that government agencies develop and maintain strategic plans and annual performance plans and reports, maintain managerial accountability, and develop performance-based budgets. The team that engaged in the initial analysis focused on reviewing individual agencies and government-wide systems such as procurement, budget, and personnel.

GPRA requires agencies to maintain and update their plans over time, and to actively pursue better government initiatives. With regard to project management, this law put into place a framework for programmatic accountability, performance measurement, and an accompanying culture change that has sustained itself across much of the federal government.

## Federal Acquisition Streamlining Act of 1994

Title V of the Federal Acquisition Streamlining Act (FASA) required all federal agencies to establish and maintain cost, schedule, and performance goals for major acquisitions. Agencies must achieve, on average, 90 percent of these goals. Major acquisitions involving capital assets must be justified by the agency strategic goals and business needs, and must incorporate acceptable acquisition and capital planning processes. Under FASA Title V, ongoing acquisitions must report progress against baseline performance measures and provide an explanation for any deviation from those goals, along with corrective action plans.

FASA Title V sought to cut the costs of acquisition by addressing capital planning and budgeting. Title V provided the legal wherewithal for OMB to begin migrating toward a true enterprise system of program and project management. FASA Title V also stipulated that agency heads report on programs not meeting 90 percent of their performance objectives, with a justification of the need for the project and a recommendation for remedial action.

## Information Technology Management Reform Act of 1996

Also known as the Clinger-Cohen Act, or the CIO Act, this law formalized the federal government's approach to technology acquisition, management, and use. Like the CFO Act, this law stipulated that agencies establish a chief information officer role to be accountable for the successful use of technology within the agency. The law further strengthened OMB's role by giving the director of OMB the authority to oversee all capital planning with respect to IT. The CIO Act emphasized the acquisition aspects of IT, requiring that OMB establish processes for evaluating the risks and results of major IT acquisitions. The act also required agencies to develop policies and procedures for integrating their systems and exercising oversight of IT.

The CIO Act advanced project management in the federal government by focusing on the importance of information technology, which was already a target-rich environment for project management. The act created a justification and a path forward for formalizing project management methodologies and tool acquisitions in the IT arena.

## E-Government Act of 2002

The E-Gov Act gave form and substance to the notion of an overarching federal IT strategy. Arising from the reinventing government initiative, *e-gov* was initially defined in a 2001 report issued by the Council for Excellence in Government. President Clinton's e-gov framework included strategies for increasing access to government (including ensuring privacy and security), increasing agency use of automation to deliver services, and adopting government-wide electronic government initiatives. Passed into law in late 2001, the E-Gov Act prescribed the use of technologies that improve efficiencies, reduce costs, eliminate paperwork, and automate routine administrative processes.

This mandate led to innumerable initiatives and played a tremendous role in advancing project management for IT projects. Leading up to and following the massive effort surrounding the year 2000 (Y2K) technology threat, many federal agencies sought refuge in project management. Project management methodologies began to be introduced and PMOs started to spring up. PMI's project management professional (PMP) certification began to be recognized in procurements more often. The E-Gov Act supported this trend by providing more justification for IT project management.

## DIRECTIVES AND REGULATIONS AFFECTING FEDERAL PROJECT MANAGEMENT

Project management is a difficult concept to legislate because it is a highly contextual method for getting things done. Although no laws directly address the management of projects, a host of regulations and agency policies shape the ways project management is conducted. The most prolific source of information related to project management is the Federal Acquisition Regulation (FAR).

Oversight of project management is woven into the FAR, reflecting the view that project management is more an extension of the acquisition process than a set of stand-alone practices. Outside the U.S. federal government, in state and foreign governments, project management is regarded as a stand-alone discipline that uses the acquisition lifecycle to accomplish its goals. The federal sector is acquisition-centric, however, so the FAR provides a consolidated channel for establishing and maintaining projects.

In addition to the FAR, certain laws and regulations have shaped project management in the federal government in recent years. These regulations have laid the groundwork for the current environment of project management by formalizing the concept of increased accountability and more specific work products. Yet, projects in the federal government are subject to myriad forces, including current administration priorities, congressional priorities, and a host of regulatory and decision chains. In some cases, the laws themselves have driven innovations in project management. In other instances, the laws have simply recognized trends that already were emerging in the project management field.

Many of the directives and regulations relevant to project management emanate from OFPP, within OMB, where Lesley Field champions project management from her office overlooking the White House. Lesley and her team own the development and improvement of government-wide project management, and they have promulgated greater levels of accountability and precision in project management through a variety of methods. OFPP has worked to institute a framework of regulation that integrates project management into the overall acquisition lifecycle. OFPP is also seeking to develop effective methods for detecting problems on projects early. The basic idea is that small problems are easier to fix than large projects. To accomplish this, OFPP is working to improve both agency performance reporting and large-project reporting so that action can be taken earlier.

A number of laws and regulations shape the way the federal government implements project management practices.

## OMB Circular A-109, Major Systems Acquisitions

The original Circular A-109, dated April 5, 1976, addressed the management effectiveness of major programs and the use of cost schedule control system criteria (C/SCSC), the precursor to earned value management. This circular is important because it was the first set of guidance from OMB on managing major systems development efforts. Circular A-109 includes a requirement to "assess acquisition cost, schedule and performance experience against predictions, and provide such assessments to the agency head at key decision points."[5]

A-109 defines the need for a "program manager" but does not include any mention of project manager. Yet the concept is clearly evolving as a singular role to lead the overall planning and implementation of a major system acquisition. Thanks in part to this early work, civilian agencies are required to use earned value management systems (EVMS) on large acquisitions. This policy was overhauled in 1996 by a group of more than 14 agencies[6] that converted C/SCSC to the industry standard EVMS model.

## OMB Circular A-11, Part 7, Capital Programming Guide, and Exhibit 300

Circular A-11 was originally developed in 1996 to address the preparation, submission, and execution of the federal budget. This circular plays a central role in federal project management by defining many of the requirements related to the management of projects. Part 7 sets forth a policy on the planning, budgeting, acquisition, and management of capital assets and requires that business cases be developed for major capital acquisitions. A supplement to Circular A-11, "The Capital Programming Guide," affirms the need for effective program and project management on IT and large non-IT projects.

The guide focuses on an important document, Exhibit 300 (E-300). Major acquisitions and investments across the federal government must be reported through E-300; this format allows OMB to coordinate collection of agency data as required by the Federal Acquisition Streamlining Act of 1994 and the Clinger-Cohen Act of 1996. Exhibit 300 ensures that investments under consideration are connected with agency "mission statements, long-term goals and objectives, and annual performance plans developed pursuant to the GPRA."[7]

E-300 documents are designed to consolidate the myriad issues attendant to IT asset management by leveraging business cases for investments. E-300 also brings together a host of other mandates required by federal legislation, including implementation of the E-Gov Act, Clinger-Cohen Act, and Government Paperwork Elimination Act, as well as IT security reporting, agency modernization efforts, and overall project investment management.

E-300s are business cases that form one element of an agency's budget submission. The exhibit allows agency leadership and OMB to compare different projects using a common format and rating criteria. Exhibit 300 asks for information from the gamut of project planning, staffing, risk management, lifecycle management, acquisition, earned value, and more, and thus can serve as a valuable communication tool. The document provides an opportunity for the project team and agency leadership to demonstrate to OMB that the disciplines of good project management are in place on major projects. As the most recent E-300 (issued August 2009) explains, "OMB uses the exhibit 300 to make both quantitative decisions about budgetary resources consistent with the Administration's program

**CHAPTER 3** Regulations and Legislation

priorities, and qualitative assessments about whether the agency's programming processes are consistent with OMB policy and guidance."[8]

Whereas the E-300 document was originally a nicety that an agency could complete without entering much information, the current version demands real answers to hard questions. For example, if a project suffers from one of the following, it could very well be removed from the budget submission:

- The project has not made significant progress in resolving Federal Information Security Management Act (FISMA) security requirements.
- The project is seriously over budget.
- The project is seriously behind schedule.
- The project fails to provide the basic functionality identified in the requirements analysis.
- A qualified and experienced project manager is not in charge of the investment.
- The project is no longer a priority for the agency mission and budget.[9]

One recurring criticism of the federal government is that problems are not uncovered until it is too late. In some instances, programs have overrun by more than 100 percent before any real problem is recognized and addressed. Schedules and budgets are not adjusted for risk, and data collection is often limited. Both Circulars A-11 and A-109 begin to address the issues of planning and early detection. The new E-300 tools and processes provide OMB with the necessary framework for early detection.

## Program Assessment Rating Tool

Many federal programs are simply collections of activities designed to address a specific governmental function. Medicare is a program, for example, as is consumer protection. Numerous other laws and regulations address accountability and results within such programs. Recently, however, specific tools have been developed to evaluate the outcome of federal programs. For example, the program assessment rating tool (PART), developed as part of the Bush administration's GPRA initiative, was designed to address the output of these programs and to evaluate them based on their results and their ability to perform their intended function. (In this instance, program refers both to a collection of projects and to a service or outcome produced by the federal government, such as Medicare.)

Established in its present form in 2007 under Executive Order 13450, Improving Government Program Performance, the PART is a questionnaire and process designed to evaluate the results of a particular program. The PART supports an annual quality improvement effort undertaken across the government. Each year, agencies complete PART drafts. The agency performance improvement officer and other agency staff conduct an assessment with representatives assigned by OMB. The PART assessment addresses program results in the context of long-term goals, annual performance, and efficiency measures. The PART influences project management in that it requires many of the basic preconditions of project management, including accountability, clear roles, a predefined schedule, and a set of deliverables. Most important, the PART demands results. The results of a PART assessment can greatly influence future funding decisions on the program in question.

Successful project management practices in the federal environment must operate within a larger federal context, including a wide array of laws, regulations, and directives. Most agencies have specific guidance for managing projects, in the form of methodologies, policies, and standards. As OMB and GAO develop tools and processes that enable government-wide portfolios of tools, it is incumbent upon individual agencies to understand the requirements that are being placed on their project and program managers and to ensure that major acquisitions are following the best guidance available.

## NOTES

1. *National Review,* http://www.quotegarden.com/government.html (accessed November 2, 2009).
2. http://www.gao.gov/about/history/index.html (accessed November 2, 2009).
3. http://caoc.gov/index.cfm?function=projectmanagement (accessed November 2, 2009).
4. http://www.fai.gov (accessed October 29, 2009).
5. OMB Circular A-109, Section 7, Part G.
6. "Earned Value Management and Past Performance," presentation by David Muzio at the NCMA Suncoast Chapter, December 2006.
7. OMB, Exhibit 300, OMB Circular A-11 (2008), p. 7.
8. OMB Circular A-11, Part 7, Exhibit 300 (August 2009), p. 12.
9. "Strong Project Managers Can Ace the Exhibit 300 Process," *Federal Sector Report,* July 2006, P2C2 Group, Inc., http://www.p2c2group.com/jul06nws.html (accessed April 29, 2009).

# Chapter 4
# Building Strong Teams: The Vehicle for Successful Projects

> *Teamwork is the ability to work together toward a common vision. The ability to direct individual accomplishments toward organizational objectives. It is the fuel that allows common people to attain uncommon results.*
>
> —Andrew Carnegie

Managers cannot do all the work of their teams; if they could, there would be no need for teams. Even the 19th century industrialist Andrew Carnegie knew that, as much as he would have liked to do everything himself, he needed others. One of the project manager's or leader's key responsibilities in both the federal government and the private sector is to ensure that team members work well with each other and are able to perform their individual jobs.

## TEAM TYPES AND STRUCTURES

The particular structure of the team will depend in large part on the task, the organization or agency, and the people available (see Figure 4-1). The ideal staffing for a task or project simply may not be possible.

**FIGURE 4-1:** Project Team Structure

One immediate issue is team size. A small team will generally be easier to manage effectively because the project manager will be able to get to know team members better. In the initial phase of the project, the manager will be seeking team member "buy-in" to the project's goals and objectives. With fewer team members, the manager may be able to link team goals to individual goals more effectively.

Technical project realities may necessitate a large team, which is by definition more complicated to manage: the more people, the more possible interrelationships. As the number of team members expands arithmetically—1, 2, 3, 4—the number of possible interrelationships expands geometrically—2, 4, 6, 8—creating more and more relationships and therefore potential complications.

The project manager has to take the "math" of interrelationships and communication into account when forming the team. First and foremost, managers have to consider whether they can handle a large team. Will the project manager be spending so much time managing interrelationships and communication that there will be little time left to manage the project? Forming project subteams around major tasks is an effective method for harnessing large teams, with the managers of those subteams reporting directly to the overall project manager. Selecting the right team type or structure is an important consideration for the project manager.

Most projects use a matrix team construct, employing a cross-functional team comprising resources temporarily assigned from other parts of the organization. Many organizations find that this structure promotes cross-functional solutions and enhances professional growth opportunities. As with any construct, however, the matrixed team has its challenges. Project staff who are "borrowed" for the project have to answer to multiple managers, work with new team members, and balance the work of the project with their "day job." For project managers, getting the right personnel resources when they're needed from other units in the organization can be a real challenge. On the flip side, the resource's functional (or line) managers often lament the loss of control over their direct reports' assignments and professional development.

While the matrixed team is common for federal projects, two other team structures seen with growing frequency in the federal environment are the integrated project team and the virtual team. Each offers unique contributions to success in an increasingly complex project environment.

## Integrated Project Team

Use of an integrated project team (IPT) is growing across civilian federal organizations, mirroring the growing complexity of projects in the federal government. Project managers using an IPT structure will need to advance their fundamental skills as they build new competencies to be successful in the evolving project management environment.

IPTs can be formed at two "levels": project-based, with representation from all teams responsible for the execution of a project or program; and functionally based, with representation from all key stakeholder groups. The Department of Energy (DOE), in Order 413.3A, adopted a project-based approach, defining IPTs as "cross-functional groups of individuals organized for the specific purpose of delivering a project to an external or internal customer."[1] DOE's related guidance on IPTs aptly identifies them as "the crossroads where the technical, management, budgetary, safety, and security meet."[2]

In 2003, DOE decided that "all acquisition programs and projects shall use an integrated project team approach to managing projects." DOE promoted IPTs as the "core of project management implementation," coordinating all essential acquisition activities "through the use of multi-disciplined teams, from requirements definition through production, fielding/deployment, and operational support in order to optimize design, manufacturing, business, and supportability processes."[3] The idea of the IPT is to integrate and coordinate activities and to maximize overall project performance rather than performance in particular functional areas.

Key factors that affect the structure and membership of an IPT among the 24 identified in the DOE order include:

- Size, cost, and complexity
- Number or organizations involved and their geographic separation
- Number of organizational approvals needed
- Degree of organizational independence
- Whether the different organizations and functional disciplines share a similar objective
- Political and market conditions
- Stakeholder involvement
- Degree of consensus on methodology and what is an acceptable end product
- Awareness and commitment of organization top management.[4]

The IPT is intended to be flexible; thus, DOE's 2003 regulations did not call for specific team membership and organization. DOE did remind project and IPT managers, however, of three basic core elements: "(1) the PD [project director] is in charge of their own project; (2) IPTs are responsible to and empowered by the PD; and (3) communication between IPTs, the PD, the Program Manager and all levels of acquisition is encouraged to exchange information, build trust, and resolve issues—ideally at the lowest possible level."[5]

The 2010 census provides an example of functionally based integrated project teams. Every ten years the Census Bureau executes a monumental effort to count every American. This critical endeavor provides the basis for a wide variety of important actions, from federal funding to the apportionment of representation in Congress. The structure for the 2010 Census includes the use of IPTs to execute the project.

Figure 4-2 provides a snapshot of several of the IPTs that support the 2010 census, highlighting their relationship with a "master" IPT, the Census Integration Group (CIG). The CIG, which is composed of leaders from organizations responsible for executing the decennial census, performs high-level integration of plans, processes, and products across divisions and functional teams. Key CIG functions include identifying, coordinating, and resolving issues that are escalated by subordinate working groups or business units.

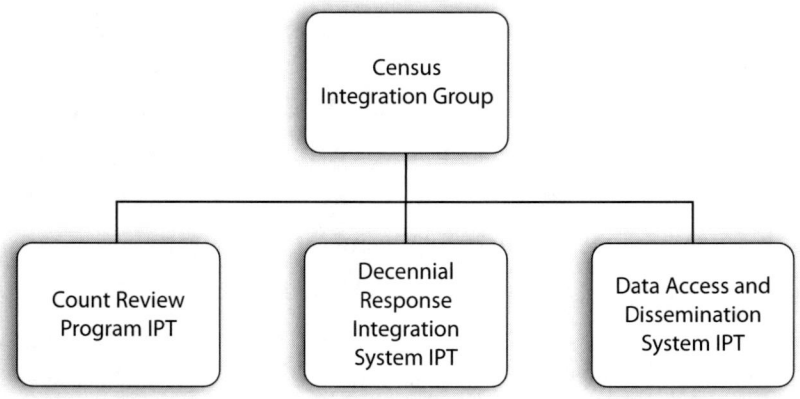

**FIGURE 4-2:** Integrated Project Teams Supporting the 2010 Census

The IPTs under the CIG are a representative sample of the various management units that are working to conduct the 2010 census. They are made up of representatives of the organizations and "systems" that own some part of the overall process or have subject matter expertise critical to the project.

## Virtual Team

A virtual team comprises members "linked via the Internet or media channels to each other and various project partners, such as contractors, customers, and regulators. Although physically separated, technology links these individuals so they can share information and operate as a unified project team."[6] As large projects and the federal agencies that execute them tend to be geographically dispersed, virtual teams are being relied on increasingly. On the plus side, day-to-day annoyances and distractions may be minimized with a virtual team. But how, for example, can meetings be scheduled in different time zones? What is lost when face-to-face contact is not possible? In addressing issues like this, project managers must remember that the goal is not just to design and structure the team well, but also to get the team to function well.

Dr. Deborah L. Duarte, an expert in organizational behavior, and Nancy Tennant Snyder, Vice President for Leadership and Strategic Competency Creation at the Whirlpool Corporation, have come up with some useful criteria for managing virtual teams. They point out that the business justification for virtual teams is strong. These types of teams increase speed and agility and leverage expertise and vertical integration between organizations to make resources readily available. Virtual teams also lessen the disruption of people's lives because they can use technology instead of requiring team members to travel to meet in person. Team members can broaden their careers and perspectives by working across organizations and cultures and on a variety of projects and tasks.[7]

Duarte and Snyder explain that virtual teams are more complex to manage. They point out that the effective use of communications technology is not the only criterion for success:

> Although the effective use of electronic communication and collaboration technologies is fundamental to the success of a virtual team, virtual teams entail much more than technology and computers. When virtual teams and their leaders are asked about successes and failures, they rarely mention technology as a primary reason for either. . . .
>
> There are seven critical success factors for virtual teams, of which technology is only one. Others are human resource policies, training and development for team leaders and team members, standard organizational and team processes, organizational culture, leadership, and leader and member competencies."[8]

Interestingly, these success factors are fundamentally the same as those for the more common, co-located teams. Like many project teams, those that are virtual tend to have a matrix structure, comprising members from various elements of the organization. In addition, virtual teams benefit from a solid project foundation and the leadership of a strong project manager.

Project managers have to be able to adapt to working in a virtual environment. Important skills and actions include:

- Coaching and managing performance without the traditional forms of feedback.

- Selecting and appropriately using the right electronic communication and collaboration technologies. (Specific technologies are discussed in Chapter 5, Leveraging Technology for Project Success.)

- Leading in a cross-cultural environment by understanding the impact of various team members' cultural characteristics on the virtual team setting. The relationship between the project organization's culture and the deployment of virtual teams should also be considered.

- Facilitating team members' transition into the virtual work environment. Work standards will likely be more complex than those in a conventional office.

- Building and maintaining trust, to an even greater degree than on a conventional team. The initial project buy-in will have to include work methods as well as project goals.

- Networking across standard organizational and hierarchical boundaries. The result may be breaking through organizational boundaries and increasing cross-departmental collaboration.

- Developing and adapting organizational processes to meet the expanded demands of the team.[9] One method to consider is allowing virtual team members to determine their own reporting schedules and methods.[10] Before doing so, however, project managers must obtain (or validate that they have) the necessary authority to make process changes. Rejected process changes can result in a loss of credibility.

- Communicating the value of the virtual team to stakeholders while communicating the value of the project itself.

## Other Team Types

Other team types that are often used to manage projects in both the public and private sectors include projectized, co-responsibility, customer-focused, surgical, and self-managed teams[11] (see Table 4-1).

| Type | Description | Strengths | Challenges |
|---|---|---|---|
| Projectized | ■ Team members assigned to work full-time for the duration of a project<br>■ Project manager has some control over budget, material resources, and team member evaluations<br>■ Typically team members are physically co-located | ■ Establishes a stable project environment for conducting work<br>■ Provides the project manager some authority over team members and with other projects or peers in the organization | ■ Obtaining necessary personnel for the duration of a project<br>■ Team members' concern about being separated from their functional organizations |
| Co-Responsibility | ■ Led by two project managers, one with technical skills and the other with business skills relevant to the project's objectives | ■ Two managers with complementary skills and capabilities, filling any gaps that a single project manager may have | ■ Difficulty determining who is in charge |
| Customer-focused | ■ Comprises members from different specialties that collectively manage complex projects<br>■ Project manager serves as a facilitator who is first among equals, rather than an authority figure | ■ Provides multidimensional view of the project<br>■ Promotes strong stakeholder representation and buy-in | ■ Lack of team stability resulting from reassignment of team members to address crises on other projects |
| Surgical | ■ Project manager has full control to produce the project's deliverables<br>■ Provided with solid administrative and technical support | ■ Team members execute on deliverables or project types they know best<br>■ Appropriate for projects requiring highly specialized or unique skills | ■ High risk to count on a single resource for key deliverables<br>■ Project manager gets all the glory; may foster team resentment |
| Self-Managed (or Self-Directed) | ■ Team members collectively assume decision-making authority<br>■ Project manager provides guidance and coordinates decision-making | ■ People who make their own decisions are likely to have a greater commitment to executing them effectively<br>■ Team members closest to the work have a better understanding of how to perform the tasks | ■ Team members may be reluctant to make major decisions<br>■ Effective self-managed teams take time to develop<br>■ Achieving team consensus may delay decision-making; compromise solutions may not yield best results |

**TABLE 4-1:** Characteristics of Types of Teams

## ESTABLISHING THE PROJECT TEAM

*Teamwork* can be defined as a "cooperative effort by the members of a group or team to achieve a common goal."[12] In general, team members contribute to project success by bringing different and complementary skills to the effort to achieve project goals. One of the project manager's critical first tasks is to choose the personnel best suited for the task and to get them to "sign on" to the task, that is, to make the project's goals their goals.

The first step, after the project itself is created, is to select and establish the team. The project manager may not have the option to fully determine who will join the team and may have to work with staff already on hand. Ideally, the project manager should be able to select individuals who have the technical skills to contribute to the team and who can work well with each other. Highly skilled prima donnas may have skills that contribute to the general work of an agency, but they are best suited to work on projects that can be done independently.

In *The Everything Project Management Book,* Rick A. Morris[13] offers some simple criteria for determining the right and wrong team members. He notes that the right team members are reliable, trustworthy, available, flexible, have something to contribute, make an effort to get along with others, abide by the project's rules and parameters, and ask for help when needed. The wrong team members show up only when they feel like it, are not honest about their skill level, must do everything their own way, make no effort to work as a team, complain frequently, and think they know everything. Some of these criteria may seem obvious, but one trap we all can fall into is overlooking the obvious and focusing too much on the subtle and obscure. The project manager can share these characteristics with the team members to set expectations for their behavior and participation.

Interestingly, the characteristics of a good team member are also the characteristics of a good project manager. The team will reflect the leader who formed the team:

> Forming a strong team is the best first step a manager can take toward executing vision and strategy...your team should become an extension of your personal leadership, a force that projects your vision, values, objectives, and requirements....The team you construct will magnify your management methods and your message. Who you are and how well you recognize the strengths and weaknesses in your skills will directly affect how effective your team is. In fact, everything about your team is a reflection of you—for better or for worse."[14]

The Bureau of Indian Affairs PMO (IAPMO) within the Department of the Interior supports its projects by getting teams off to a good start. To kick-start projects, the IAPMO conducts three-day project development workshops (PDWs) that include the development of key initiating documents such as the charter, initial project plan, work breakdown structure, risk assessment, and schedule. These workshops have contributed to effectively forming the team and led to an increase in successful project execution across the project's lifecycle.[15]

The value of this approach was confirmed in an interview with Lesley Field, Director of the Office of Procurement Policy at OMB.[16] Field believes in getting outside "business advisors" who represent the functional program or their customers (often the taxpayers) involved at the beginning of any project. She suggests that these advisors include representatives of all relevant stakeholder groups, especially in the program area, acquisition, and information technology, creating a team that is "cross-functional and holistic." Ultimately, the organization's leaders must be held accountable for the success or failure of the effort.

This is also an opportunity to look for support networks outside the project team, those undertaking similar or complementary functions. This information exchange builds a bridge between the team, executives, and other key stakeholders. Incorporating these stakeholders in relevant team activities provides an opportunity to demonstrate leadership. Executives must lead by setting the example and expectation for the flow of information, while managers must lead by engaging all key stakeholders in the execution of projects.

Don't forget that the project manager is also a member of the team. The project manager will have to look for people with complementary strengths, people who bring skills that the project manager might lack. Team assignments should include backups for key roles, including that of project manager. This calls for some duplication of skills, as well as meeting the fundamental objective of obtaining team members with complementary skills. Also, project managers must set an example by their own actions and should demonstrate behavior consistent with the statements and policies they expect others to follow. A particular job for project managers is to run political interference for team members, to free them from bureaucratic constraints to enable them to do their jobs. The team leader, to use an analogy, has to be the lightning rod for the team.

## Set Team Rules

Perhaps the best first step in establishing a project team is to develop clear rules of engagement for the team. The "ground rules" of the project should support an effective project environment. Effective projects maintain a culture of their own, and these rules will help create a project culture quickly. Sample ground rules include:

- Everyone has an equal opportunity to influence the final outcome. The project manager must protect the "playing field" with this rule of engagement. The culture and progress of the project depend on honest, vigorous debate. This rule of engagement does not mean that everyone has an equal vote, but that all participants should enthusiastically participate in the process. Team member roles will determine who gets to vote on particular matters.

- Issues get resolved through pre-defined channels. Issue resolution is most often ignored on projects because issues tend to cause discomfort. Effective issue resolution requires an established escalation process.

- Individuals are accountable. Projects are premised on people following through on commitments. Team members must clearly understand that they are accountable for results and their own participation.

- Team members listen to each other. Projects are energetic places, where new ideas and innovations are debated every day. In this exciting atmosphere, it is easy to adopt your own line of thinking and stop hearing the other ideas in the room. Effective project managers and stakeholders maintain the humility of listening first.

## Define Roles and Responsibilities

Providing clear definitions of team members' roles and responsibilities, even generic definitions, establishes a framework for the project manager to set expectations and to foster teamwork and team building. The roles included on a given project team and the number of people filling those roles depend on a number of project variables, including size, scope, complexity, and budget. Project managers on larger efforts may consider commissioning a project "core team" composed of key task or functional roles. Members of the core team form the standing team that works most directly for and with the project manager.

Common roles on projects include the following, all or some of which may serve on a core team:

- *Executive sponsor.* This is a critical role on any project. The executive sponsor must provide leadership in support of the project's vision and goals. The executive sponsor needs to actively and visibly promote the project, obtaining the resources required and removing obstacles to successfully achieving the project objectives. A project with multiple sponsors may establish an advisory board comprising executives from organizations with a significant stake in the project's outcome.

- *Project director.* On larger projects, the project director may perform some of the responsibilities usually performed by the executive sponsor. In organizations where the executive sponsor supports many projects, the project director is the conduit for communication, status, and issue escalation between the sponsor and the project manager.

- *Project manager.* In the context of the core team, the project manager may need to play the role of facilitator (see Chapter 9, Project Management Competencies and Skills), serving in an impartial role in core team meetings and other stakeholder interactions.

- *Business expert.* The primary responsibility of the business expert is to make sure that the organization's business interests are appropriately represented. The business expert typically serves as the translator between the business' interest and any technology-based project products or outcomes. Depending on the scale and scope of the project, the team may include one or more business experts. This core team member actively participates in the design and development of the project's outcomes, whether they are processes, policies, programs, or technology. The business expert is also often responsible for protecting or projecting the interests of the project's ultimate customers.

- *IT expert.* The IT expert on the project core team provides insight into the options and risks associated with possible technological solutions. Effective IT experts are able to translate technical issues and risks into plain English for the project manager, project team, and key stakeholders. For projects with IT vendors, the IT expert represents the government's interests and provide independent and objective evaluation and validation of each vendor's deliverables and final product.

- *Financial/budget expert.* Often overlooked on the project core teams, the financial/budget expert can provide the project manager and executive sponsor critical analysis of financial data, tracking actual costs against the budget. Early in the project's life, this team member can provide the financial justifications as part of the business case. The financial expert can also provide an early warning of cost overruns and determine impacts and "what-ifs" related to possible cuts to the project budget.

- *Contract specialist.* The growing emphasis in the federal government on acquisition and contract management makes the contract specialist a potential key player on a project core team and an important asset to the project manager. This role can include evaluating vendor performance and tracking compliance with contract terms and conditions, alerting the project manager to any deficiencies before minor issues become front-page news.

- *Subject matter experts* (SMEs). Throughout the life of any project, experts from a wide array of specialties may be needed. Their tenure on the project may be only as long as it takes to answer a specific question or, if they represent a unique specialty that is required for the project, the entire project lifecycle. The project manager should work with the business and IT experts to identify the need for SMEs as early in the project as possible so these experts will be available when needed.

## DEVELOPING THE PROJECT TEAM

Teams, like people, go through various growth stages. The manager has to take the stages of team development and the needs of individual members into account when forming the team. Bruce Tuckman's seminal group theory identifies those stages as forming, storming, norming, performing, and adjourning.[17] Well known for its simplicity, this theory has been taught widely in project management (and human resource development) courses since it was first set forth over 40 years ago.

Table 4-2 describes actions and behaviors of the project manager and team members across the various project and team development phases. Suggested project manager actions for successfully developing a team are highlighted.

| Project Phase and Key Management Tasks | Team Stages and Team Behaviors | PM Actions |
|---|---|---|
| *Initiation* – Project manager identifies, selects, or recruits team members and defines roles and responsibilities. | *Forming* – Team defines purpose, composition, leadership patterns, and life span. | *Implement Structure* – Organize and direct work, and define team members' roles and responsibilities; get them off to an efficient start. |
| *Planning* – Project manager and team collaborate on developing key project management deliverables and establishing the appropriate project framework. | *Storming* – Team members experience "natural" conflict and tension as they work to establish and understand their roles. | *Coach* – Set high standards and clarify expectations, working collaboratively with the team; coach individuals on team participation. |
| *Early Implementation* – Negotiate changes and refinements to the project plan; develop project details. | *Norming* – Team members achieve greater levels of openness, trust, and confidence in each other and the group's ability to succeed. | *Encourage "Ownership"* – Empower team members to structure work and find ways to collaborate and solve problems independent from the project manager. |
| *Implementation* – Execution of project plan begins. Project manager's role shifts toward coordinating and integrating the project tasks. | *Performing* – Team has "matured" and is operating efficiently; project execution is smooth. In some cases, teams will achieve the status of "high performing" by becoming self-managing and self-motivating. | *Delegate, Coordinate, and Integrate* – Assign task responsibilities and ownership. Coordinate subteam activities and integrate project with internal and external elements. |
| *Closeout* – Project manager performs administrative wrap-up of the project. Assists or manages the reassignment of team members, as appropriate. | *Adjourning* – Team is anxious over the end of project and the uncertainty of next assignments. | *Coaching* – Conduct formal project closure for the group, celebrating success. Provide feedback on team members' performance and promote next project. |

**TABLE 4-2:** Stages of Team Development

In fostering the team's development, the project manager should keep in mind three facets of members' needs: physical, professional, and personal. Simply stated, the team members should have an appropriate physical space conducive to work effectively and the necessary tools to do their jobs. In the case of virtual teams, the project manager should make sure that the critical technology is in place and is working to support the team's efforts across geographical and time zones. Professional growth on the job is a key facet of an individual's full participation on a team. Challenging and interesting work, with commensurate support and training, will motivate team members and return dividends to the project in terms of greater commitment and loyalty to the project and higher-quality results. The personal facet refers to the project manager's responsibility to support each team member's job satisfaction and to foster a positive team environment.

## MANAGING THE PROJECT TEAM

Specific methods for managing project teams will be driven by the unique circumstances of the project. Methods are important, but they are secondary to basic leadership, management, and communications principles. Two key aspects of managing a project team are initiating the team and responding when the team runs into trouble.

Knowing when a team isn't performing optimally or is regressing to a previous developmental stage is a critical skill for the project manager, as is seeking help before the situation deteriorates. When project teams experience challenges at NASA, project managers can seek the support or intervention of the organization's Academy of Program/Project and Engineering Leadership (APPEL). The academy conducts team assessments to uncover issues and enhance performance. Approximately 120 teams (out of about 300 NASA-wide) were provided assistance in fiscal year 2008. Roughly 70 percent of the requests for assistance were for team building rather than technical skills training. APPEL's approach addresses:

- *Team effectiveness* through an assessment that includes eight questions and is based primarily on behaviors, not technical issues (and can be performed on-line).
- *Individual effectiveness* through a similar assessment to the one performed for the team.
- *Team workshop* to review the results of the assessment. The three-day workshop supports team development, addresses specific issues, and builds a plan for "how will the team work together differently" going forward.
- *Sustained change in performance* through coaching activities following the assessments and workshop.
- *Identification of trends on team and individual performance* based on the initial assessments, workshop, and coaching. Reassessments track progress toward the goals established in the plan developed in the workshop.[18]

## **WORKING WITH CONTRACTORS**

Project managers in the federal government often have to work with outside contractors. The project manager must understand the contract as it relates to the project, particularly the timing and quality of deliverables. The project manager also has to keep in mind that contractors are from the private sector, where they may be accustomed to working in less procedurally restrained environments. In most cases, project managers will be able to rely on their organization's contract specialists or, if their project is large enough, team members with contract management responsibilities, to be the primary interface with contractor personnel (e.g., contracting officer's technical representative, or COTR). To the degree the project manager can focus on results rather than procedures, this will ease working with outside contractors.

The General Services Administration's (GSA) Public Buildings Service (PBS) and the Department of the Interior's project management office offer two different examples of the role contractors play on projects in the federal government. Increasingly, PBS project managers are assuming the role of integration or general contractor—managing, coordinating, and integrating the work of both government and contractor personnel. Since much of the construction and engineering expertise resides in the private sector, PBS integrates contractors and its own staff at all levels of the project.

The Department of the Interior's PMO operates differently. The PMO established a multivendor indefinite delivery/indefinite quantity (IDIQ) contract to enable Interior projects to access expert project management support focused on planning and conducting integrated baseline reviews (IBRs). DOI instituted a policy (OCIO Directive 2008-016, June 20, 2008) requiring "major" projects to go through an IBR process and obtain the approval of the agency's Investment Review Board (IRB). The IBR validates that before the project moves to execution, it is: (1) *aligned* with the organization's strategic plan, budget, program goals, and acquisition and contracting guidelines; (2) *realistic* vis-à-vis GAO cost estimating guidelines and other standards; and (3) *viable* based on risk assessment and sensitivity analysis of the cost and schedule. IBR products, specifically the resulting project plans, have been used as requests for proposals (RFPs) to procure support to execute projects. Further, the project management vendors' support of the IBR process supports the PMO's and wider Interior Department goals, promotes higher-quality project plans, lowers risk during the execution/implementation phase, and contributes to development of the proper project scope.[19]

While there are many different permutations of managing contractors and integrating them into project teams, a few challenges and strategies seem to be universal in the government environment.

- **Challenges**

    Vendor personnel:

    - Work for an external organization and report to different managers

    - Are subject to different expectations and are evaluated on a different scale; company job performance requirements may not be consistent with their government counterparts

    - May be assigned more interesting or challenging aspects of the project by virtue of the contract terms, their past experience, or corporate expertise or product

    - May have one year of experience 20 times over because they're constantly reassigned to perform the same task for multiple clients

    - May require special security clearances, which can be time-consuming and cause project schedule delays.

- **Strategies**

    - Avoid an "us" versus "them" mentality; integrate vendor personnel into the team and subteams and establish processes and tasks for producing deliverables collaboratively.

- Establish clear guidelines for government and vendor personnel to work together.

- Develop mutual objectives and promote the common purpose of achieving the project's goals and outcomes.

- Address any differences directly with each group, emphasizing the common purpose: a successful project outcome.

A strong project team is the foundation of most successful projects. Selecting the right team structure provides the appropriate framework for the team to form and effectively execute the project. Employing integrated project teams and virtual teams, both growing trends in the federal government, can provide project managers an effective structure for larger, more complex projects. Project managers who recognize the importance of the team and foster an effective group dynamic as well as each of the team members' individual goals will see dividends for their efforts in the form of loyalty and commitment.

> Although every team has its own way of operating, successful teams seem to share ten key characteristics:
>
> 1. *Clearly defined project goals.* Clear goals enable team members to understand why they are doing their tasks and provide meaning to their work. Clear goals also help team members ensure that their work is meeting the project's ultimate goals and enable them to make any needed corrections without always having to consult with the project leader.
>
> 2. *Clearly defined roles.* Clearly defined roles enable team members to meet their responsibilities. When team members know what is expected of them and they are able to meet responsibilities, they will have opportunities for growth and expanded responsibilities.

3. *Open and clear communication.* Clear communication is essential at all stages of the project. The team needs to remain informed. The leader needs information to monitor progress and make any necessary adjustments, as well as to convey information to upper management and other stakeholders.

4. *Effective decision-making.* Decisions should be based on as much current information as possible, using a variety of methods.

5. *Balanced participation.* All team members participate in and contribute to the work of the team, not just their own tasks. The leader needs to encourage such balanced participation.

6. *Valued diversity.* Team members are valued for what they can uniquely bring to the team.

7. *Managed conflict.* Diversity of opinions is also important to a project team. Managed conflict means that different options are discussed and the best solution is arrived at— whether it is a compromise or a particular viewpoint. Managed conflict also means that problems are addressed, not avoided.

8. *Positive environment.* The feeling that each member of the team is valued and has something to contribute creates a positive environment. This climate of trust among members of the team, including the project manager, is critical to project success. Team members need to know that their colleagues can be depended on to do their jobs—that they are both willing and able.

9. *Cooperative relations.* A team is more than just a collection of individuals. Team members have to be willing to work with each other.

10. *Participative leaders.* The leader shares responsibility and glory when things work out—and takes the heat when things don't.

The more these characteristics are present, the greater the opportunity to build and maintain a successful project team.

## NOTES

1. "Integrated Project Teams Guide for Use with DOE O 413.3A," U.S. Department of Energy, Washington, DC, September 24, 2008, pp. 1-2, http://www.er.doe.gov/opa/PDF/g4133-18%20IPT.pdf (accessed May 23, 2009).
2. "Integrated Project Teams Guide for Use with DOE O 413.3A."
3. Office of Engineering and Construction Management, U.S. Department of Energy, Project Management Practices, Rev E, June 2003, Integrated Project Teams, Office of Management, Budget and Evaluation, http://oecm.energy.gov/admin/Portal/LinkClick.aspx?tabid=358&table=Links&field=ItemID&id=451&link=Integrated ProjectTeams.pdf (accessed May 4, 2009).
4. "Integrated Project Teams Guide for Use with DOE 0413.3.A," pp. 2–3.
5. Office of Engineering and Construction Management, U.S. Department of Energy, Project Management Practices, Rev E, June 2003, Integrated Project Teams, Office of Management, Budget and Evaluation, http://oecm.energy.gov/admin/Portal/LinkClick.aspx?tabid=358&table=Links&field=ItemID&id=451&link=IntegratedProjectTeams.pdf (accessed May 4, 2009).
6. David I. Cleland and Lewis R. Ireland, *Project Management: Strategic Design and Implementation* (New York: McGraw-Hill, 2008), p. 427.
7. Deborah L. Duarte and Nancy Tennant Snyder, "Virtual Team Critical Success Factors," in Eric Verzuh, editor, *The Portable MBA in Project Management* (Hoboken, NJ: John Wiley & Sons, 2003), p. 289.
8. Duarte and Snyder, p. 289.
9. Duarte and Snyder, pp. 289–290.
10. Terrence L. Gargiulo, "The Top Ten Strategies for Managers of Mobile Workers: Surviving and Thriving in the Emerging Mobile Workforce," Makingstories.net. http://www.scribd.com/doc/8958995/THE-TOP-TEN-STRATEGIES-FOR-MANAGERS-OF-MOBILE-WORKERS-Surviving-and-Thriving-in-the-Emerging-Mobile-Workforce (accessed April 24, 2009).
11. J. Davidson Frame, *Project Management Competence* (San Francisco: Jossey-Bass Publishers, 1999), pp. 147–153.
12. "Teamwork," Answers.com, 2009, http://www.answers.com/topic/teamwork (accessed May 3, 2009).
13. Rick A. Morris, *The Everything Project Management Book* (Avon, MA: Avon Media, 2002), p. 83.
14. Thomas J. Neff and James M. Citrin, with Catherine Fredman, *You're in Charge—Now What?* (New York: Crown Business, 2005), p. 81.
15. Personal interviews with Allan Roit, former Director, Project Management Office, Bureau of Indian Affairs, September 15 and October 21, 2008.
16. Personal interview with Lesley Field, Director, Office of Procurement Policy, Office of Management and Budget, October 8, 2008.

17. Bruce W. Tuckman. "Developmental sequence in small groups," *Psychological Bulletin*, 63, 384–399. Reprinted in *Group Facilitation: A Research and Applications Journal,* Number 3, Spring 2001, available at http://dennislearningcenter.osu.edu/references/GROUP%20DEV%20ARTICLE.doc (accessed May 20, 2009).
18. Personal interview with Dr. Ed Hoffman, Director, Academy of Program/Project and Engineering Leadership, NASA, September 10, 2008.
19. Personal interview with Will Brimberry, Program Manager, Project Management Office, Department of the Interior, December 12, 2008.

## Chapter 5
# Leveraging Technology for Project Success: New Tools of the Trade

*Information is the Currency for Democracy.*
—THOMAS JEFFERSON

The federal government is utterly reliant on information technology to execute projects and programs of all shapes and sizes—from deep-sea exploration to GIS satellites and everything in between. Of the $74 billion the government spent on IT in 2009, a relatively small portion was for systems that support managing projects. These project management systems range from simple project scheduling applications to function-specific tools (like risk management) to portfolio management systems to full-fledged enterprise project management information systems. Government agencies rely heavily on these tools and systems throughout all phases of the project lifecycle.

Project management also relies increasingly on a wide range of systems, data feeds, and information channels, all of which contribute to a highly complex environment. From EVM data fields to the data required by E-300, a tremendous amount of source data is needed to adequately address the complexities of a modern project. Today's systems link directly into budgeting, human resources, information security, and other internal sources. And systems must extend beyond the firewall as well.

Federal and vendor-managed systems are more interrelated than ever. For example, the typical contractor EVM system must allow for federal access, reporting, and auditing. Project management systems must account for integrated governance processes, distributed teams, cross-border currency exchanges, and automated risk analysis. The project management software marketplace is as active as it ever has been. Commercial software is integrating more features into systems such as risk management, links to agency budgets, and automated E-300 submission to be responsive to the needs of the federal market.

## INFORMATION TECHNOLOGY IN THE FEDERAL ENVIRONMENT

The federal government is undergoing significant changes in how it plans and deploys technology. In early 2009, President Barack Obama named Vivek Kundra to serve as his chief information officer. Kundra has proven to be a champion of project management and portfolio management tools, investing in government-wide systems and seeking to establish accountability for the government's massive outlay of IT dollars. In speaking about a new Social Security data center, he said:

> What we want to do is look at the entire portfolio to ensure that as we make this investment we're looking at them across the federal government and saying, you know what, if we're investing right now to

## CHAPTER 5  Leveraging Technology for Project Success

build a whole new data center how does that play into the larger vision of federal IT and how does that play into leveraging that investment for other functions beyond the Social Security Administration.[1]

This line of reasoning is pervasive in the federal environment, with agencies seeking to leverage single applications of technology across multiple organizations or functions. The concepts of reuse and scaling of technical platforms to accomplish project objectives are transforming both IT and non-IT projects. Project management systems must similarly scale up to integrate across and beyond project boundaries.

In writing about trends in the federal government, Mark Abramson, Jonathan Breul, and John Kamensky from the IBM Center for the Business of Government recently discussed six trends transforming government.[2] One of those trends involves the availability of governmental services "on demand":

> In terms of responsiveness, government organizations across the world know they have to be much better at sensing and responding to economic, social, technological, and health changes or crises—be they terrorism, mad cow disease, or the processing of drug benefit claims. Those forces, coupled with new technical possibilities, are driving different choices about program design and operations—and their underlying computing infrastructures. These challenges require a deep and potentially difficult transformation: moving from business as usual to what is increasingly being characterized as performing "on demand."[3]

This on-demand feature extends to project technologies as well. Project teams are often scattered across the country, indeed the world. Repositories, project portals, and core reporting systems must be accessible across all time zones, in a secure fashion. Today's government workers are not 9- to 5ers, and neither are the contractors who are employed by the government. The authors went on to note the key characteristics of on-demand government:

> On demand government has four major characteristics. The first is *responsiveness:* Whatever the legislative, organizational, or operational change, governments are able to react quickly to meet present or potential needs. The second is *focus:* As organizational processes are transformed and the roles of key players, including suppliers, are optimized, governments have greater insight into what functions should be done by the government itself or could be done by other institutions, public or private. The third is *variability:* Open, integrated technology infrastructures foster collaboration and the creation of services to meet evolving needs, enabling governments to deliver the right service, at the right place and time, to the right degree. The fourth is *resilience:* Governments can maintain their service levels no matter the impediment or threat. While technology has always supported governmental operations, in on demand it is the prime enabler of resilience.[4]

The evolution in technology is enabling government projects to reach beyond the typical set of stakeholders. Consider this executive example: Less than a month into his term, newly elected President Barack Obama signed into law the American Recovery and Reinvestment Act of 2009 (ARRA), the largest public spending measure ever undertaken by the U.S. government. The law promised to create three to four million new jobs, refurbish our nation's public school facilities, overhaul the transportation infrastructure, make leaps in healthcare recordkeeping, increase college affordability, and develop a renewable energy infrastructure. ARRA promised to deliver funds to state and local governments to spur innovation and economic growth through public works projects. In typical Obama style, the President promised complete transparency of the spending through a new website called "recovery.gov."

With nearly half the funds in the stimulus bill being administered by nonfederal entities,[5] the need for oversight and accountability was clear. Less than a year later, the White House has rolled out a website designed to track ARRA dollars at work across the country. The site provides information from a variety of perspectives: investments, opportunities, tracking and oversight, and impact. In addition, www.data.gov delivers data feeds from a wide variety of government sources in easy-to-navigate formats, fulfilling the promise of the President's open government initiative.

For all its promise of transparency, however, the recovery.gov website still lacks one key element: project data. One blogger commenting on the website had this to say:

> In my view. . . the ability to track projects in real-time and to evaluate their impacts. . .holds both the greatest promise and also the greatest challenge. Releasing official project-level data and providing metrics and tools for analysis (e.g., jobs created per dollar spent) would be a good first step. Open-sourcing this process as much as possible would be even better.
>
> One opportunity is to gather more local intelligence about which projects are positively impacting citizens and the economy and which ones are wasting money. Naturally, these assessments would be more subjective, but not necessarily less reliable than the official data, which we know can be manipulated to hide any signs of poor performance.[6]

## **TECHNOLOGIES IN THE PROJECT ENVIRONMENT**

Every federal agency deploys project management technologies differently. Some have a barebones setup, which may consist of a few licenses of scheduling software, while others maintain enterprise-wide systems. Each level of project management "maturity" exhibits certain characteristics in terms of project management technology.

## Basic Project Management

The "basic" project management environment makes limited use of formal project management processes and tools. Organizations in this category see little value in investing in a tool that their agency may or may not adopt. Microsoft Project continues to be a staple on many federal project managers' desktops. Agencies that have yet to jump into formalized project management will often begin with simple spreadsheets and a scheduling application. Even the low-end scheduling software on the market today can accomplish a lot by incorporating resources, dependencies, effort and duration, and milestones.

Agencies can work successfully within this paradigm to the extent that the scale and scope of the project do not exceed the capabilities of the tool. There is tremendous value in mastering the basics of project scheduling and maintaining simple spreadsheets. Yet the project schedule represents one small slice of the project management pie.

## Intermediate Project Management

The "intermediate" environment describes agencies that have implemented project management methodologies and have established a robust culture of project management. These agencies will either adopt a tool that can be scaled up later or select a tool geared to a specific type of project, such as a scheduling tool that helps them manage large projects. Intermediate-level tools often provide portfolio management capability.

Agencies in this environment would do well to standardize their use of tools. For example, scheduling standards should be implemented to ensure that reporting is based on a similar set of assumptions across the agency. It is also important to create an environment of accountability, which can be fostered by the PMO owning the tool.

### Advanced Project Management

A select few agencies that have embraced project management and its technological underpinnings have adopted project management information systems (PMIS) that incorporate broad and deep project management functionality. For example, one major vendor provides data feeds to and from federal budgeting software, E-300 feeds, and links to human resources, as well as massive amounts of functionality for risk management, portfolio management, and resource management. PMIS solutions tend to be modularized, with major areas addressing contract management, risk, and portfolio management.

Advanced tools require significant investment. Agencies that rely on and use these tools successfully conduct extensive modeling, analysis, and pilot-testing before going live with a real system.

## ASSESSING PROJECT NEEDS

Agencies need to balance their current project management requirements with their aspirations for the next generation of project management in selecting IT tools. Project management should begin with a set of business requirements and processes from which tool use is derived and shaped. The agency's level of project management maturity should guide the acquisition of a new tool.

Projects, like any other major organizational activity, have embedded business functions that drive the need for technology. Project management has four major functions: planning, executing, measuring, and reporting. Two of the functions—planning and executing—are time-phased: Planning happens earlier, executing happens later. (To be clear, this examination is focused on functions, not the phases of a project lifecycle. A function fulfills a basic business need, whereas a project phase is a time-bound set of activities.) The remaining two functions—measuring and reporting—occur across all phases of a project.

Within each function, certain technologies must be used if the function is to be fully realized. Technology's role is to support the execution and scaling of those business functions. Figure 5-1 maps the project management applications or technologies that support each function.

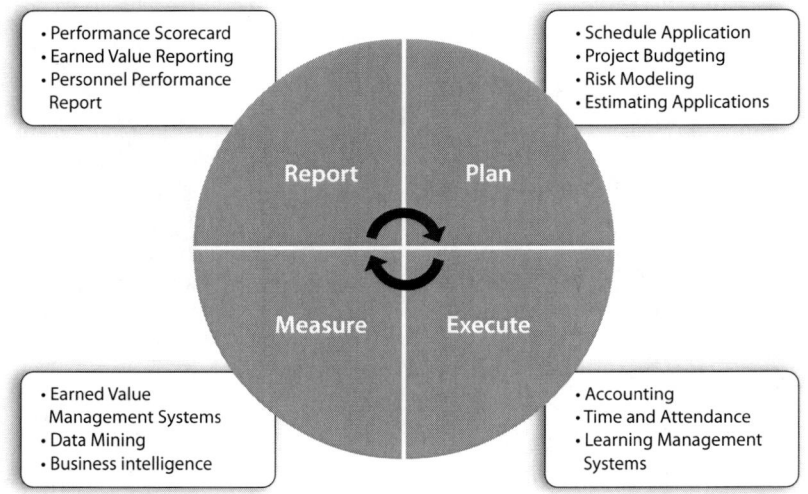

**FIGURE 5-1:** Role of Technology in Supporting Major Project Management Functions

## Planning

In the definition phase of a project, more is unknown than known. Early planning efforts are usually formed through basic word processing. Planning is also supported with scheduling applications, as well as budgeting and risk applications. In engineering and construction-oriented organizations, formal estimating software may be used in the planning stages. Many agencies engage in common preplanning activities, such as developing charters and scope statements. These types of project deliverables often follow templates.

As the work breakdown structure (WBS) is developed, the team needs to understand which tools will support the progression of this information from a WBS into the schedule. Early WBS information may also be incorporated into a solution in the discovery stage. Initial schedules are formed using scheduling software, and budgets are developed in spreadsheets or in agency-approved accounting software.

## Executing

As projects move into execution, more transactional data (including materials use, time and attendance, and inventory tracking) will need to be captured. As execution is the most frenetic project phase, systems should be uploaded and ready to go. Some PMIS systems offer a robust, government-centric application that can track project requirements, schedule, cost, scope, and earned value.

Often, projects require more specialized tools that work in concert with the particular line of business. For example, GSA's Public Buildings Service uses an automated workflow system for its construction project management. This system helps GSA work with its numerous vendors more effectively and efficiently. Contractors can submit plans and revisions directly into the system, reducing paperwork significantly. As project documents are drafted, reviewed, finalized, and released, the system tracks these events and ensures that the documents follow predefined workflows.

## Measuring

Measurement incorporates data gathering, analysis, and evaluation. Performance data (including EVM and non-EVM data such as contract milestones) are processed and displayed against performance baseline data. Typically, the measurement is a processing-intensive effort, and the output is only as good as the data going in. (See Chapter 14, Managing Project Performance, for a more thorough discussion of this concept.)

Systems that measure need to directly access meaningful data, such as time and attendance data, schedule and EVM data, and financial data. On large projects, measurement can involve a staff of IT professionals.

## Reporting

Reporting plays an important part in communicating the status of projects. Projects also play an important part in an agency's reporting. Technology that can deliver fast, accurate reports across large, complex projects is finally coming of age.

The George W. Bush administration used a scorecard approach to report on projects across the entire federal government. These scorecards had limited depth of information but provided a quick reference to the status of various initiatives. Under Obama, the new tool is VUE-IT. Available on the OMB website (www.whitehouse.gov/omb/egov/vue-it/index.html), this tool provides charts and graphs associated with agency spending on projects and programs. The underlying data are provided by project management and accounting systems, such as earned value reporting and budget appropriations.

VUE-IT is a good example of how technology supports the dissemination of project information. Another example is E-300. OMB now

CHAPTER 5  Leveraging Technology for Project Success

requires that all agencies post their E-300s on their websites. While previously preparing an E-300 may have been a paperwork exercise that was limited to a bureaucratic reviews, today's E-300s are free and open to the public, driving new levels of accountability in the reports.

## GOVERNMENT 2.0

Project managers in the federal sector face the same sorts of communication challenges as in the private sector. With so many stakeholders, what are the best methods for disseminating information? Some agencies have begun using Web 2.0 technologies, such as Twitter and Facebook, to manage communications. These technologies provide a central hub through which communications and dialogues are channeled. These tools are searchable, and they can be monitored. Federal agencies are adopting Web 2.0 technologies at a rapid pace.

Government 2.0 is the general term being applied to government efforts to use the web to open up government to the public. According to a May 12, 2008, article in the *Wall Street Journal*:

> You don't need to have a Facebook account, or to have edited a Wikipedia entry, to understand that the Web is in another highly disruptive period. Online tools under the rubric Web 2.0 are changing how information flows, with social networks letting people communicate directly with one another. This is reversing the top-down, one-way approach to communications that began with Gutenberg, challenging everything from how bosses try to manage to how consumers make or break products with instant mass feedback.
>
> The institution that has most resisted new ways of doing things is the biggest one of all: government. This is about to change, with public sector bureaucrats the new targets for web innovators. . . .[7]

This particular article focuses on the "wiki" concept, the idea of putting information out to the general public through the web and asking for public comments. The most widely known example is the website Wikipedia.com, where people can post articles and others can edit those articles. Wikipedia gets bad press for its less-than-perfect accuracy, but the concept is solid. Putting information out to the public can serve to elicit ideas and solutions that might not be available through conventional channels.

The federal government has launched its own wikis, allowing federal employees to post and expand on information until consensus is reached. There is even a wiki called "intellipedia" that allows information sharing, with proper security controls, among the 37,000 employees of various American intelligence agencies. The Department of State sponsors a similar site.

## TECHNOLOGY TRENDS IN PROJECT MANAGEMENT

New software being developed for project management in the federal government includes recordkeeping and access, accounting, website, and document-sharing programs. The project manager need not be an expert in these systems but should have a handle on their basic capabilities. Some of the new tools being developed are driving a new age of project information. A project manager's job involves communication to a large degree. Many new technologies focus not only on getting the information into the tool, but also on making the data accessible to a variety of audiences.

Three examples of new project technologies in the federal environment are:

- *Predictive project management.* Newer project management solutions deliver a predictive project management capability to enhance the task-estimating process. This type of software tracks planned and actual time spent on tasks and uses the data to build estimates. Some vendors build estimates using thousands of data points from all their customers. So when an individual inputs a task called "conduct kickoff meeting," the tool can find other instances of kickoff meetings and estimate the time required.

- *Process-oriented project management.* As methodologies mature, agencies are struggling with how to integrate various lifecycles into one project. New process-oriented tools provide a robust interface that focuses on managing the process and workflow associated with project management.

- *Hosted solutions.* Many project solutions now offer a web interface. These solutions allow project teams to connect from anywhere, enter task information, retrieve reports, and more. In some instances, these solutions can be cheaper than a server-based option; however, security concerns may render a hosted solution infeasible unless it is hosted within the firewall.

Hundreds of project management packages are available in the marketplace today. Agencies should spend the time to gather and evaluate their requirements thoroughly before investing in any one system. Understanding current project management needs and capabilities, as well as the organization's direction, will help agency leadership invest in the right set of tools going forward.

> Recovery.gov and data.gov are emblematic of the government's embracing new ways to reach out to citizens. In projects, similar technologies and approaches are being used to communicate with and manage project stakeholders. Used properly, technology can prove invaluable to government. Technology can make it easier for citizens to participate in government. It can enable them to use the government

services they need efficiently and thereby get fuller value from their tax dollars. A good experience may encourage citizens to become better informed about the working of their government at all levels.

Technology is a tool designed to serve the project manager and project team. The particular circumstances of a project will call for a balance between locating and obtaining appropriate new technologies and making the best use of available technologies. The effectiveness of the selected hardware and software technologies will need to be monitored just as the entire project is monitored. The project manager and team will need to anticipate and make adjustments as necessary.

Particularly useful emerging technologies are recordkeeping and access technologies, which will enable project managers to take advantage of institutional memory, culling lessons learned from past projects and storing them for the future benefit of new project managers. Used appropriately, technology is a tool that will enable government project mangers to better serve the public.

## NOTES

1. Timothy M. O'Brien, "Vivek Kundra: Federal CIO in His Own Words," March 5, 2009, http://radar.oreilly.com/2009/03/vivek-kundra-federal-cio-in-hi.html (accessed March 5, 2009).
2. Mark A. Abramson, Jonathan D. Breul, and John M. Kamensky, "Six Trends Transforming Government" (Washington, DC: IBM Center for the Business of Government, 2006).
3. Abramson, Breul, and Kamensky, p. 17.
4. Abramson, Breul, and Kamensky, p. 17.
5. GAO Report 09-580, "As Initial Implementation Unfolds in States and Localities, Continued Attention to Accountability Issues Is Essential," April 2009.
6. Anthony D. Williams, "Recovery.gov: Off to a Slow Start," www.wikinomics.com (accessed February 20, 2009).
7. "From Wikinomics to Government 2.0," *Wall Street Journal,* May 12, 2008, A13.

## Part 2

# People

The second pillar of project management in the federal government is people. Projects are simply impossible to deliver without effectively managing, motivating, directing, and leading skilled staff. This part focuses on project management practices that engage government personnel and stakeholders in projects and improve the quality of their participation.

In Chapter 6, *The Crucial Role of Communication: Telling the Story*, we go into some depth on the project manager's role and the importance of context in communication, highlighting the successful efforts of various government agencies. This chapter includes models for organizing and executing successful communications throughout a project's lifecycle.

Chapter 7, *Leadership and the Project Manager: Bearing the Brunt of the Storm*, illustrates how today's federal project managers must expand their capabilities to include effective management *and l*eadership. In the context of balancing the different roles of manager and leader, the chapter introduces a variety of roles that successful project managers fulfill during a project and when dealing with various stakeholders.

In Chapter 8, *Engaging Stakeholders: Establishing Effective Project Relationships*, we describe the practical side of this critical project management component. In addition to identifying and seeking to understand stakeholders, this chapter offers examples of how to assess various stakeholders and their impact on a project, as well as how to work effectively with stakeholders in a complex and challenging environment.

Chapter 9, *Project Management Competencies and Skills: Success through Experience*, focuses on critical project management skills for today's federal project managers, with emphasis on communication skills. The chapter also introduces emerging skills that complement core capabilities; we believe these are essential to future project managers in the evolving federal project management environment.

In Chapter 10, *Project Manager Professional Development: Building the Project Management Corps*, we discuss the rise of professional certifications as a differentiator, if not a growing requirement, in the federal project management arena. Industry-based certifications and the recently implemented federal acquisition certification for program and project managers (FAC-P/PM) are highlighted in this chapter.

# Chapter 6
# The Crucial Role of Communication: Telling the Story

> *The speed of communications is wondrous to behold. It is also true that speed can multiply the distribution of information that we know to be untrue.*
>
> —EDWARD R. MORROW

On April 7, 1865, two days before the American Civil War ended, Abraham Lincoln sent a telegram to his commanding general, Ulysses S. Grant. The telegram read, "Gen. Sheridan says 'If the thing is pressed I think that Lee will surrender.' Let the thing be pressed."[1] This is a masterful example of concise communication. Lincoln—upper management—conveyed to his project manager, Grant, exactly what he wanted done. He also conveyed his reason, even though Grant likely knew that Lee and his formerly fearsome army had been forced to flee their Petersburg and Richmond defenses and should be caught. Two days after Grant received Lincoln's message, Lee surrendered.

Project managers are not likely to have their communications studied a century and a half after they are made. Project managers will also not likely be working for the same high stakes that Lincoln and Grant were. However, even seemingly small projects aimed at solving more mundane problems may well serve to prevent major future problems. As Lincoln showed in the entire body of his Civil War communication, "telling the story," or setting the project in context, is an important contributor—perhaps the most important contributor—to project success. This remains true today.

## THE PROJECT MANAGER'S ROLE IN COMMUNICATION

"Ninety percent of a project manager's time is spent communicating" is a common maxim in the project management realm. How can this be? When you think about the complexity of communications in terms of content and channels (or paths), this scenario begins to make sense. PMI's *A Guide to the Project Management Body of Knowledge (PMBOK® Guide)* uses the formula $n(n-1)/2$ to determine the total number of potential channels, where "$n$" represents the number of stakeholders. So if your "small" project has 20 team members, the executive stakeholders number about 5, and 3 project managers from other divisions are interested in your progress, your project has 378 potential communication channels [$28(28-1)/2 = 378$]. The *PMBOK® Guide* suggests, "A key component of planning the project's actual communications, therefore, is to determine and limit who will communicate with whom and who will receive what information."[2]

# CHAPTER 6 The Crucial Role of Communication

Communication is essential to secure buy-in from stakeholders throughout a project's life. The project manager is typically the person responsible for selling the project vision, as well as the methods used to implement that vision. At the start of the project, the federal project manager should establish a communication program that reflects three basic purposes:

1. *Disseminate and receive information.* The foundation of the communication program is a plan for what will be communicated, how, by whom, and to whom. Just as important is what information the project manager or team expects or needs to receive from stakeholders.

2. *Achieve support for the project.* The project manager and team should use the content and context of the messages communicated to build and maintain support for the project and its outcomes. People cannot support what they don't know about.

3. *Comply with federal reporting requirements.* Project managers must be cognizant of reporting requirements internal to their organization, the larger department, or federal policy agencies such as OMB and EPA. Multijurisdictional projects may also require reporting to state and local or even international government authorities.

## SETTING THE CONTEXT

The key to fulfilling the purpose of communication is context. Why is context important? Try to identify the two missing numbers: <u>0</u> <u>7</u> <u>0</u> <u>4</u> <u>1</u> <u>7</u> _ _. Some people immediately try to figure a mathematical solution, while others try to discern a pattern. However, if additional information is provided, for example "American history," it becomes easier to determine that **7** and **6** are the last two numbers, completing the date the Declaration of Independence was signed.

Communication is all about context. The message must be relevant to the circumstance or framework within which it is received. The project leader has to be able to explain the context of the project, how the project fits into organization, agency, or department plans and goals, and how it meets the needs of the stakeholders. The appropriate context means that the message is delivered using the language, vocabulary, or common lexicon of the audience.

For a project with a wide variety of stakeholders, the project manager has the added complexity of communicating in a context that is appropriate for each distinct group. Although the audience and the context may vary, consistency in the message is critical to the credibility of the message and the messenger. Successful communication can be defined as getting the right message to the right people at the right time, using the right delivery methods and the right language.

Ed Hoffman shared a good example of context and how NASA applies a "storytelling" approach[3] to communication within its training and consulting activities. NASA's APPEL supports communication activities within and across projects through a variety of methods, including masters forums, lessons-learned sessions, and other "campfire" events for the NASA project management community. A key objective of these communication activities, particularly in sharing lessons learned, is to shift the focus from specific teams and projects to the "greater good," making the lesson about the practice of project management rather than about an individual's or team's failure. This method enables constructive reflections at the individual, project, and community levels on "How are we doing?" and "Where are we going?"

# CHAPTER 6 The Crucial Role of Communication

As described in Chapter 7, Leadership and the Project Manager, the vision the project manager conveys has to sync with the goals and perspectives of the organization, including all its stakeholders. This vision has to take into account the diversity of missions across the organizations within a federal department, recognizing that the project team will have to work with different teams that have different overall objectives.

Effective communication enables the project manager to maintain support throughout the project, particularly in the (likely) event that things do not go exactly as planned. The two-way aspects of communication give the project leader the information needed to detect and solve problems early, and to recognize and keep doing what is going well. Moreover, continuing open communication helps buy the project manager time to solve problems when they occur.

## COMMUNICATION MATRIX AND PLAN

Communication can be internal or external, with gradients and interconnections (see Figure 6-1). Agency upper management, for example, can be considered either an internal or an external audience. Media is external, while customers might be considered internal or external. Communication can also be formal or informal. For example:

- *Formal external communications:* OMB Exhibit 300 (about as formal as a government report can get), Freedom of Information Act (FOIA) requests, and requests from Congress.

- *Formal internal communications:* Memoranda, budget exhibits, status reports, project presentations, and scope statements.

- *Informal external communications:* Phone calls from citizens or other agencies, e-mail inquiries, and news reports and articles.

- *Informal internal communications:* "Water cooler" meetings, e-mails, and even the project manager's behavior (which sets an example for team members).

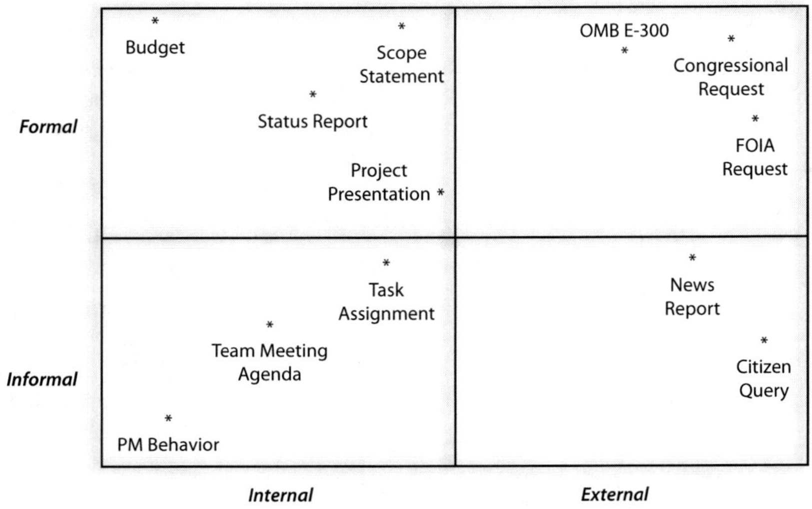

|  | Internal | External |
|---|---|---|
| **Formal** | * Budget　　* Scope Statement<br>* Status Report<br>Project Presentation * | OMB E-300　　* Congressional Request<br>* FOIA Request |
| **Informal** | * Task Assignment<br>* Team Meeting Agenda<br>* PM Behavior | * News Report<br>* Citizen Query |

**FIGURE 6-1:** Types of Communication

For example, a budget is usually a formal internal communication, occasionally shared formally or informally with external recipients. By comparison, Freedom of Information Act (FOIA) requests and citizen queries are always external, with the latter varying in its formality. The relationship among internal/external and informal/formal is important because it indicates the level of effort required to develop, review, and disseminate the message, as well as the message itself and the communication method.

Finally, communication can be verbal or in writing. The most appropriate form of communication (e.g., e-mail, phone call, report) should be chosen for each audience. Even though communication should be tailored to the audience, the project manager should be careful not to deliver an inconsistent message by telling different audiences different things (or different versions of the same thing). Tailoring the context and message for audiences still requires consistency in content and intent.

Knowing the formality, source, and destination of various communications helps project managers allocate time and attention appropriately. Thus, the development and implementation of a formal communication plan is a critical tool. Project managers might create a matrix for each form of communication, including the following key elements:

- *Information need/message.* Description or outline of the specific information (e.g., project status, specific risk, upcoming event) that is the focus of the communication. If feedback is required, describe what information is expected and how it will be gathered.

- *From.* The individuals who will be the source or signatory of the message or information.

- *To.* The stakeholder groups or individuals who will receive the message or information.

- *Delivery method/communication medium.* The communication tool (e.g., e-mail, report, broadcast) or activity (e.g., meeting, demonstration, training) used to deliver the message or information.

- *Frequency/delivery date.* Timing of the contact (e.g., one time, weekly, monthly) and the delivery date.

- *Prepared by.* The person responsible for preparing the message (not necessarily the person named in "From"; this category may also identify the person required to approve the message or information to be disseminated.

The communication plan should be as detailed and specific as possible, including the names of the stakeholders and others responsible for particular areas. Effective communication plans are developed using the results of a thorough stakeholder analysis (described in Chapter 8, Engaging Stakeholders).

No matter the format or the specific content, the key is that a structured, documented plan for project communication will continually pay dividends. A project communication plan will facilitate the engagement of all key stakeholders, actively engage team members, and ensure that important messages are delivered and information is shared.

## A MODEL FOR COMMUNICATION (AND CHANGE) MANAGEMENT

Projects are structured vehicles that introduce change. Whether the change is a new system, a new organization, new processes, or new responsibilities, many inherently fear change. A variety of government organizations, including elements of the Federal Aviation Administration (FAA), have used the ADKAR[4] model for their communication planning. ADKAR was initially designed as a tool to assess whether change management activities like communications and training were having the intended results in an organization.

Table 6-1 shows the primary project manager actions as they relate to the ADKAR phases (shown in bold caps), highlighting the communication emphasis for each phase. A wide variety of communication tools (e.g., e-mails, meetings, presentations, brown-bag lunches, focus groups) can be employed for any of the phases, depending on considerations such as project scope, organizational culture, and the physical location of stakeholders.

| Project Manager's Actions | Communication Emphasis |
|---|---|
| Make those involved or affected **AWARE** of the project's plan and the need for its intended outcomes and impacts. | - Develop effective messages to communicate the compelling business reasons for the project and the expected outcomes.<br>- Ensure that all stakeholders are aware of the project, with an emphasis on "over-communicating" to primary stakeholders.<br>- Consider "branding" the project and establishing regular communication vehicles (e.g., project newsletter, blog, web portal). |
| Build and promote support for the project. Foster a genuine **DESIRE** among the project's team members and customers for the successful completion of the project. | - Focus on communicating the benefits and improvements the project will yield.<br>- Customize messages to relevant individuals, roles, functional or geographic areas, and the organization as a whole. |
| Provide stakeholders with the relevant **KNOWLEDGE** on how to prepare for the project outcomes and to learn what the project will accomplish. | - Communicate to stakeholders their shared responsibility for the success of the project and realization of the project's benefits.<br>- Provide instruction or training to key stakeholders to serve as change agents in their organization for the project. |
| Train, inform, orient, and mentor relevant stakeholders on the skills and **ABILITIES** needed to implement the project outcomes through new skills, behaviors, and processes. | - Describe and model the specific actions and behaviors they will need.<br>- Conduct training and orientation sessions for key stakeholders on the new operational or organizational context that will be established with the successful completion of the project. |
| Establish the processes and structures to sustain and **REINFORCE** the changes resulting from the project. | - Establish communication mechanisms to collect and report feedback on implementation or use of the project's products.<br>- Empower the change agents to serve as front-line eyes and ears to listen for informal information on the results.<br>- Conduct lessons learned to improve the next project and to identify and define the necessary fixes to the project outcomes. |

**TABLE 6-1:** ADKAR Phases

Additional considerations for communication related to the ADKAR model include:

- *Communicating for team member buy-in.* Project leaders cannot just order their team members to do their jobs. Team members will not buy into goals unless they understand the goals. Steve Flannes and Ginger Levin, in their book *Essential People Skills for Project Managers*, recommend not just asking if team members understand, but asking them to restate the goals in their own words.[5] Getting and keeping team members involved provides more meaning to their work and gets them more engaged in the process. When team members know the purpose behind instructions, they are more motivated to carry them out and to take the initiative to make appropriate adjustments in urgent situations when higher management is not available.

- *Communicating by example.* Effective communication requires leaders and project managers to set an example through their actions. A leader has to walk the walk as well as talk the talk, to use a trite but expressive modern cliché. Leaders have to take both explicit and implicit communications into account. Explicit communications are things said, or written, with the intent to communicate a message or information of some sort. "Implicit communications are the subtle, unspoken signals sent by your actions."[6] In one organization, for example, the leadership talked about the importance of project management and they supported the establishment of a PMO. However, their actions demonstrated that this was truly a low priority: The PMO director was not provided any additional project manager resources nor the authority to carry out her responsibility for improving project success in the organization. Leadership's actual lack of support was solidified when, in a subsequent reorganization, the PMO was absorbed by another business unit.

- *Status reporting.* Management experts suggest that project participants talk with customers and stakeholders to ensure their understanding of a project's goals, including the sometimes subtle details of the goals.[7] This conversation should be the start of continuing interactive relationships with various stakeholders. It can even be beneficial when a manager does not have all the answers to stakeholder questions. Getting back to the questioner with the requested information will demonstrate to stakeholders that their concerns are being taken seriously.

Lesley Field, Director of the Office of Federal Procurement Policy at OMB,[8] agrees. Field has her staff provide regular reports to various groups of stakeholders, starting (but not ending) with higher-ups within the particular organization. Preparing the reports requires project managers to keep an eye on potential problems and to receive information on a regular, if not constant, basis.

Since communication is an operational as well as an informational tool, receiving information on project progress will let leaders and managers move to correct minor problems before they become major problems. Regular reports also provide a good opportunity to seek further input from stakeholders. The project manager should ask them not just if they like how things are going, but how things might be improved. This is also the time to look for support networks outside the project team, perhaps those undertaking similar or complementary functions. Effective information channels can only benefit project management.

## THE ROLE OF THE MEDIA

Failed projects apparently make good headlines. Communicating with the media is an issue for any federal project manager who is senior enough to have authority to talk with the media. It is hard to argue against openness. Maintaining good relations with the media, when things are going well and even when they are not, buys the benefit of the doubt. This approach may secure the project manager time to correct problems if things do go wrong. News reports of problems, legal or otherwise, are bad enough. But when they end with "refused to comment," whatever the reality, it looks like the project manager is trying to hide something. All too often, managers and leaders, including elected political leaders, have in fact been trying to hide something.

Management and leadership experts Thomas Neff and James Citrin summarize the case for having good and open relations with the media.

> If you have damaging information it is imperative to get it out and communicate it immediately...especially during difficult times. After all, when you talk to the press, you have the opportunity to tell your story. You can use the occasion to try to have them share your perspective. If you are in a leadership position in a visible company [or the federal government], especially in a time of crisis, stories will be written regardless of what you do. Reporters have a job to do, and they will do it whether you like it or not. Treating them forthrightly, consistently, and with facts is considered best practice in crisis situations.[9]

How to deal with the media should be planned at the start of the project and consistently implemented during the project. At the outset, project managers should consider the potential media interest in their project. If the project has high visibility and may garner press attention, project managers should work with department executives, the media office, and legal counsel to determine an appropriate approach. The results of discussions (e.g., plans for press releases, interviews, town hall meetings) with the internal players should be integrated into the project communication plan.

## INFORMATION ACCESS AND SECURITY

Federal officials have two additional factors to consider in dealing with the flow of information: access and security. First, the Freedom of Information Act (enacted in 1966) requires that certain materials be made public. In 1996 the act was amended to facilitate "public access to information in an electronic format."[10] As a practical matter, project managers should be aware of their organization's policies and procedures associated with FOIA requests. In most situations, the office responsible for the department's FOIA process will inform the project manager when a request warrants action. Project managers should also consider the potential for future FOIA requests when determining the type of information and the method for archiving it once the project is complete.

Second, national security concerns require that certain materials not be made public. In consultation with upper management (possibly including the FOIA, security, legal, and inspector general offices), the project manager will to have to decide what information, if any, needs to remain confidential throughout the project, what information will need to remain confidential during certain phases of the project but can later be released, and what information should be totally open. Confidential or "classified" information may include private information about citizens (e.g., social security numbers, tax data) as well as national security information. Every federal agency is staffed with experts who are fully knowledgeable about information security and classification; the project manager should call on their expertise in establishing appropriate and legally compliant information security policies and procedures for the project.

> Effective communication can save a troubled project while poor communication can threaten a project that is on the path to success. Successful federal project managers will find that a significant portion of their job requires them to communicate—to executives, team members, the interested public, probing media, and even a concerned Congress. Increased access to information, both accurate and inaccurate, will only increase the pressure on project managers to keep the information flowing both to and from the project's stakeholders. Employing technology will address part of the challenge, specifically methods, timing, and frequency. But at the end of the day, the project manager must have a sound communication plan, an effective approach to developing messages, a clear process for obtaining feedback, and a deep understanding of the project's context from the stakeholders' perspectives.
>
> Neff and Citrin provide a concise summary of ten guidelines that a project manager should follow to communicate effectively:[11]
>
> 1. Know your audiences so you can tailor your message and your style to their readiness and to what *they* care about.
>
> 2. Tell stories to establish an emotional connection to your point.
>
> 3. Make sure communication is two-way. Effective communication is more than promulgating a message; it is a continuous give and take in which ideas are explored, assimilated, and adapted before being locked in.
>
> 4. Use and reuse your communication in various forums and formats both to reinforce your message and to leverage your time.
>
> 5. Make sure the message fits the context. Communicating is intimately intertwined with organizational culture; adapting an organization's language and shorthand—or introducing a new and agreed-upon language—will help transform that culture.

6. Know the communication settings that you are most comfortable in—be it stirring a large crowd to action or working in small groups—and play to your natural strengths.

7. In a crisis, get the information out as quickly as possible. Acknowledge the challenges of the situation to establish credibility, and then act as a "shock absorber" between the uncertainty of the situation and employees' deep-seated desire for stability.

8. Be conscious of the signals you are sending, whether the message is delivered verbally, in writing, in a video, or through nonverbal or nonvisual methods.

9. Allow people to see you listening and assimilating their information. Having all the answers is usually the wrong approach. If you don't pause to ask questions and circle back when you have more data, you will lose credibility, trust, and the audience.

10. Get direct input from the field; while this requires making a significant time investment, it will pay back many times in enhanced credibility, trust, and stakeholder investment.

Even the best project managers rarely are able to implement every one of these communication elements. The good news is that communication success can be achieved by effectively executing just a few. Project managers can apply their past experiences and their insights into their current project to determine the appropriate mix and emphasis of their communications.

## NOTES

1. Abraham Lincoln to Ulysses S. Grant, April 7, 1865, *The Literary Works of Abraham Lincoln*, selected, with an introduction by Carl van Doren and with illustrations by John Steuart Curry (NewYork: The Heritage Press, 1942), p. 276.
2. Project Management Institute, *A Guide to the Project Management Body of Knowledge—Fourth Edition* (Newtown Square, PA: Project Management Institute, 2008), p. 253.
3. Personal interview with Dr. Ed Hoffman, Director, Academy of Program/Project and Engineering Leadership, NASA, September 10, 2008.

4. Adapted from Jeffrey M. Hiatt, *ADKAR: A Model for Change in Business, Government, and Our Community* (Loveland, Colorado: Prosci, 2006).
5. Steven W. Flannes and Ginger Levin, *Essential People Skills for Project Managers* (Vienna, VA: Management Concepts, 2005), p. 26.
6. Thomas J. Neff and James M. Citrin, with Catherine Fredman, *You're in Charge—Now What?* (New York: Crown Business, 2005), p. 222. © 2005 by Esaress Holding, Ltd. Used by permission of Crown Business, a division of Random House, Inc.
7. Flannes and Levin, p. 26.
8. Personal interview with Lesley Field, Director, Office of Procurement Policy, Office of Management and Budget, October 8, 2008.
9. Neff and Citrin, p. 221.
10. General Services Administration, *Your Right to Federal Records: Questions and Answers on the Freedom of Information Act and Privacy Act*, May 2006, p. i.
11. Neff and Citrin, pp. 230–231.

# Chapter 7

# Leadership and the Project Manager: Bearing the Brunt of the Storm

> *I believe the techniques and principles that work are timeless. It's all about collaborating with people, building trust and confidence, and making sure you take care of the followers. You also need to give them what they need to do their work well, solve problems, face reality, create opportunities and monitor risks.*
>
> —GENERAL COLIN POWELL (U.S. ARMY RETIRED)[1]

The harsh and cynical view, regretfully often fact-based, is that the difference between leadership and management is that leaders motivate people to follow while managers force people to follow. A somewhat less harsh statement is that "Good managers do things right. Good leadership does the right thing."[2] As well as being cynical, for good leaders and managers, this view is oversimplified. A team needs both leaders and managers, and they can—even should—be the same people.

People running organizations, from the small work team assigned a task to the entire U.S. government, need to act as both leaders and managers, with strong elements of facilitator and mentor thrown into the mix. These are all different roles, but they are compatible and complementary—and all essential. Today's federal project managers must expand their focus to include both leadership and management elements[3] (see Figure 7-1).

| Management Focus | Leadership Focus |
|---|---|
| Goals and Objectives | Vision |
| Telling how and when | Selling what and why |
| Shorter range | Longer range |
| Organization and structure | People |
| Autocracy | Democracy |
| Restraining | Enabling |
| Maintaining | Developing |
| Conforming | Challenging |
| Imitating | Originating |
| Administering | Innovating |
| Directing and controlling | Inspiring trust |
| Procedures | Policy |
| Consistency | Flexibility |
| Risk-avoidance | Risk-opportunity |
| Bottom line | Top line |

**FIGURE 7-1:** Project Management vs. Leadership

Leaders on projects are known by many names, commonly project or executive sponsor and project director. More important than their title, however, is their role. In federal projects, the role of leadership often transcends titles, falling to individuals with longevity, experience, or specific expertise. A critical attribute on any project, leadership cuts to the heart of project success in the federal sector. Consider the term *federal project leadership*. Each word suggests a universe of experience, know-how, and education. Combined, these three words suggest a challenging, complex work environment.

Leadership is often distributed across large projects, forming pockets and divisions within stakeholder groups. Some leaders in the federal environment come equipped with budgets; others arrive with nothing more than a vision. Regardless, it is critical to establish and cement leadership early on in a project setting.[4]

## LEADERSHIP IN A PROJECT CONTEXT

The role of leadership can be described as creating, conceptualizing, and articulating a vision, which is sometimes described as the "why" of the project. The scope of that vision will vary according to the project, its tasks, and the nature of the group involved. The project manager will likely have been given an overall goal, and perhaps some parameters regarding methodology. He or she may have had input into creation of the overall vision.

As the de facto project leader, the project manager will not just run the project but will represent the project to stakeholders outside the organization, to other levels within the organization, and to the team members. The project vision has to sync with the goals and perspectives of the organization, including employees, and the stakeholders. Developing and promoting a vision must take into account the diversity of missions within federal departments and recognize that team members' "day jobs" may have different (even conflicting) objectives from those of the project.

The project manager is the primary person responsible for "selling" the project's vision—the necessary first step to getting stakeholders and team members to buy into the need for the project. This common analogy to sales takes on a literal meaning to some of the stakeholders of government projects, particularly taxpayers, whose money is funding the project. In the current economy and for the foreseeable future, taxpayers are likely to demand increased assurance that they are getting their money's worth.

Project leaders cannot just instruct their team members to do their jobs. Team members simply will not buy into goals unless they understand those goals. To ensure their understanding, Steven Flannes and Ginger Levin, in their book *Essential People Skills for Project Managers*, recommend not just asking if team members understand, but asking them to restate the goals in their own words.[5]

Getting and keeping team members involved provides more meaning to their work and gets them more engaged in the process. Unlike in the days of what might be called command management, when team members know and actively support the team's goals, they are not only more motivated to do their jobs but are also better equipped to do them. For example, when team members know the purpose behind instructions, they are better able to carry them out and are more likely to take the initiative to adjust those instructions appropriately when higher management is not available. This is a continuous process, with the team leader needing to constantly look after the team members as well as stakeholders.

Tending to team members' and stakeholders' needs is one way a project manager can demonstrate leadership. The team leader, in essence, has to be the lightning rod for the team—taking the heat for team members. Situations that require leadership action can include:

- Resolving conflicts among team members or between project stakeholders fairly and professionally

- Running political interference for team members, freeing them from bureaucratic constraints and thereby enabling them to do their jobs effectively

- Raising and promoting concerns raised by team members and stakeholders to the project sponsor or the organization's executives

- Actively fighting the inevitable resource battles, showing your team that you're willing to go to the mat to secure the personnel or material the project needs to be successful.

Leaders must set an example by their own actions, demonstrating behavior consistent with statements and policies they expect others to follow. A leader has to walk the walk as well as talk the talk. And just as leadership includes being a mentor to team members, the leader should find a mentor to provide an outside and objective view (see Chapter 9, Project Management Competencies and Skills, for more on mentoring).

## **BALANCING LEADERSHIP AND MANAGEMENT**

In a government project setting, where dotted lines of responsibility prevail and roles are often unclear, the project manager must strike a balance between leadership and management. In this context, leadership means creating and adjusting the vision and management means executing projects and carrying out daily operations to achieve the vision. In an organization, executives are responsible for strategic, vision-oriented action; project managers lead teams to deliver projects and operational managers lead personnel to deliver services. In the project context, the project manager must perform both leadership and management tasks to be successful. The federal government is seeing an increase in the emphasis on the project manager as leader as well as a need to improve or expand the project manager's skills and capabilities.

According to Vijay Verma and Max Wideman in their paper, "Leader vs. Manager":

> The old image of a powerful project personality with a burning vision of the future state rounding up the troops and charging off to Nirvana, is hardly consistent with modern management thinking. Consequently, some of the current concepts of leadership and attributes required of the leader of an enterprise need to be carefully rethought when applied in the project context.[6]

In the current federal environment, the project manager must shift from the hierarchical, leader-follower model to leading the team to achieve goals by applying a mix of leadership and management skills: collaboration, negotiation, and decisiveness. Jerry Harper, former director of a Department of Commerce PMO, highlights the intersection of leadership and management in relation to project managers dealings with executives; he expresses this intersection as "courage." Harper's specific example is the responsibility of project managers to address cuts to project budgets. He asserts that project managers must employ key management skills to explain, honestly and directly, to executives that if resources are limited, the project's original goals will not be met and the organization's mission may not be fulfilled. Management without vision, and vision without management, are equally useless.[7]

But vision and management skills are not enough; project managers also need to serve in the roles of facilitator and mentor to their teams, as well as change leaders in their organizations.

## Facilitator

Perhaps to a surprising extent, leadership skills in the federal government focus on building consensus and creating pockets of support. Eliciting project support demands that project leaders step in front of stakeholders and facilitate the process.

Facilitating is an important project management skill. In this role, the leader/manager does what is needed to enable team members to act with skill, confidence, and efficiency for the sake of the project, the organization, and themselves. The facilitator both models and creates methods for ending conflict within the team and between the team and stakeholders. He or she also works to secure needed project resources. (See Chapter 9, Project Management Competencies and Skills, for more details on facilitation.) To carry out these facilitation functions, the manager must to be able to communicate, in writing and verbally, with clarity and efficiency. (See Chapter 6, The Crucial Role of Communication.)

## Mentor

As a mentor, the team leader models appropriate organizational and professional behavior for team members. He or she helps team members identify possibilities for problem solving and career path development. As a mentor, the team leader should display genuine personal interest in each team member's performance and development. From a practical perspective, projects serve as an excellent proving ground for leadership and an effective opportunity to develop an organization's next generation of leaders. (The project manager's role in mentoring and training is discussed further in Chapter 9.)

## Change Leader

Projects are about change, yielding a new or improved process, service, or product. Project managers in the federal government must be prepared to accept the additional mantle of change leader. John Kotter, in his book *A Force for Change*, describes key characteristics across the spectrum of management to leadership.[8]

- *Resource linker.* Coordinates the right people, in the right place, at the right time; identifies and uses resources (including logistics, workflow, and facilities); prepares and anticipates needs; networks and shares information and resources across organizational units; facilitates wider and more substantive stakeholder participation in the project.

- *Problem solver.* Listens actively to all; contributes to problem resolution; shares lessons learned within and across organizational units; mediates and resolves conflicts; communicates; facilitates; educates and coaches colleagues and team members.

- *Process helper.* Keeps project and change moving forward, removing obstacles and promoting the project and its anticipated results; provides real-time support for colleagues; answers process/technical questions; coaches; monitors and views progress of others; looks for opportunities to continuously improve project and process.

- *Catalyst.* Makes things happen; identifies problems, fears, and resistance; initiates corrective action; instills urgency and personal ownership among team members and stakeholders; motivates others to step up and succeed.

- *Leader.* Provides vision and direction; shows personal commitment; communicates consistent, clear, and frequent messages; leads by example; models behavior; focuses on stakeholders' needs; has a positive and unifying influence on others.

## CHARACTERISTICS AND TRAITS OF PROJECT LEADERS

"Safety first has been the motto of the human race for half a million years; but it has never been the motto of leaders. A leader must face danger. He must take the risk and the blame, and the brunt of the storm." This quote from Herbert Casson, an author and writer on topics including management in the early 20$^{th}$ century, suggests that bravery is an important element of leadership. To be effective in their roles as facilitator, mentor, and change leader, project managers must exhibit certain key characteristics and traits. These include understanding (and demonstrating) the difference between authority and responsibility, displaying confidence, and recognizing and facing reality.

### Authority vs. Responsibility

Authority and responsibility are related, but they are not the same. Authority means having the power to get a task done whereas responsibility means having to accomplish a goal. Authority and responsibility are also related to the ability to get a task done. Authority without responsibility is useless. Responsibility without authority is equally useless, and far more frustrating.

Responsibility has another meaning. A project manager can assign an aspect of a project to a team member, giving that person authority to get the job done. The team member is then responsible to the project manager for getting the job done. "If you put someone in charge of a particular aspect of a project. . .that person is responsible to you. . . .Because you are in charge, you cannot blame your team members for things that go wrong."[9] The person doing the delegating remains responsible to his or her bosses for accomplishing the assigned task.

The project manager can delegate what might be called functional responsibility, but not ultimate responsibility. The leader/manager's role as facilitator involves obtaining the proper resources to enable the project staff to do their jobs. Appropriate authority to do the job is one of those resources. Any limits on authority, including spending, can affect the team member's ability to carry out the project. Subordinate task managers cannot be blamed if these limits hamper task success.

## Confidence

Management coach and writer D. A. Benton has an interesting chapter title in her book *CEO Material: How to be a Leader in Any Organization*: "You Feel Broadly Adequate."[10] Her point is that a leader needs to demonstrate confidence in his or her ability to do the job, regardless of how the leader might actually feel. Benton offers some ways a leader can look at the record and find reasons to be confident. "Confidence is the driver behind everything. . . .People are drawn to you; they want to be around you, do like you, learn from you, and be highly thought of by you. People are happy to follow you because you are more fun to be around."[11]

Confidence also signals the leader's conviction that the job can and should be done. One way a leader expresses confidence is by enlisting others with skills in which the leader might not be as strong. For example, ideally the leader should also be a manager. But a realistic leader will have assessed, both formally and informally, his or her abilities and perhaps found less skill in, say, administration. An effective and confident leader will then select a number two person for the project who is a good administrator.

### Recognizing and Facing Reality

Referring to the people running projects as the "leader" or the "manager" is just convenient shorthand. The person running the project should actually be called the "leader/manager/facilitator/mentor." The leader has to be all four at once, calling up whatever skills are needed for the particular situation. As General Colin Powell noted, this ability starts with knowing and facing reality.

Some of the basic leadership functions, in particular regular interaction with stakeholders and staff members, can give the leader a crucial heads up in determining and recognizing reality—and any changes in reality. For example, facing reality may require a project manager to take the unpopular, but necessary step of informing executives that the project will be delayed or will exceed the budget. Particularly when the facts are uncomfortable or bad, facing reality is a prominent trait of leaders.

## THE ROLE OF LEADERSHIP

Leaders have to manage as much as managers have to lead. Successful management on the part of leaders (e.g., executives and sponsors in the project context) is seen in their willingness and ability to participate in relevant project management activities, remove barriers (e.g., organizational, political, resource), and support the development of their project managers.

Dr. Ed Hoffman, Director of NASA's APPEL, offers advice on "how to get project management right."[12] He suggests that project managers, sponsors, and the organization's leaders ask themselves the following questions:

- Are we addressing project management from the perspective of leadership and the organization?
- What is the strategy, and what are the priorities resulting from the strategy, for the agency?
- Does the agency have a policy or strategy for selecting, starting, stopping, executing, and managing projects or programs?
- Does the executive level of the agency "get it"—understand what is needed to be an effective project manager?
- Has management established a direct line from strategy to policy to projects and programs?
- Do the executives want to build project management capabilities and competencies or do they regard project management solely as necessary to satisfy an external requirement?

Hoffman believes that "Government must shift their mindset to the 'project age' in support of customers." He sees this shift in varying degrees of maturity on project management across the federal government. He further suggests that the increasing complexity of projects demands greater emphasis on leadership (see Figure 7-2). We would add to Hoffman's advice that the executives demonstrate their understanding of effective project management by providing training, staffing, and material support to project managers.

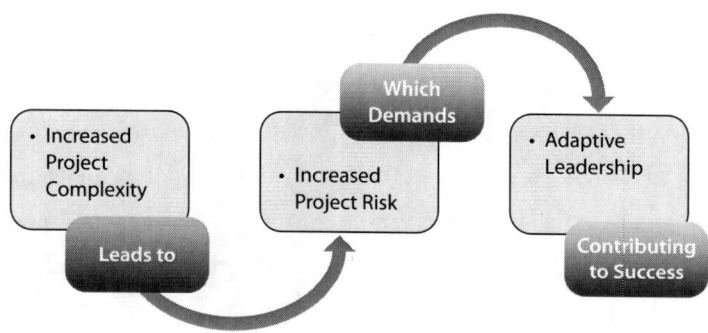

**FIGURE 7-2:** Relationship between Project Complexity and Leadership

In a 2008 study of corporate culture, psychiatrist and management consultant Judith Bardwick provided an incisive and valuable summary of the most effective form of leadership/management for the future, in both the private and public sectors:

> The ideal style of leadership for today's organizations involves inclusion, greater personal responsibility, a greater sense of belonging, team collaboration, coaching and mentoring, and listening seriously to others' ideas because their knowledge and experience can enable them to make important and unique contributions. . . .Employees need "yes" answers from executives, leaders, and project managers, notably their boss, to each and every one of the following questions: Do you need me? Do you recognize me? Will you reward me? Will you invest in me? Will you support me? Do you expect more from me? When all the answers are affirmative, the response of people at all levels is "count me in!"[13]

## LEADING AND MANAGING PROJECTS IN THE FEDERAL GOVERNMENT

Project managers in the federal government face all the demands and realities that project managers in the private sector face, including (especially in the current economic environment) responsibility for the bottom line: delivering projects on budget and on time. The 2009 American Recovery and Reinvestment Act (ARRA) raised the bar on both leadership and management by federal government project managers. The ARRA funds allocated to projects come with requirements for new or expanded management controls and increased reporting, requiring project managers to demonstrate that their projects are returning value for the money spent. This is a clear, current example of the demand on federal project managers to lead as well as manage. Project managers must give their subordinates the resources needed to carry out assigned tasks, along with the authority (with any limits clearly stated) to do their jobs.

Federal government project managers face at least one more challenge than project managers in the private sector do. They have a far larger number of outside stakeholders: the entire tax-paying population of the United States. The federal government does not just have to work effectively and efficiently, but it also has to be perceived as working effectively and efficiently. In his foreword to a new book on government human resources management, former Chairman of the Federal Reserve Board Paul Volcker writes, "The stakes in terms of government that can command the trust and confidence of the American people has never been higher. Success in meeting that challenge has to start with the people who make up the public service today and tomorrow."[14] Trust in the government's ability, dedication, and honesty is nothing short of critical in today's environment.

**CHAPTER 7** Leadership and the Project Manager

The general state of project management in the federal government, as with any other large organization, is mixed. The government is developing a crop of generally first-rate project managers, through recruitment as well as internal training programs. According to an April 2009 analysis by Michael O'Brochta, a former project manager and contracting officer's technical representative (COTR) at the Central Intelligence Agency:

> These project managers are much more knowledgeable about best practices and much more knowledgeable about the kind of supportive work environment they need to achieve success. These project managers are quite capable of identifying the executive actions they need to achieve success.[15]

Upper management within the federal government, regretfully, does not always keep up with the "state of the art" in project management. O'Brochta continues:

> Unfortunately, it seems that a majority of organizations still don't get it. According to the December 2008 "Improving Government Performance and Delivery" report by the Council for Excellence in Government in cooperation with the Office of Management and Budget, approximately 80% of the Federal program managers surveyed reported that they receive little support from their executives.[16]

A good example of project management in the federal government is the Department of the Interior's Bureau of Indian Affairs (BIA).[17] Allan Roit, former director of the Indian Affairs PMO, which handles IT and construction, says that project development within his office is designed to be flexible, involving careful monitoring of project progress and regular interaction with staff and stakeholders. BIA's system allows for flexible adjustment to changing circumstances. Two key lessons that BIA's PMO has learned from experience are:

- *Leadership and upper management support are key to project success.* Leadership at BIA, and the overall Department of the Interior, supports program and project management and managers. They provide alignment and structure throughout projects by formulating visions and setting goals and objectives to reflect these visions.
- *The result of this leadership and support is loyalty.* Project managers are loyal to the project and the organization, and leaders are loyal to their projects and programs.

One final example of the pinnacle of leadership and management is the Department of Energy's Office of Environmental Management (OEM). Despite winning PMI's coveted "Project of the Year" award two years in a row (in 2006 and 2007), Jim Rispoli, the former Assistant Secretary of Energy for OEM, explains that DOE/OEM is "not a success story as much as an example of an organization that has succeeded."[18] In our interview with Secretary Rispoli, he pointed out that the efforts he led at Energy to go from an underperforming organization (less than 50 percent of projects on time and budget) to one winning awards for project management efforts (90 percent on time and budget) required effective management *combined with* bold leadership to achieve success.

> The challenge for federal project managers starts with the continuously evolving view of the role of the federal government, along a spectrum from "the source of all problems" to "the solution to all problems." In reaction to the major financial crisis that began in 2008, the idea of a federal government actively involved in monitoring the private sector has gained far more support than it had just a few years ago. The public is demanding not just that the government do more—this pendulum will likely swing back—but that it do what it does better. This is not likely to change.

**CHAPTER 7** Leadership and the Project Manager

A second issue within the government is that there are really two types of government employees, career civil servants and political appointees. The former are likely to be in government until retirement. The latter are in government, for the most, just during the time in office of the current administration. The civil servants are the repository of institutional memory. Political appointees tend to see themselves as agents of change.

In addition to exercising good management and leadership, political appointees can ameliorate this natural tension by recognizing and crediting the institutional memory and experience of career civil servants, rather than regarding them as hidebound bureaucrats. Reciprocally, career federal employees should regard, and judge, political appointees as agents of refreshing change rather than as political hacks seeking change for the sake of change.

## NOTES

1. "Lessons in Leadership," *PM Network*, vol. 22, issue 6, August 2008 (interview with Colin Powell), p. 61.
2. Vijay K. Verma and R. Max Wideman, "Project Manager to Project Leader? and the Rocky Road Between…" rev. 3 (06-11-02), presented at PMI's 25th Annual Seminar and Symposium, Vancouver, BC, Canada, October 17, 1994.
3. Verma and Wideman.
4. Verma and Wideman.
5. Steven Flannes and Ginger Levin, *Essential People Skills for Project Managers* (Vienna, VA: Management Concepts, 2005), p. 26.
6. Verma and Wideman.
7. Personal interview with Jerry Harper, program manager, U.S. Department of Commerce, September 15, 2008.
8. John Kotter, *A Force for Change* (New York: The Free Press, 1990), pp. 79–88.
9. Rick A. Morris, *The Everything Project Management Book* (Avon, MA: Avon Media), 2002, p. 97.
10. D.A. Benton, *CEO Material: How to Be a Leader in Any Organization* (New York: McGraw Hill, 2009), pp. 69–78.
11. Benton, p. 69.
12. Personal interview with Dr. Ed Hoffman, Director, Academy of Program, Project, and Engineering Leadership, NASA, September 10, 2008.
13. Judith M. Bardwick, Ph.D., *One Foot Out the Door* (New York: AMACOM, 2008), p. 89.
14. Hannah S. Sistare, Myra Howze Shiplett, and Terry F. Buss, *Innovations in Human Resource Management* (Armonk, NY: M.E. Sharpe), 2008, pp. ix–x.

15. Michael O'Brochta, PMP, "Federal Project Manager Momentum," *PM World Today*, April 2009, volume XI, issue IV, http://www.pmforum.org/viewpoints/2009/PDFs/apr/Federal-PM-Momentum.pdf (accessed October 27, 2009).
16. O'Brochta.
17. Personal interviews with Allan Roit, former Director, Project Management Office, Bureau of Indian Affairs, September 15 and October 21, 2008.
18. Personal interviews with James Rispoli, Assistant Secretary, Office of Environmental Management, U.S. Department of Energy, October 3 and October 20, 2008.

## Chapter 8
# Engaging Stakeholders: Establishing Effective Project Relationships

> *... I have found no greater satisfaction than achieving success through honest dealing and strict adherence to the view that, for you to gain, those you deal with should gain as well.*
> —ALAN GREENSPAN, FORMER CHAIRMAN OF THE FEDERAL RESERVE[1]

The Office of the Chief Architect at GSA's Public Buildings Service (PBS) is a busy place. With such mandates as improving border security checkpoint structures, creating innovative new workspaces, and retrofitting government buildings to increase energy efficiency, there is no shortage of work to do. Whether constructing new buildings or refurbishing existing structures, PBS interacts with a wide range of stakeholders across a complicated mix of regulations, laws, industry standards, historical precedents, and other constraints. PBS project managers must deliver construction projects on time and on budget, and often in the face of conflicting demands from stakeholders. With each new project comes a new set of local, regional, and federal partners that must support the project, at least nominally.

PBS's challenge of addressing stakeholder needs while conforming to all the requirements of the project is commonplace among government agencies. Consequently, PBS, like other agencies, is seeking innovative new tools and methods for accessing and influencing stakeholders.

In the 21$^{st}$ century world of work, the term *stakeholder management* is almost an oxymoron. In so many situations, stakeholders try to manage the managers. Stakeholders maintain a distinct advantage, with up-to-the-second communications, extensive media outlets, and instant links to diverse constituencies through collaborative websites. Information simply flows too fast for any project team to be able to control or even manage it. In most cases, the best a project manager can hope to do is stay abreast of the information and try to shape it toward a successful project conclusion. Nevertheless, project managers are often asked to do more than just keep up with the information.

Understanding the power, influence, and importance of the project's relationships with various stakeholders is key to obtaining and maintaining support, buy-in, and participation. In short, vigorous stakeholder management is critical to the success of a project.

## WHO ARE THE STAKEHOLDERS IN FEDERAL PROJECTS?

Federal projects bring together diverse constituencies and powerful people. For federal project managers, getting stakeholders to believe in the project is a key, and challenging, success factor. The best project managers have a story to tell; for their project to be successful, stakeholders need to believe that story. For the U.S. Census Bureau, for example,

CHAPTER 8 Engaging Stakeholders

the story is about an informed citizenry. But the story could be about defending the nation from attack, cleaning up nuclear waste, or putting a space station into orbit. Federal projects serve the national interest, and stakeholder management should originate from that connection.

Project managers must view stakeholder management as more than just a set of tasks to be accomplished, but rather as a channel for promoting the project. Stakeholders should understand why a project is important. They also need to understand the rationale behind the project approach and methodology.

Internally, stakeholders include the project manager, customer, project team members, and sponsor, as well as the organization carrying out the project. In many projects, the most significant (and immediate) stakeholders are the relevant senior leaders in the organization. The level at which the project is performed (e.g., department-wide or within a subordinate agency), as well as the project manager's chain of command, determines who the project's executive stakeholders are. Project managers should not forget that the agency's Inspector General might be an important stakeholder as well.

Stakeholder groups on federal projects include a wide range of constituents, from federal employees to local governments to industry groups (see Figure 8-1):

- *Congress.* As the ultimate stakeholder, Congress, through committees and oversight activities, has the power to fund, continue, increase, modify, or eliminate most federal government projects. A single large project may fall under the purview of one or several congressional committees. Congressman Elijah Cummings (7th District, Maryland) is a senior member of the House Committee on Oversight and Government Reform, the main investigative committee in the U.S. House of Representatives. He identifies a "lack of oversight" as a consistent theme across the projects and programs that have come before his committee. Increased oversight by Congress and executive branch agencies is a likely outcome of dramatic and public failures of government projects.

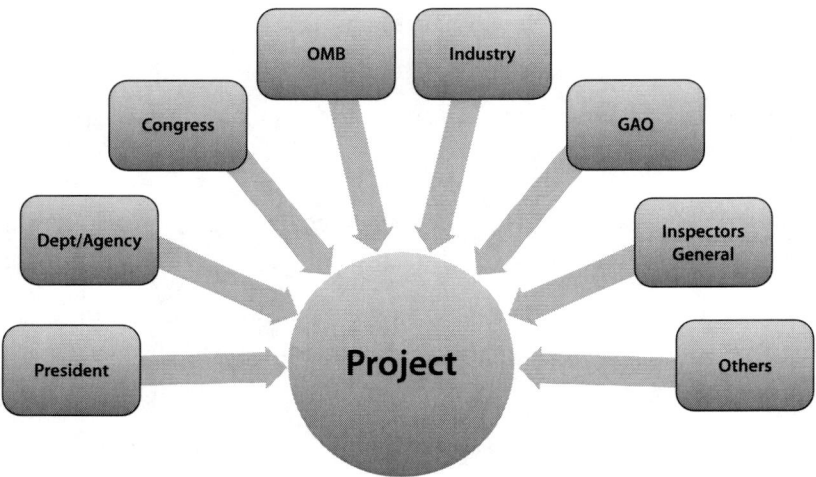

**FIGURE 8-1:** Federal Project Stakeholders

The message for federal project managers is to be aware of stakeholders' interests and power to affect the project and to actively engage stakeholders throughout the project. One stark (and infamous) example Cummings provided was the Federal Emergency Management Agency (FEMA) response in the aftermath of Hurricane Katrina regarding trailers for people displaced by the destruction. A lack of oversight and a "culture of mediocrity" led to the delivery of trailers that were poorly constructed and had toxic components that sickened the people who lived in them. Besides the human toll, as Congressman Cummings put it bluntly, "Mediocrity is expensive!"[2]

**CHAPTER 8** Engaging Stakeholders

- *The President and agency leaders.* Elected and appointed leaders often bring with them a specific agenda and have limited windows of opportunity for introducing change. If elected and appointed leaders fail to achieve the necessary buy-in and cooperation from civil servants, they may find that a project is implemented to its minimum requirements and is not "owned" by the stakeholders. Civil servants, on the other hand, provide continuity across administrations, legislative cycles, and priorities. Civil servant leaders have the power to resist change, knowing that time is on their side for any given mandate. This inherent difference in perspective between appointed leaders and civil servants could become either a strong catalyst for effective project management or a war of wills.

- *Office of Management and Budget.* OMB plays a leadership role in defining the priorities, policies, and direction of the executive branch. A variety of OMB's policies are directly related to the practice of project management in the federal government. As an interested stakeholder, OMB gains insight into major projects through E-300. Further, FAC-P/PM is the training framework OMB has established in its effort to improve project management in the federal government.

- *Government Accountability Office.* GAO is the investigative arm of Congress. Every two years since 1990, GAO has reported on high-risk areas to bring attention to opportunities for improving government performance. The "high risk" GAO identifies is commonly related to "vulnerabilities to fraud, waste, abuse, and mismanagement." Through GAO's work, a deep well of lessons learned has emerged, uncovering both the failures and successes of projects and programs across the federal government. Like OMB, GAO is an interested party in project performance. Projects executed by organizations on the high-risk list are clearly under more scrutiny. Furthermore, its government-wide view gives GAO status as a stakeholder in some projects.

- *Department and interagency stakeholders.* Perhaps the most common and direct stakeholders are the department staff involved in a project—whether as team members or as internal customers. Typically, these stakeholders have a significant vested interest in the outcome of the project, often as owners of the new processes, systems, tools, or products. Proactively managing and actively engaging this stakeholder group will likely yield the greatest benefit, ideally by gaining their enthusiastic support or at the very least by overcoming their resistance.

- *The public.* Although in theory the ultimate source of government power in a democracy lies with the people, the public often has very little visibility in federal projects. Nonetheless, through their representative bodies and public hearings, individuals and organizations may participate directly in project reviews as well as in lobbying efforts for and against particular projects and project alternatives.

- *Opposition stakeholders.* Although not found in every project, this is a special class of stakeholders who perceive themselves as being harmed if the project is successful. An example might be a community that opposes a new government facility being built. Early involvement of opposition stakeholders may result in a more positive outcome; conversely, neglecting these stakeholders can doom a project.

- *Media.* The media generally pays attention to major projects with large budgets. The press has a duty to report objectively but often focuses more on problems than successes.

- *Vendors/suppliers/industry.* In the procurement process, vendors and suppliers are often important stakeholders. Besides selling products or services, this stakeholder group puts its reputation and future business on the line with nearly every project. The tangled web of procurement policies and practices creates a complicated relationship between the companies (large and small) that "play the game" of government contracting and the federal departments and agencies that own the projects. Government project managers treat vendors at times as adversaries and at other times as partners, but in each case they must be managed appropriately as stakeholders.

- *Future generations.* During its limited tenure, each administration has a responsibility to future generations regarding long-term debt, viable and affordable infrastructure, and a healthy environment. Interest groups that lobby for or against a project's outcomes often represent these stakeholders. The Department of Energy's Office of Environmental Management, for example, finds that its projects sometimes draw both—those anxious to rid their communities of toxic facilities and those opposed to the residual waste being interred in their communities.

Effective stakeholder management in the federal sector begins with identification of the individuals, organizations, and markets that will have a bearing on the project. Working with these various, often disparate, groups requires a set of skills that has emerged from the new age of information technology. Treating stakeholders like static entities that need the occasional information update is a mistake. Instead, stakeholders should be viewed as dynamic groups that form, congregate, and separate easily. The federal project manager should strive to build partnerships between the project and stakeholder groups by understanding their concerns and goals related to the project and through effective communication that invites their active participation in the appropriate elements of the project.

## STAKEHOLDER MANAGEMENT IN ACTION

The performance of the decennial census is a highlight of American democracy, providing the data and information essential for our democratic processes to function properly. Since 1941 the Census Bureau has occupied a group of buildings on the 226-acre Suitland federal campus, southeast of Washington, D.C. Recognizing the need to consolidate and streamline operations, the Census Bureau and GSA's PBS worked together to design and build a 1.5 million-square-foot building.

Designed as a "complex among the trees," the Census headquarters building was envisioned as an example of sustainable and functional space that would support effective operations for many years to come. PBS worked closely with Census Bureau staff, designers, architects, and construction engineers to develop the initial concepts. To accomplish the daunting task of designing and constructing a new office building next to the existing structure, PBS developed effective techniques for working with stakeholders.

Whether the structure is a new courthouse in an urban setting or a building situated on a federally owned suburban campus, PBS faces the significant challenge of reviewing and approving hundreds of thousands of pages of project documentation from myriad internal (within GSA and PBS) and external stakeholders. Each project must adhere to federal guidelines as well as state and local building statutes. Stakeholder man-

**CHAPTER 8** Engaging Stakeholders

agement must incorporate historic preservation groups, local entities, and even foreign governments.

PBS has been implementing the use of electronic project management software that will enable faster review of documents by the various stakeholders. As envisioned, architects and builders will no longer need to submit or review paper-based architectural plans. All plans will be available electronically, with interfaces for comment, review, approval, and other elements of workflow.[3] This process reflects key stakeholder management tenets: engaging stakeholders in the project and communicating effectively with them.

PBS's operational environment and experience managing and balancing a wide variety of stakeholders comes with an equally wide variety of issues and needs. For example, PBS has found that some stakeholder groups have become increasingly savvy and interested in the construction process, like judges who have expressed very specific recommendations for new courthouse designs.

To further illustrate the challenges of managing stakeholders, let's shift from the example of GSA's PBS and construction of the Census Bureau building to execution of the 2010 census, one of the largest projects the federal government has ever undertaken. Understanding each stakeholder's issues and interests mitigates the risks associated with their participation in the project and interaction with the project team. Using the census as an example, the matrix in Table 8-1 outlines how a project may engage its key stakeholders from the perspective of each group's issues, concerns, and needs.

| Stakeholder Group | Sample Issues, Concerns, Needs | Engagement Methods |
|---|---|---|
| **President** | - Producing a fair and accurate count | Briefings and reports |
| **Congress**<br>- House Subcommittee on Information Policy, Census, and National Archives | - Accurate and timely execution<br>- Adherence to budget<br>- High-quality data<br>- Remediation of issues cited for correction | Status reports and briefings, responses to requests for information, committee hearings |
| **Commerce Department and Commerce Secretary** | - Accurate and timely execution<br>- Adherence to budget<br>- High-quality data | Status reports and briefings |
| **Census Bureau and Census Bureau Director** | - Managing a highly complex, labor- and technology-intensive project across the U.S. and its territories<br>- Gathering accurate and complete census data<br>- Improving on performance of prior census efforts<br>- Meeting mandated deadlines (constitutional and congressional) on time and within budget<br>- Engaging the public and achieving a high rate of participation | Meetings, project communications, briefings, project team membership, task responsibilities, internal employee communications |
| **Census Project Management Organizations**<br>- Decennial Leadership Group<br>- Census Integration Group<br>- Census operations and systems teams<br>- Regional centers and local offices | - Internal communications and coordination challenges<br>- Identifying and managing risks to schedule, cost, and operations<br>- Making timely policy decisions and resolving issues<br>- Managing resource, schedule, and budget requirements | Status reports, meetings, project communications, interviews, briefings, project teams, task responsibilities, policies and procedures, operational plans and instruction |
| **Census Advisory Committee**<br>Provides recommendations to the Director of the Census Bureau from the data user community | - Availability and accuracy of data<br>- Type of information collected<br>- Economic and demographic trends | Meetings and briefings |

*(continues)*

## CHAPTER 8 Engaging Stakeholders

(continued)

| Stakeholder Group | Sample Issues, Concerns, Needs | Engagement Methods |
|---|---|---|
| State and local governments | ■ Need to understand population dynamics<br>■ Completeness and accuracy of count in their jurisdictions<br>■ Count's impact on funding for programs and representation in Congress | Targeted communications and solicitations |
| U.S. Government Accountability Office | ■ Assessment of effectiveness of programs and efficiency of processes to achieve an accurate count | As requested, based on inquiries by members of Congress |
| Public | ■ Count's impact on funding for programs and representation in Congress<br>■ Concerns about privacy and how the information will be used | Media campaigns, public outreach through local government and public interest groups |
| Political Parties | ■ Concerns about completeness and accuracy<br>■ Potential impact on legislative redistricting | Indirectly through public communications and congressional updates |

Note: The information in this table is intended as an illustration and is not a product of the Census Bureau or the project management organizations conducting the 2010 census.

**TABLE 8-1:** Sample Stakeholder Engagement Matrix: 2010 Census

## MANAGING STAKEHOLDERS IN A COMPLEX ENVIRONMENT

GAO offers one of the most complicated cases in stakeholder management. Known as the "congressional watchdog," GAO conducts about 1,000 "engagements" each year to evaluate the performance or processes of government projects, programs, or operations. More than 90 percent of these engagements are initiated by Congress (almost entirely by requests from committees) or by a legal mandate. The remaining 10 percent of GAO's work is initiated at the discretion of the Comptroller General, typically in response to issues that cross the jurisdictions of multiple congressional committees. When GAO is called in, it is usually to investigate a perceived problem. These projects are often politically charged from the outset, with various stakeholder groups fortifying their positions in preparation for the perceived battle to come.

Steve Backhus, Director for Quality and Continuous Improvement at GAO, explains that throughout the life of an evaluation project, a primary activity for the project manager and team is to carefully and skillfully navigate around the perspectives, expectations, and biases of the stakeholders. For a GAO team, the key stakeholders in the agency that is the focus of the evaluation are often not voluntary participants in the project. Backhus attributes GAO's success in large part to its project management processes and its approach with stakeholders.[4] That approach is characterized by the following guidelines:

- *Objectivity.* Approach projects and stakeholders with a sincere desire to do good and to correct, not to find fault. Clear, well-grounded questions and objectives enable team members to focus on actual rather than preconceived outcomes.

- *Communication.* Communicate across a wide variety of stakeholders with disparate objectives while striving to protect the interests of all parties: Congress, the agency, and GAO. Constant communication with each ensures that there are no surprises regarding the evaluation process or findings.

- *Expertise.* Operate with "contextual sophistication"—a true appreciation by GAO team members and experts of the technical, operational, and organizational complexity of the agency or program being studied. When agency stakeholders see that evaluations include team members with relevant expertise, they give greater credence to the process and results.

## CONDUCTING A STAKEHOLDER ASSESSMENT

Increasing access to information and the growing number of sources complicates stakeholder management. Given the overabundance of information available today, project managers must assume that stakeholders believe they know as much, if not more, than the project team members. Lacking any real control over the flow of information, the project manager, sponsors, and team members must try to harness the forces that influence stakeholder behavior and attitudes.

An effective tool for managing stakeholder involvement in a federal project is the stakeholder assessment. A stakeholder assessment can be used to gauge the dimensions that drive stakeholder behavior, such as attitudes and biases toward the project, extent of influence over the project team members, averseness to conflict, and geographic factors. The assessment will provide important information that will help the project manager and team develop an approach to managing stakeholders effectively.

Stakeholder assessments can take a variety of forms and can involve various tools and methods. Simplicity and utility are the keys to performing the right level of analysis. The assessment should be simple to understand and execute, and should be designed to provide information that the project manager and team members can use to communicate effectively with stakeholders and achieve the shared project goals. Key elements of any stakeholder assessment should include the group (or individual), their concerns/issues/goals, a description of their influence/impact on the project, and actions to manage/engage them. A straightforward worksheet (see Table 8-2) will suit the needs of most projects.[5]

| Stakeholders (Individuals or Groups) | Involvement/ Role | Priorities/ Concerns | Level of Support Needed | Current Level of Support | Influence Strategy |
|---|---|---|---|---|---|
| Department CIO | Resource supplier | Clear requirements, solution uses existing technology, user adoption | 3 – Needs to promote project and secure needed resources | + | CIO is the chair of the project's advisory board. Keep CIO informed of status and any issues – "no surprises." |

**TABLE 8-2:** Stakeholder Assessment Worksheet

Definitions of the columns in the worksheet are:

- *Stakeholders (individuals or groups)*: These individuals or groups include those requesting the project; those the project manager must go through for resources, approval, guidance, etc.; those that will use the product/service; and others who can influence the project.

- *Involvement/role*: Based on the stakeholder description, identify their role or involvement—sponsor, requestor, owner, resource supplier, customer, or end-user.

- *Priorities/concerns*: What are the important or risky areas of this project from the stakeholder's perspective?

- *Level of support needed*: "1" = Their support is not necessary now; "2" = Helpful to have their support; and "3" = Critical to have their support."

- *Current level of support*: "+" = Actively supports the project; "0" = Neutral to the project; "-" = Opposes the project and may work against it; and "?" = Unknown level of support.

### CHAPTER 8 Engaging Stakeholders

- *Influence strategy*: Methods for engaging and managing the stakeholder's participation on the project.

Another, more complex assessment tool, originally developed in the adult education arena, addresses the "influence" and "interest" relationships between stakeholders and the project (see Figure 8-2).[6] This tool guides project managers and team members in the tactics they can employ to manage the relationships with their stakeholders. Evaluating influence and interest relationships is in line with advice from Michael O'Brochta, a former senior program manager and author of many project management articles: "Project managers can use sources of power to influence executive actions (or counter-actions) and increase the odds of project success."[7]

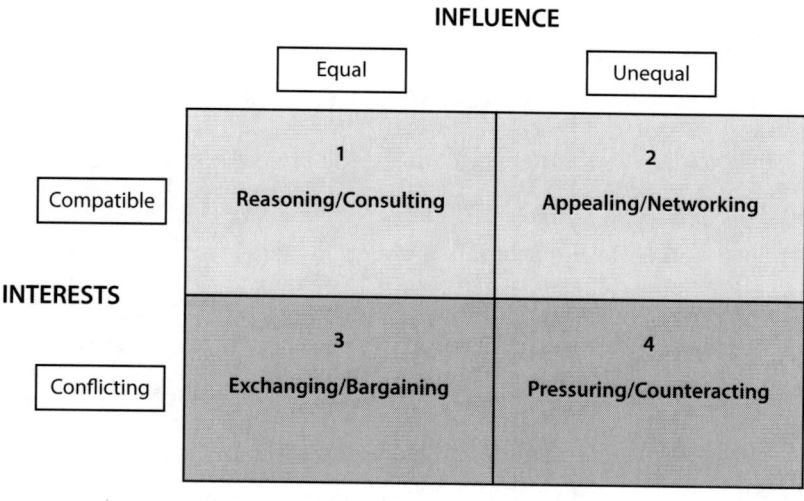

**FIGURE 8-2:** Stakeholder Influence-Interest Relationship

Why use such an involved technique? For complex or politically charged projects (common in the federal government), a more detailed stakeholder assessment tool can guide project leaders toward specific actions that will enable them to manage stakeholders more effectively. In addition, team members will gain a greater appreciation for the interests and concerns about the project from the stakeholders' perspectives. The project manager and team members will then be able to adjust their behavior, the information they provide, and the methods they use to communicate with each stakeholder accordingly.

Each quadrant in Figure 8-2 describes the techniques a project manager should employ depending on the extent of agreement or conflict between the project and each stakeholder (individually or as a group). For example, alignment of interests and influence allows the project manager to be more consultative or collaborative, while misalignment requires escalating levels of action on the part of the project manager—either more diplomacy or the engagement of other stakeholders to appeal or apply pressure as needed.[8] This approach enables the project manager to communicate effectively with stakeholders and provides the team the information needed to meet the stakeholders' expectations.

Stakeholders with influence equal to the project manager's and with compatible interests (cell 1) are important allies to a project. The project manager and team should maintain a good working relationship with these stakeholders; the communication plan should reflect methods for keeping them informed and supportive, and they should be encouraged to champion the project.

Stakeholders with unequal influence and compatible interests (cell 2) are allies of the project and should not require a high level of resources to enhance their relationship with the project; however, a project team member could be designated to address their needs. The project communication plan should include methods for keeping them informed.

# CHAPTER 8 Engaging Stakeholders

Stakeholders with equal influence but conflicting interests (cell 3) may pose a limited risk to the project. The risk plan should include an item that addresses monitoring these stakeholders in case their level of influence changes. They should also be kept informed about project progress through general communications.

Stakeholders with unequal influence and conflicting interests (cell 4) may pose a significant risk to the project and therefore require active management throughout the project. The risk management plan should include a mitigation plan with regard to these stakeholders. The communication plan should include ways to keep them appropriately informed as well as ways to persuade them to take ownership and to gain their support. These stakeholders will need to be monitored closely. If these strategies fail, the project manager may be faced with giving in to their demands.

Table 8-3 applies the Stakeholder Influence-Interest Relationship (Figure 8-2) assessment to the groups identified in the Stakeholder Engagement Matrix (Table 8-1). While the groups in this example are at a fairly high level, this type of assessment can be applied to any stakeholders that a project manager or team must engage to achieve project success.

| Stakeholder Group | Interest | Influence |
|---|---|---|
| President | H | M |
| Congress/House Subcommittee on Information Policy, Census, and National Archives | H | M |
| Commerce Department and Commerce Secretary | H | H |
| Census Bureau and Census Bureau Director | H | H |
| Census Project Management Organizations | H | H |
| Census Advisory Committee | H | L |
| State and local governments | H | L |
| U.S. Government Accountability Office | M | L |
| Public | L | L |
| Political Parties | M | L |

**TABLE 8-3:** Sample Power/Influence Matrix: 2010 Census

The result of the analysis can yield a better understanding of the relationships between stakeholders and the project manager, and can also improve the quality of interactions with each group. Above all, project managers and team members must remain focused on constructively engaging stakeholders as part of their efforts to achieve project goals and outcomes.

## MANAGE STAKEHOLDERS (OR BE MANAGED BY THEM)

Living in this complex world and engaging in multilayered, complicated federal projects means adopting a vigorous approach to managing stakeholders. Kathleen Hass, in her book *Managing Complex Projects: A New Model,* describes the following key elements.[9]

- *Establish positive relationships with key stakeholders.* Use stakeholder assessment and management techniques to help create a positive relationship with key stakeholders. In addition, build and maintain a direct one-on-one connection with the most critical stakeholders by calling (not e-mailing) them on a regular basis. Do not shy away from adversaries; engage them in constructive conversations in an effort to mitigate their influence or turn them into allies.[10]

- *Involve customers and users in every aspect of the project.* Avoid the urge to limit interaction with customers and users in the time between soliciting their needs and delivering the project results. Maintain their active participation throughout the project in order to uncover unexpected impacts or identify opportunities to improve the project results.

- *Establish and manage virtual alliances.* In the federal government, engage a variety of external stakeholders—political or interest groups, other agencies, suppliers, or industry—to form alliances and thereby provide support, help identify potential issues, or secure needed resources for the project.

- *Establish and manage expectations.* At the outset, as well as throughout the project, document, understand, and address expectations, including resolving unreasonable expectations. Without clearly establishing or managing stakeholders' expectations, a project manager is almost guaranteed to fail to satisfy them.

The most effective federal project managers develop an approach to stakeholder management that incorporates the nature of the team (collaborative, virtual, command and control, etc.). Projects tell stories, and the best people to tell them are the stakeholders—the people who have come to believe in the objectives of the project.

> Today more than ever, it is important for project managers in the federal government to understand a project's relationship with executive stakeholders and the considerable power and influence they wield. Project managers can employ a structured stakeholder management approach and skills to lead the relationships with their stakeholders and maintain their support. Project managers must work closely with stakeholders, listening to their wants and needs and employing techniques to advance their support. This two-way communication is a key ingredient of effective project management.

## NOTES

1. In remarks made May 13, 2004, before the Federal Reserve Bank of Chicago's Smart Money Conference, https://fraser.stlouisfed.org/historicaldocs/ag04/download/29216/Greenspan_20040513.pdf (accessed May 12, 2009).
2. Personal interview with Congressman Elijah Cummings, Maryland 7th District, January 12, 2009.
3. Personal interview with Bill Guerrin, Assistant Commissioner, Office of Construction Programs; AnnMarie Sweet-Anshire, PMO Director, Office of the Chief Architect; and Arnold Hill, Architect/Project Manager, General Services Administration, October 3, 2008.

4. Personal interview with Steve Backhus, Director, Office of Quality and Continuous Improvement, Government Accountability Office, November 24, 2008.
5. Kathleen B. Hass, *Managing Complex Projects: A New Model* (Vienna, VA: Management Concepts, 2009), p. 218. Adapted with permission.
6. Ronald M. Cervero and Arthur L. Wilson, "The Politics of Responsibility: A Theory of Program Planning Practice for Adult Education." *Adult Education Quarterly* 45 (1) (Fall 1994): 261.
7. Personal interview with Michael O'Brochta, former senior program manager, Central Intelligence Agency, November 5, 2008.
8. David I. Cleland and Lewis R. Ireland, *Project Management Handbook: Applying Best Practices Across Global Industries* (New York: McGraw Hill, 2008).
9. Hass, pp. 219–224. Adapted with permission.
10. Brian Irwin, *Managing Politics and Conflict in Projects* (Vienna, VA: Management Concepts, 2008). Adapted with permission.

# Chapter 9
# Project Management Competencies and Skills: Success through Experience

> *Our job as a federal agency is management and oversight, to be responsible stewards of the public's trust and resources. Therefore, we must have a highly qualified and technically proficient management team and staff. My aim is to have a high performing organization, sustained by a career oriented workforce, driven to produce results that are important now and into the future.*
> —JAMES A. RISPOLI, FORMER ASSISTANT SECRETARY,
> U.S. DEPARTMENT OF ENERGY[1]

Numerous surveys and assessments conducted by OMB, GAO, and individual agencies in cooperation with industry have shown that project management, and in particular the skills associated with being a successful project manager, are critical to agencies achieving their missions.[2] The practice and discipline of project management has been institutionalized on the defense side of the federal government for years. The Defense Acquisition University (DAU) and the Defense Acquisition Workforces Improvement Act (DAWIA) certification in a variety of project- and program management-related areas are clear examples of this commitment to the development of project management skills and competencies. In the past few years, the practice and discipline of project management have been expanding by leaps and bounds across the civilian side of the federal government as well.

OMB and a growing number of agencies have recognized and begun to realize the benefits of a formal approach to building and maintaining project management competencies and skills as part of their goals to improve the quality and success rate of projects in the federal government. Nonetheless, recent studies indicate that formal training lags behind the increased demand for, and the responsibility and accountability of, project managers. A joint study commissioned by OMB and the Council for Excellence in Government, for example, found that up to half of the project managers surveyed had not received training in critical project management areas. Most who had received training rated it "moderately" to "highly" valuable.[3]

The emergence of project management as a core competency in the federal government signals a shift in the career paths and opportunities for government personnel. Agencies across the government are establishing programs to identify, train, and certify individuals as project managers. OMB has further confirmed the arrival of project management on the federal scene with the development and implementation of the federal acquisition certification for program and project managers

(FAC-P/PM), which requires agencies to train and develop program and project managers (see Chapter 10, Project Manager Professional Development). Agencies that have already started down the project management path are now working to comply with this standard, while others with less mature project management capability must build programs to meet the FAC-P/PM requirements.

## WHAT ARE THE CRITICAL SKILLS?

Interviews, literature reviews, and surveys indicate that successful federal project managers possess a wide variety of skills. Although the emphasis differs from agency to agency, most share a fairly consistent set of skills. Project management in the federal government is moving beyond what are commonly thought of as "traditional" skills. Many organizations are focusing on a more comprehensive set of skills and competencies, including core project management skills, communication skills, emerging project management skills, and subject matter expertise. Table 9-1 compares the skills in these categories with traditional project management skills.

Every two years, the federal CIO Council updates the core competencies associated with the Clinger-Cohen Act. In addition to the core project management competencies, the list includes emerging competency areas like leadership, change management, and performance assessment that require skills not normally found in project managers who rise through the technology ranks in the federal government. The emphasis on these Clinger-Cohen competencies further suggests that successful federal project managers must expand their capabilities beyond their technical expertise.

| Traditional Emphasis → <br> New Emphasis ↓ | Scheduling | Budgeting | Quality Management | Risk Management | Facilitation | Communication | Leadership | Business Writing | Management | Negotiation |
|---|---|---|---|---|---|---|---|---|---|---|
| Integration/Coordination | | | | | ✓ | ✓ | | ✓ | ✓ | |
| Supervision | ✓ | | ✓ | | ✓ | ✓ | ✓ | | ✓ | |
| Analysis | ✓ | ✓ | | ✓ | | | | | | |
| Contractor Management | ✓ | ✓ | ✓ | ✓ | ✓ | ✓ | | | ✓ | ✓ |
| Lessons Learned/Knowledge Management | | | ✓ | ✓ | | ✓ | | ✓ | | |
| Negotiation | ✓ | ✓ | | | ✓ | ✓ | ✓ | ✓ | | ✓ |
| Teaching/Mentoring | | | | | ✓ | ✓ | ✓ | ✓ | ✓ | |
| Framing | ✓ | ✓ | ✓ | ✓ | ✓ | ✓ | ✓ | ✓ | | ✓ |
| Messaging/Context | | | | ✓ | ✓ | ✓ | ✓ | ✓ | | |
| Integration | | | | | | ✓ | ✓ | | | |
| Workflow | | | | | | ✓ | ✓ | | ✓ | ✓ |
| Facilitation | ✓ | ✓ | ✓ | ✓ | ✓ | ✓ | | | ✓ | ✓ |
| Integrity | ✓ | ✓ | ✓ | ✓ | | ✓ | ✓ | | ✓ | ✓ |

**TABLE 9-1:** Comparison of Traditional and New Project Management Skills

## CORE PROJECT MANAGEMENT SKILLS

The core set of skills needed for success as a project manager in a federal agency derives from the primary knowledge areas described in PMI's *A Guide to the Project Management Body of Knowledge (PMBOK® Guide)*.[4]

## Leadership

Government project managers are increasingly relied on to fill a leadership role in their organization. As the primary person responsible for the use of an agency's resources to achieve goals and introduce improvements to the organization, the project manager is increasingly being brought into the decision-making process to contribute to setting strategic direction, allocating resources, and defining goals.

The rising prominence of project managers (and project management overall) is evident in organizations where the project management office resides at the C-level (e.g., chief information officer, chief financial officer) in the organization and is actively involved in setting policy and providing guidance on executing projects. The Department of the Interior's PMO, for example, is part of the CIO structure and is involved in developing and implementing policies related to project planning throughout the organization. (See also Chapter 7, Leadership and the Project Manager.)

## Coordination

The increasing complexity of projects and the dispersion of tasks, resources, and stakeholders across organizations make coordination high on the list of key skills. Project managers at GSA's Public Buildings Service are evolving into a role that requires tight coordination as a result of the involvement of multiple stakeholders (federal, state, and local government representatives), execution of tasks across various disciplines (construction, contracting, security, real estate, and technology), and compliance with myriad regulations and standards. The coordination role is especially critical because PBS project managers are regionally dispersed and nearly 95 percent of project staff are contractors. PBS operates effectively in this environment by providing clear and regular communications to stakeholders and, even more critically, conducting formal project reviews at regular intervals, typically in conjunction with major project phases.

## Supervision

Project management involves the supervision of resources to achieve the project's outcomes. Strong project management practices provide a solid structure that project managers can rely on to ensure that their team gets the right tasks done right. One common challenge identified in our interviews and research was the lack of supervisory experience among people thrust into the project manager role. In many agencies, project managers rise through technical career paths and have little if any experience supervising a team. To develop in their new role, they require greater guidance and support as "new" supervisors. For example, the Bureau of Indian Affairs is building a cadre of project management mentors who are helping project managers, mostly from the IT ranks, improve their "people" skills, including building their supervisory competence. (See also Chapter 4, Building Strong Teams.)

## Risk Assessment/Management

Effective risk analysis is key to successful project planning. The results of this analysis should trigger changes to project plans or baselines, as well as the development of mitigation plans. Jerry Harper, a senior program manager in the Department of Commerce, notes that, in his experience, projects succeed when thorough risk assessments are performed. Following an assessment, project managers must ask themselves, "What can be done to adjust the project plan, schedule, work breakdown schedule, and budget in response to the risk assessment?"[5] The answer to this question should be documented and communicated, especially to the executive

CHAPTER 9  Project Management Competencies and Skills

sponsor and any oversight or guiding organizations. These stakeholders should be made aware of necessary changes to the project and their potential impacts—and asked to approve those changes. Early information on risk minimizes surprises later in the project.

## Project Analysis and Requirements Definition

The effort involved in project analysis and requirements definition (which involve an iterative process that goes deeper and deeper to get to exact project needs) is universally underestimated. Project managers need to be able to link good analysis—business, technical, and economic—with project communications, understanding and conveying requirements from the customer's perspective. Thorough planning should be conducted at the front end of the project, and all key stakeholders should vet the resulting plans.

The Department of the Interior's PMO, for example, focuses on excelling in the planning phases, emphasizing project analysis and requirements definition. DOI has instituted a policy (OCIO Directive 2008-016) requiring "major" projects to go through an integrated baseline review process and obtain the approval of an investment review board (see Chapter 11, Governance and Project Portfolio Development).

## Contractor Management

Managing contractors is a critical skill in agencies where outsourcing is prevalent. Successful project managers integrate contractor personnel fully into their project teams. The choice of contract type can assist in effective contractor management and thereby contribute to project success. The Energy Department's Office of Environmental Management, for example, favors the use of cost-plus award or incentive fee (CPAF or

CPIF) contracts, which promote efficient execution by contractors to meet established performance goals.

## Stakeholder Management

Project managers must work within and across multiple groups of stakeholders who may control or influence funding, personnel, key resources, legislation or regulation, and decision-making authority. One agency with a complicated set of stakeholders is GSA's Public Buildings Service. PBS's projects include the usual internal stakeholders (executive sponsor, contractors, and the project team), but the project manager must also manage relationships with local and state jurisdictions, historic preservation groups, and in some cases foreign governments. (See Chapter 8, Engaging Stakeholders.)

## Schedule, Scope, and Change Management

The criticality of the fundamental skills associated with managing the project schedule and scope is common across organizations and projects. In addition, throughout a project's lifecycle, the project manager must continuously identify, assess, and manage the impacts of changes, answering the question, "If this change occurs, what impact will it have on the project scope, schedule, budget, and requirements?"

Formal change processes enable project managers to clearly communicate the facts of potential impacts to the relevant stakeholders, limiting the emotion associated with altering anticipated outcomes. In one case, a federal project manager was able to show an irate executive sponsor the change requests he had approved, along with the associated analyses and impact descriptions that had been presented verbally and in writing. The project manager was able to keep the project moving forward and demonstrated to his team and other managers the value of this critical project management process.

## Lessons Learned

Although most organizations identify gathering lessons learned as a critical skill, few take the appropriate time to perform the function. Two examples of organizations that implement effective systems to make the most of lessons learned are GSA's Public Buildings Service and NASA:

- GSA's PBS maintains an online project management methodology that enables near real-time improvements to project management practices based on lessons learned. Project practitioners who access the online project portal are encouraged to document, post, and share their lessons learned and to recommend improvements to the organization's methodology. These recommendations are considered as they are submitted, and adjustments to the methodology are implemented as appropriate.[6]

- NASA applies robust lessons learned processes to its projects. Unfortunately for the project managers and teams, failures in NASA projects are usually quite public. As a result, NASA actively gathers and analyzes lessons learned on all of its projects and programs, taking the time to formally conduct and document those lessons.

  As part of its core business and its organizational culture, NASA fully investigates failures to understand, analyze, and communicate what happened, why, and what should be changed to prevent a recurrence. In NASA's "masters forums," senior project personnel and outside experts typically present the lessons in a story format. Through its defined lessons learned process, NASA makes it clear that the organization trusts its people to learn from failures, make the necessary corrections, and fix the mistakes.[7]

## Financial Analysis and Budgeting

Frequent budgetary fluctuations increase the challenges of managing projects in the federal government. The current fiscal crisis is compounding the ever-present stress on project managers to deliver projects with limited financial resources. The need to be efficient with the taxpayers' money, particularly in the current fiscal environment, has increased the importance and need for project managers to have strong financial analysis and budgeting skills. Among the key skills needed are:

- *Budget forecasting and financial projections.* What is the potential cost of the project over the life of the effort and into the operations and maintenance phases? At a minimum, project managers in the federal government should be adept at building a cost estimate that takes into consideration the budgetary and spending cycles and presents a "total ownership cost" figure. (See Chapter 13, Aligning Federal and Project Planning Cycles.)

- *Financial and economic analysis.* An understanding of the internal and external conditions that will influence the project is critical for project managers. For example, GSA's PBS seeks to learn local economic conditions and drivers on projects to be sure that the location, design, and function of new buildings are consistent and support local goals. In one case, a building concept called for a new building to be located on the outskirts of town. However, local leaders wanted to locate the building where it would increase the flow of traffic through the center of town and thus support local businesses.

- *Budget control/cost management.* Project managers must be able to use tools and methodologies, such as earned value, that can enhance cost control over their projects. They need to have adequate experience, exposure, and training in financial analysis and measurement to support their responsibility to report project performance accurately.

## COMMUNICATION SKILLS

Communication skills are universally recognized as essential for successful project managers. Because communication is the foundation for virtually all project management activities, some have even suggested that if a person lacks innate communication skills, he or she should be dissuaded from pursuing the project management career path. Several key aspects of communication skills are critical to project management success.

### Information Sharing

In the absence of information, people will fill the void with assumptions, guesses, and their own biases. The project manager's ability to communicate effectively (both providing and receiving information) with key stakeholders and constituencies is a critical success factor on most projects. Key to successful communication is the ability to ask the right questions.

Steve Backhus, Director of the Office of Quality and Continuous Improvement at GAO, explains that project managers in his organization must possess the ability to communicate with a wide variety of stakeholders with disparate intents and objectives. At the same time, project managers must constantly consider the interests of all parties—Congress (GAO's customer), the agency or program being evaluated, GAO team members, and the taxpayers. Constant communication with each group is necessary to ensure that there are no surprises regarding the evaluation process, findings, or resulting recommendations.[8]

## Engaging Executives

A primary role of the project manager is to protect the project—its funding, resources, scope, and schedule. Communicating effectively with executives is critical to ensuring project progress. To that end, project managers must engage executives to obtain agreement, support, guidance, and decisions. Those who successfully communicate with executives establish clear expectations at the outset of a project. They ask executives their preferred method, timing, and content of communication throughout the project and also outline the project's needs and expectations in terms of communication with the executive.

## Negotiation

Negotiation is the process whereby two or more parties with different needs and desired outcomes work to find a mutually acceptable solution. Since negotiating is an interpersonal process, each negotiating situation is different, influenced by each party's skills, attitudes, and style. People often regard negotiating as unpleasant because it suggests conflict. Understanding more about the process enables project managers to conduct negotiations with confidence and increases the likelihood that the outcomes will be positive for both parties.

For organizations where most project staff is contracted, negotiation is a very practical project management skill, allowing the government to obtain the needed resources for the best price. On a more operational level, project managers spend most of their day negotiating—with other project managers to obtain resources, with executives to obtain approvals, with team members on tasks and schedules, and with vendors on pricing.

## Communicating with Clarity

The most carefully thought-out communication plan and the best communication methods and tools will be worthless if the message is not clear. The project manager's goals are to understand and to be understood. To achieve these dual goals, the project manager must have the ability to communicate (in person and in writing) from the perspective of the project's constituents and stakeholder groups (e.g., IT, construction, budgets, contracts). This skill can be particularly challenging for project managers who come from technical areas, where writing clearly and succinctly may not have been as valued a skill. Developing a formal communication plan and using standard templates for communication activities (such as reporting status) allow the project manager to focus on the message content and the recipient. (See Chapter 6, The Crucial Role of Communication.)

## Teaching and Mentoring

The ability to teach or mentor is an important skill that project managers must possess to support their projects. Regardless of their project management maturity level, most organizations rely on experienced project managers to teach and mentor rising project managers, team members, and even executives on project management practices and value. In some cases, the project manager provides "just-in-time" training on project management tasks and technical project elements.

## EMERGING PROJECT MANAGEMENT SKILLS

The growing prominence of project management as a discipline and career path has led to the emergence of a host of new skills that the federal project manager needs to be successful. The current pace of change, volume of information, crisis-driven environment, and increased emphasis on project management require the development of skills not traditionally associated with project management.

### Framing

The ability to define the boundaries of a problem or opportunity and derive its core is the central component of framing. With the proper frame, the project manager is able to inventory the relevant elements required to address the problem or opportunity—the people, processes, tools, information, and actions—while simultaneously eliminating the extraneous items that distract from achieving a resolution.

### Messaging and Context

The ability to distill, organize, deliver, and receive information goes beyond the traditional skill of communicating information about a project. Effective messaging and context require project communications from each stakeholder's perspective, translating concepts and jargon across the multidisciplinary personnel who make up today's project teams. This skill is about telling the story in a way that is relevant and compelling to the audience.

NASA has turned structured "storytelling" into an effective part of improving project performance across the organization. Through masters forums, lessons-learned events, and other "campfire" activities for the project management community, NASA has been able to shift the focus from specific teams and projects to the "greater good." This shift enables project teams to reflect constructively on "How are we doing?" and "Where are we going?" The project manager draws on specific recent or historical examples to create a relevant metaphor for the project team and stakeholders.

## Integration

The growing diversity and complexity of projects and project teams call for managers to have the ability to integrate unconnected systems—not IT systems, but people, processes, resources, information, and technology. For the project manager this is akin to leading a symphony, integrating the sweeping sections and balancing the delicate solos to deliver a harmonious result. GSA's Public Buildings Service, for example, is preparing for the evolution of the project manager role as an integrator. PBS project managers must integrate all the disciplines involved in building development—design, construction, contracting, personnel, safety, environmental, financial, political, regulatory, marketing, and more—to create a masterpiece, a facility that will endure the pressures of time, weather, and aesthetics.

## Workflow Management

Information overload is a common challenge for today's project manager. In the face of increasing project complexity and stakeholder diversity, project managers must gain control of the flow of work and information associated with their projects. The ability to control information inputs and subsequently direct, defer, disseminate, and delegate differentiates the successful project manager from the rest. Workflow control enables project managers to focus on the critical elements of a project when attention is required and to empower members of the project team to own their respective project tasks. Further, many projects that involve the improvement or automation of core business processes require project managers to have a grasp of defining and documenting workflow.

The Treasury Department's Bureau of the Public Debt Administrative Resource Center (ARC) manages projects by executing a series of interlaced workflows to support the conversion of its customers' data onto its back-office systems. These workflows include activities related to discovering customer requirements, documenting business processes, performing data conversion, conducting training, and implementing contracts. ARC project managers are most successful when they can effectively control these various workflows.

## Facilitation

More than managing effective meetings, project managers must have the ability to lead groups of people (e.g., teams, stakeholders, the public) through the process of achieving specific results. At any time during a project, the project manager may need to conduct a structured, facilitated session to address a problem, complete a deliverable, or solicit input from key stakeholders.

Designing, delivering, and documenting a facilitated session involves more than drafting an agenda and putting out meeting minutes. Successful facilitators prepare scripts for their sessions that describe the specific activities and outcomes needed to reach a final result. While conducting a session, the facilitator must have the ability to respond to situations that require adjustments to the activity or process to produce a useful outcome. Effective facilitated sessions yield more solid and sustainable results, engage stakeholders, and make efficient use of time and resources.

## Curiosity and Imagination

Skills such as "thinking outside the box" and defining and solving problems are becoming more and more critical for project managers. By seeking to understand why a problem has occurred and developing alternative solutions, project managers are able to look beyond specific barriers, anticipate potential problems, and make recommendations for correcting systemic issues.

Project managers at GAO are responsible for leading their teams in efforts to understand issues affecting the programs they analyze. This effort requires critical listening and analytical skills, as well as the ability to think beyond traditional causes in formulating recommendations to address identified problems. Project managers in scientifically oriented organizations such as NASA and the National Institute of Standards and Technology thrive in an environment that encourages curiosity and imagination.

## Integrity

The PMI® "oath" includes the "courage" to speak the truth about real impacts on projects driven by executive decisions or external factors (e.g., legislation, regulation, crises). For example, project managers must respond appropriately to executive sponsors and other key stakeholders when the budget is cut. They need to be honest and direct about the impacts, including what can't be done unless the budget is restored. Solid project information provides the foundation for a project manager to communicate clearly and rationally to executives in these situations.

## SUBJECT MATTER EXPERTISE

The importance of a project manager's expertise in the project's "subject" depends on many factors, including the organization, the individual, the project team, and the project's level of complexity (see Figure 9-1).

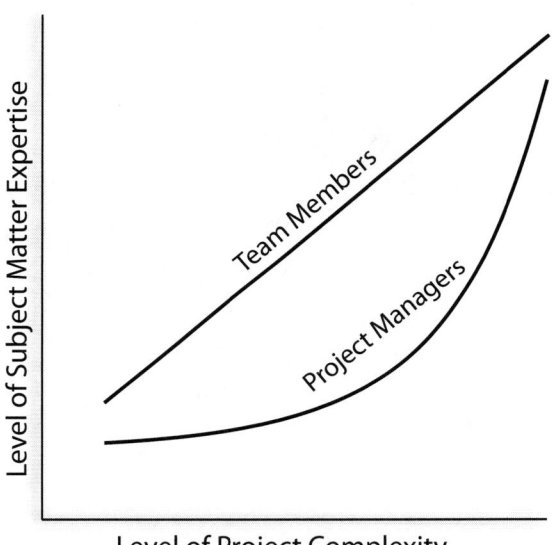

**FIGURE 9-1:** Influence of Project Complexity on the Need for Subject Matter Expertise

At GSA's PBS, project managers must understand the fundamentals of constructing a building. Since 95 percent of construction is contracted out, GSA serves as "owner representative" and facilitator. The project manager and team need to understand a wide array of technical areas, including contracting, environmental, safety and security, and construction costs.

On the other end of the spectrum is a greater emphasis on the core project management skills. At the Bureau of the Public Debt's ARC, the project manager's role is to lead the experts (technical and business owners) through structured project management processes to achieve project goals.

More in the middle of the spectrum is "contextual sophistication." The best example of this perspective is GAO team members and experts who must appreciate the technical, operational, and organizational complexity of the agency or program being reviewed in each of their assessment engagements.

> Organizations today face challenges when they assign technical experts to manage projects or skilled project managers to manage highly technical projects. Technical experts may not have the increasingly necessary soft skills to manage the people and processes on a project. Conversely, a nontechnical project manager may have limited ability to deal with technical experts or elements on a project. This need to balance technical expertise with management skills can be addressed by clearly defining and agreeing on roles and responsibilities, including who has the final decision-making authority.
>
> The role of the project manager is evolving into that of a "project integrator," which requires new or increasingly emphasized skills. This shift is reflected in the use of matrixed organizational models, where resources and responsibilities are shared across business units, projects, and project managers, with PMOs serving as the coordination point.
>
> The emergence of new skills that integrate with traditional skills will place increasing demands on federal project managers to adjust and adapt to new project environments. Acquiring and honing these skills will differentiate successful project managers and projects throughout the federal government.

## NOTES

1. Statement of James A. Rispoli, Assistant Secretary for Environmental Management, U.S. Department of Energy, before the Subcommittee on Strategic Forces Committee on Armed Services, U.S. House of Representatives, March 1, 2006.
2. Many GAO assessments and reports include references to management or project management practices. See GAO-08-1051T for several relevant citations in the information technology arena. Also, see the survey on project management skills, "The Council for Excellence in Government Program Management Survey Data Report" (Vienna, VA: Management Concepts, 2008).
3. "The Council for Excellence in Government Program Management Survey Data Report" (Vienna, VA: Management Concepts, 2008).
4. *A Guide to the Project Management Body of Knowledge—Fourth Edition* (Newtown Square, PA: Project Management Institute, Inc.), 2008.
5. Personal interview with Jerry Harper, Office of the Chief Information Officer, U.S. Department of Commerce, September 15, 2008.
6. Personal interview with Bill Guerrin, Assistant Commissioner, Office of Construction Programs; AnnMarie Sweet-Anshire, PMO Director, Office of the Chief Architect; and Arnold Hill, Architect/Project Manager, General Services Administration, October 3, 2008.
7. Personal interview with Dr. Ed Hoffman, Director, Academy of Program/Project and Engineering Leadership, NASA, September 10, 2008.
8. Personal interview with Steve Backhus, Director, Office of Quality and Continuous Improvement, Government Accountability Office, November 24, 2008.

## Chapter 10

# Project Manager Professional Development: Building the Project Management Corps

> *Successful advancement of project management requires the sponsorship and commitment of management. Specifically it is the duty of project managers to establish advancement processes and to manage the initiative. Accomplishing this objective requires the effective allocation of time for project owners, project managers, and project participants to acquire the required competencies.*
> —DAVID CLELAND AND LEWIS IRELAND
> PROJECT MANAGER'S HANDBOOK: APPLYING BEST PRACTICES
> ACROSS GLOBAL INDUSTRIES

The increased demand for project managers, particularly in light of the growing number of retirements from the federal government, presents a challenge for the next generation of project managers. Many are stepping into a void in organizations where the project management environment is immature and the discipline and practices are informal at best. As part of the maturation process, organizations need to design and implement programs to support the emergence of the project manager "class" and individuals need to develop the relevant skills through formal training, certification, and mentoring.

A 2008 study on program management conducted by OMB and the Council for Excellence in Government revealed that a "large majority of survey respondents do not currently hold certification from a professional organization" such as PMI or DAU (for DAWIA-related specialties) and are not formally trained, coached, or mentored as project or program managers. Many respondents reported that the most valuable training they received was in the area of "soft" skills—strategic planning, leadership, human capital, and performance measurement. They noted that they had not received much training in other, seemingly critical areas such as budgeting, risk management, and requirements development.[1]

## PROJECT MANAGEMENT CERTIFICATION

Numerous certification programs are available to today's project manager. Determining which certifications are most appropriate for a particular project manager depends on a variety of factors, including organizational requirements for professional progression, job relevance, personal and intellectual interest, and accessibility.

The Project Management Institute (pmi.org), Carnegie Mellon University's Software Engineering Institute (sei.cmu.edu), the American Society for the Advancement of Project Management (www.asapm.org), and the Construction Manager Certification Institute (cmaanet.org/cmci) are examples of organizations that offer certifications relevant to project management. PMI's core certifications include the Certified Associate of Project Management (CAPM) and the Project Management Professional (PMP), which require experience in the project management role as well as project management training. The Program Management Professional (PgMP) certification is the most "advanced" certification PMI offers, and it is intended for individuals who have extensive experience managing portfolios of projects. Additional PMI® certifications focus on the specific areas of scheduling (PMI-SP) and risk management (PMI-RMP). PMI® certification remains the gold standard for project management professionals, with few alternatives offering the same level of standards and rigorous testing and education.

As the name implies, the Software Engineering Institute's individual and organizational certifications are mostly technology-oriented. Best known for its Capability Maturity Model Integrated (CMMI®)[2], SEI has developed a variety of models intended to help organizations improve software and systems development processes and practices. An outgrowth of this work has been the development of related models; the two models most relevant to the project management discipline are the CMMI® for Acquisition and the People CMM®. For the individual project manager, a potential benefit can be gained through training in industry-driven best practices and processes. In particular, the CMMI® for Acquisition is applicable to the government environment (predominantly defense) and is particularly relevant in light of OMB's focus on acquisition (evidenced by the FAC-P/PM certification).

Another project management organization charged with promoting the discipline is the American Society for the Advancement of Project Management (asapm), the U.S. member organization of the International Project Management Association (www.ipma.ch). This organization provides a four-level competency-based certification for project and program managers, called USA National Competence Baseline, version 2.0. Asapm is also developing an organizational-level certification for project management competency called the asapm Performance Rated Organization, or aPro. While asapm and IPMA do not have the same level of prominence in the United States as PMI does, their competence-oriented philosophy offers a valuable paradigm for training and certification.

Industry-specific certifications can also be appropriate for federal project managers. For example, the Construction Management Association of America grants a Certified Construction Manager (CCM) certification. Project managers at GSA's Public Buildings Service need to be adept at the construction process; certifications such as the CCM, as well as the PMP, provide them with the framework for managing their projects effectively.

Training and certification in the six sigma methodology has recently gained some traction, primarily in the private sector. This methodology employs management practices and techniques targeted at improving existing business processes and creating new process designs. While there are certainly six sigma–trained practitioners (called green belts, black belts, or master black belts) in the federal government, there seem to be few coordinated efforts.

Perhaps the best-known application of six sigma in the federal government is the Department of Defense's continuous process improvement/lean six sigma (CPI/LSS) program, codified in DoD Directive 5010.42, issued May 15, 2008. This directive "establishes policy and assigns responsibilities to institutionalize CPI/LSS as one of the primary approaches to assessing and improving the efficiency and effectiveness of DoD processes in support of the Department's national defense mission."[3] As a result of this directive, organizations like the Army Materiel Command have implemented a six sigma training and certification program for their personnel. These certified personnel lead projects employing the six sigma approach, as well as train and mentor others.

A growing number of universities offer advanced degrees in project and program management. These degree programs are typically offered through the institution's business school or engineering school.

## ORGANIZATIONAL CERTIFICATION

Similar to the certifications that individuals can earn, organizations can achieve recognition for their level of project management maturity. PMI and SEI have developed "maturity models" to provide a structure for organizations to measure and improve their project management capabilities. Official assessors designated by PMI and SEI conduct a formal evaluation to determine an organization's maturity level and recommend actions to achieve, maintain, or increase its maturity. Project managers can benefit from becoming familiar with the two most relevant maturity models: PMI's Organizational Project Management Maturity Model (OPM3®) and SEI's Capability Maturity Model-Integration for Acquisition (CMMI®-ACQ). (See Chapter 13, Aligning Federal and Project Planning Cycles, for more information.)

Many organizations choose to start with a less formal internal self-evaluation using the guidelines established by these organizations. A self-assessment can provide a useful baseline for identifying areas that need improvement. One agency we interviewed was in the process of conducting an internal assessment that was to yield a "road map" for improvements in the project management environment. The assessment included a review of strategic alignment of projects to the agency's mission and how the agency's organizational structure, business processes, policies, tools, personnel skills, and metrics affected the project management environment. Overall, this assessment and roadmap effort were expected to last about nine months.

## FAC-P/PM PROGRAM

OMB has developed and maintains a variety of certifications under the auspices of the Federal Acquisition Institute (FAI). In 2007 OMB launched the federal acquisition certification for program and project managers (FAC-P/PM). The certification is required for program and project managers who are assigned to major acquisitions as defined in OMB Circular A-11, Part 7, Exhibit 300 – Planning, Budgeting, Acquisition, and Management of Capital Assets. This required certification is most relevant to program and project managers in the federal government and represents the potential emergence of a more formal career path.

Although the FAC-P/PM certification is clearly acquisition-oriented, it is generally related to industry standards for project management skills, particularly those promoted by PMI (see Table 10-1). In fact, FAI established a "letter of understanding" with PMI in December 2007 to accept the CAPM® and PMP® credentials "as satisfying the coursework areas and experience" for the entry/apprentice and mid/journeyman levels of the FAC-P/PM.

Certification under FAC-PP/M is purposely not centralized, in recognition of the "local" characteristics at the department and agency levels. Each agency is responsible for implementing a program that complies with the FAC-P/PM requirements, providing the necessary training, work experience, and skill development for its project managers.

# CHAPTER 10  Project Manager Professional Development

| Project Manager Entry/Apprentice | Program/Project Manager Mid/Journeyman | Program Manager Senior/Expert |
|---|---|---|
| ■ Knowledge and skills to perform as a team member and manage low-risk and relatively simple projects with supervision | ■ Knowledge and skills to manage program/project segments of low to moderate risk with little or no supervision | ■ Knowledge and skills to manage and evaluate moderate to high-risk programs or projects and create an environment for program success |
| ■ Overall understanding of project management practices, including acquisition | ■ Ability to apply project management processes, including requirements and acquisition | ■ Ability to manage and evaluate the requirements development process, overseeing junior team members |
| ■ Ability to develop project management documents with supervision | ■ Ability to identify and track action to initiate an acquisition program/project using cost/benefit analysis | ■ Ability to use, manage, and evaluate management processes and techniques |
| ■ Knowledge of and involvement in the project requirements process | ■ Ability to support baseline reviews and total ownership cost estimates | ■ Ability to manage and evaluate the use of earned value management as it relates to acquisition investments |

**TABLE 10-1:** FAC-PP/M Levels and Skills[4]

For some agencies with robust or well-structured project management training programs, this may not be a difficult task. Organizations that are ready to implement FAC-P/PM tend to have the following characteristics:

- Understand their workforce, their capabilities, and relevant skills
- Can identify personnel who are eligible to be certified
- Have a reasonably mature acquisition function
- Communicate and collaborate with their organization's acquisition personnel
- Can effectively manage the certified workforce after implementation.

For example, NASA's Academy of Program/Project and Engineering Leadership (APPEL) and the Department of Energy's Office of Environmental Management (OEM) have leveraged their existing comprehensive internal training and certification programs to achieve compliance with FAC-P/PM requirements. APPEL's program/project management development model is organized into four levels and clearly identifies the experience and knowledge requirements for advancing from one level to the next. DOE's project management career development program (PMCDP), which was established by directive, recognizes "the criticality of projects to success" and notes that "project management has become a focal point of improvement efforts."[5]

DOE's program includes four certification levels for federal project directors (FPDs), with specific requirements for experience and training. DOE even specifies the certification level required given the size of a project. For example, a level 1 FPD can manage projects valued between $5 million and $20 million. Personnel at DOE who have earned their PMP® certification from PMI can apply that credential for credit toward some of the requirements for FPD levels 1 and 2. The former head of DOE's OEM, Jim Rispoli, highlighted the certification of federal project directors as the top process improvement during his tenure.

The Nuclear Regulatory Commission (NRC) has also reviewed and revised its project management training program to meet the requirements of the FAC-PP/M certification. NRC selected an external training vendor to perform the training. Managers take several courses, totaling more than 20 classroom days, over six months, and receive a master's certificate from George Washington University upon completion. "NRC decided to mandate training for all major project managers, even experienced managers, to ensure that everyone had the same skill levels. In

**CHAPTER 10** Project Manager Professional Development

addition, the master's certificate puts the managers on a path to a higher level of professional certification, giving them incentive to get additional training to become even better managers."[6]

The extensive programs in place at NASA, DOE, and NRC, as well as the fact that a high percentage of these agencies' work relates to acquisition, contribute significantly to their success in achieving compliance with the FAC-P/PM requirements. For agencies that do not have formal project management structures, standards, or training, and where acquisitions are not the normal course of business, meeting OMB's goals for FAC-P/PM will be a greater challenge.

## COMPETENCY DEVELOPMENT

Improving project management requires a commitment by the organization and its leaders to provide formal and informal opportunities to increase the skills and knowledge of project managers. NASA and DOE have comprehensive training programs that integrate practical experience with skills and knowledge, leading toward internal project management certification. These programs include core courses, electives, and continuing education. Other approaches include contracting with external vendors to provide training or combining informal internal training with outside educational activities.

For organizations that do not have a formal training or certification program, an informal approach to delivering training may be the best course to gain the executive support needed to implement a more formal program. Ideas for building momentum in the development of an organization's project management capabilities include the following areas (see Figure 10-1):

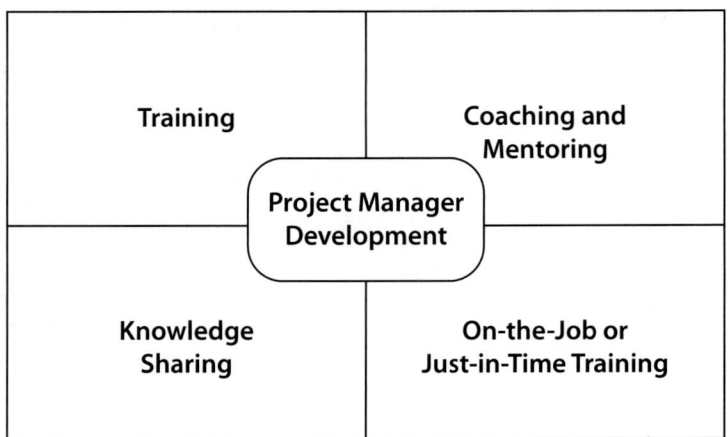

**FIGURE 10-1:** Development Methods for Project Managers

- *Training.* Successful project managers participate in a variety of training activities, including formal classroom settings, online learning, and self-study. Numerous training programs are publicly available. Many organizations have some level of internal training capability, including topics relevant to the project manager role.

- *Coaching and mentoring.* These are key components of many formal and informal training programs. The Bureau of Indian Affairs (BIA) within the Department of the Interior hired an external "coach" to build a cadre of qualified project management mentors within its PMO. The coach helped staff develop the "people" skills they need to succeed in their role as mentors.

- *On-the-job or just-in-time training.* This type of training can be delivered in a classroom setting, one-on-one, or in a brown bag lunch setting. Adult learners learn best by doing, so this can be a successful method for building individuals' and small teams' project management skills, particularly at the project level. BIA provides another good example with its project development workshops (PDWs). These three-day workshops are intended to kick-start projects by working the project team through the development of key initiating documents such as the charter, work breakdown structure, risk identification, and initial project plan and schedule. The PDWs have led to an increase in successful project execution at BIA.[7]

- *Knowledge sharing.* Establishing a project management community of practice (PM COP) is another method for sharing project management knowledge and experience. Whereas mentoring and on-the-job training reach a few practitioners at a time, establishing and building a PM COP can provide a forum for promoting best practices, sharing lessons learned, and introducing new processes and tools across an organization. Regularly scheduled meetings make sharing information a common activity and expose a wider audience to the benefits of good project management. The DoD Office of Acquisition, Technology and Logistics, in conjunction with the Defense Acquisition University, maintains an online COP for program management and other project management-related topics and practices within its acquisition community connection portal.

> The need for highly trained and certified project managers is increasing. As a project manager in your organization, you should endeavor to expand your knowledge and complement your experience with new, relevant skills, including seeking certification via your organization, PMI, or a master's degree program. Seek out and participate in relevant communities of practice, both face-to-face and online. Promote formal and information skill development in your organization; where the structures or activities do not exist, take the lead in establishing methods for improving project management skills.

Knowledge sharing is typically the most effective and cost-efficient method for developing project management skills and organizational capabilities. Instituting a local community of practice, joining industry groups or associations (e.g., PMI's Washington, D.C., chapter), establishing lessons-learned repositories, and informally sharing war stories with fellow project managers are all outstanding channels for professional growth.

Existing training programs give organizations a head start on achieving compliance with the FAC-P/PM certification requirements. Agencies without formal training programs can look to external sources or leverage the training successes across the federal government to build a program for improving project management skills and capabilities in their organizations. The cost of developing project managers can be offset by the improvements in project performance.

Of course, while obtaining a certification will certainly support career development and personal and professional growth, it is no guarantee that the person certified has what it takes to be an excellent project manager. A downside for federal employees is that the government may not pay for employees to obtain these certifications and they don't always equate to a commensurate increase in salary or a promotion to the next pay grade. Therein lies the challenge of promoting professional development for project managers.

## NOTES

1. "The Council for Excellence in Government Program Management Survey Data Report" (Vienna, VA: Management Concepts, 2008).
2. CMM and CMMI are registered in the U.S. Patent and Trademark Office by Carnegie Mellon University.
3. U.S. Department of Defense Directive 5010.42, May 15, 2008, p. 1.
4. Adapted from FAC-P/PM Draft Blueprint Version 1.2, October 15, 2007, www.fai.gov/certification/blueprints.asp (accessed February 23, 2009).
5. U.S. Department of Energy, Office of Management, Project Management Career Development Program homepage, http://www.management.energy.gov/pm_certification.htm (accessed February 17, 2009).
6. Elise Castelli, "Managers Struggle to Get New Certifications." FederalTimes.com, August 12, 2008, http://www.federaltimes.com.
7. Personal interviews with Allan Roit, former Director, Project Management Office, Bureau of Indian Affairs, September 15 and October 21, 2008.

# Part 3

# Process

The final pillar essential to achieving project management success in the federal government is process, the operational context for project management practices. Each of the chapters in this part addresses an aspect of the emergence and application of project management processes that influences and guides the execution of projects in the federal government.

Chapter 11, *Governance and Project Portfolio Development: Steering the Ship*, describes key elements in the federal project management framework, including governance and project portfolio development and management.

In Chapter 12, *Adopting and Applying Methodologies: Choosing the Right Path*, we focus on project management methodologies and product development lifecycles. The chapter provides examples of key methodologies in use across the federal government.

In Chapter 13, *Aligning Federal and Project Planning Cycles: Untangling the Knot*, we focus on the relationship between project management and external processes. At a high level, this chapter examines how government-wide planning and reporting processes like the federal budget, GPRA, and PAR affect and provide direction to the execution of projects in the federal government.

Chapter 14, *Implementing Knowledge Management Practices: Reusing the Wheel*, addresses the challenges associated with managing and sharing project knowledge. This chapter highlights practical examples of successful knowledge management practices in the federal government and discusses the direction this emerging discipline is taking.

Chapter 15, *Understanding Project Performance Management: Uncovering Success Early*, provides an overview of managing project performance in the federal government context. Examples of establishing performance measures, with an emphasis on earned value management, are presented in the context of the project performance management lifecycle.

## Chapter 11

# Governance and Project Portfolio Development: Steering the Ship

*You've got to think about the big things, so that all the small things go in the right directions.*

—ALVIN TOFFLER, FUTURIST, AUTHOR

With a billion dollar budget, the Nuclear Regulatory Commission (NRC) is a relatively small federal agency, but one with a highly critical mission. As the regulating agency for civilian nuclear activity in the United States, NRC oversees more than 350 nuclear power plants, as well as thousands of medical and commercial facilities that use nuclear materials. NRC protects people and the environment by ensuring a safe and viable commercial nuclear sector. To deliver on its mission, NRC relies on a sturdy backbone of information technology. A limited budget and IT department resources demand that NRC leadership make smart decisions at all phases of the project lifecycle. They have neither the budget for expensive mistakes nor a tolerance for lapses in service. What helps keep NRC's regulatory infrastructure on target is a robust set of project management processes.

NRC has invested in developing the framework of project management to ensure that the agency has a solid foundation for selecting, planning, and managing new projects, and then carrying those projects forward to operations and maintenance. At NRC, the Office of Information Services (OIS) relies on a strong governance process to deliver IT solutions across NRC. To accomplish their jobs effectively, OIS personnel have developed a project management framework that is accessible through the office's intranet site.

The NRC project management framework, like those established by many federal agencies, comprises four layers (see Figure 11-1):

- *Organizational governance*—provides an open, structured format for evaluating investments and executive decision-making.

- *Project portfolio management*—provides a process for managing the inventory of work associated with specific parts of the organization.

- *Project management methodology*—involves the use of approaches and standards to manage the project environment.

- *Product development lifecycle*—involves the use of industry standards in creating the products of the projects.

Collectively, these four layers form a framework for effective project management. While most federal agencies make use of all four, the degree of coordination between the layers varies by agency. In this chapter, we look at the two higher-level functions, governance and project portfolio

**CHAPTER 11** Governance and Project Portfolio Development

management. In the next chapter, we focus on the project management methodology and the product development lifecycle.

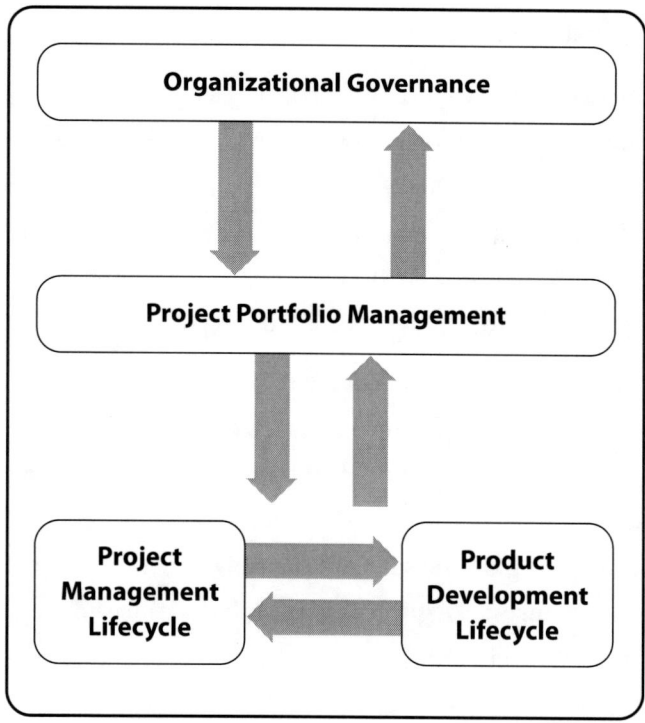

**FIGURE 11-1:** Project Management Framework

## ORGANIZATIONAL GOVERNANCE

Governance is a process that brings together agency leadership and managers to enable coordinated, open decision-making. The goal of governance is generally to provide a forum for internal stakeholders to participate in shaping the decisions and investments that will improve the performance of the organization. Governance is premised on the idea of scarcity—that there will never be enough resources to accomplish all the initiatives an agency would like to undertake. Given the dichotomy of limited resources and a plethora of good ideas, governance is a process that continually evaluates the investment portfolio to ensure that an agency is making the best choices based on a variety of criteria.

The function of governance sits above project management, spanning the full lifecycle of investment decision-making, from idea conception to evaluation, acquisition, project management, maintenance and operations, and retirement. Yet governance has a direct impact on the scope, scale, and budgets of projects. Projects are created, approved, renewed, or discontinued based on governance processes.

In the federal environment, governance takes a variety of forms. For example, governance can simply equate to a group of executives who meet regularly in the context of coordinated decision-making or it can comprise multiple layers of committees and formal processes within an agency. Depending on the scope of governance, it may be called "enterprise governance," "IT governance," or "investment review boards" (IRBs). As displayed in Figure 11-2, the typical governance structure is hierarchical, with an executive committee and multiple subcommittees. In this case, the executive committee would act as the IRB. Often, technical committees operate below the lines of business to reconcile the ideas and decisions of governance with specific implementation challenges.

Governance also operates across multiple levels of the U.S. government. For example, there are governance structures specific to directorates within an agency, governance structures that span an entire agency, and even superstructures that span the entire government (such as the CIO Council). Information technology organizations are the most prevalent arena for governance, in part because IT investments require heavy input from across the organization to ensure effective implementation.

# CHAPTER 11 Governance and Project Portfolio Development

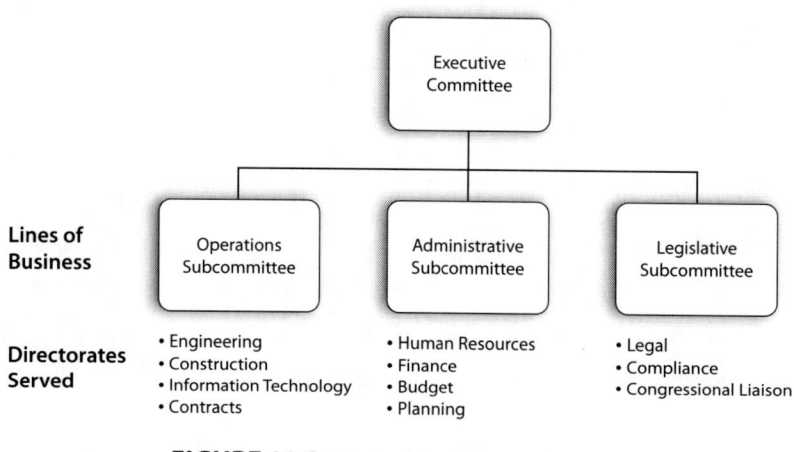

**FIGURE 11-2:** Typical Governance Structure

Governance is a balancing act that involves addressing the pressing priorities of the day while pursuing longer-term investments that will advance the agency as a whole. Often, governance makes investments from three "buckets"—*operate* the business, *improve* the business, and *transform* the business:

- *Operate.* This area is also known as "keeping the lights on." Operating the business involves maintaining the basic infrastructure of people, processes, physical plant, technology, and other areas that provide the agency with the basic tools to operate. These current, known obligations represent the largest area of expenditure for most agencies.

- *Improve.* To address current challenges, the agency must continuously improve and upgrade its physical plant, processes, technology, and people. These improvements do not represent wholesale change but are required for the efficient operation of the business. Improvements generally help keep the agency from falling behind in meeting customers' needs, and they can include upgrading technology, revising policy and procedure manuals, and modifying staffing.

- *Transform.* When an agency seeks to redesign an area of its business, it effectively transforms the business by redefining the basic assumptions, processes, and tools it uses to conduct business. Transformation may involve implementing new technologies, processes, or ways of dealing with customers. Transforming the business goes beyond improvements to existing systems, driving toward a complete rethinking of the agency's core processes.

Federal leaders must balance their investments across these three buckets, addressing the changing priorities of the organization. Within each bucket, federal governance processes should consider investments in terms of a variety of criteria, including:

- *Risk.* Agency leadership needs to understand the exposure incurred by a given investment, as well as across a band of investments. For example, investments in technology should align with the agency's overall risk profile.
- *Performance.* Projects and processes must meet performance standards, as defined by OMB, the agency, or the manufacturer (if a product is involved).
- *Transparency.* Transparency operates at two levels in governance. First, the federal agency must adhere to the letter and spirit of open government. The Presidential Memorandum dated January 21, 2009, requires executive agencies to "harness new technologies to put information about their operations and decisions online and read-

ily available to the public."[1] Second, governance provides an open forum for addressing the needs of all organizational stakeholders. This transparency is essential to ensuring that all voices are heard.

- *Legal and regulatory requirements.* According to OMB Circular A-11, Part 7:

  Agencies must develop, implement, and use a capital programming process to develop their capital asset portfolio, and must:

  - Evaluate and select capital asset investments that will support core mission functions....
  - Initiate improvements to existing assets or acquisitions of new assets only when no alternative private sector or governmental source can more efficiently meet the need
  - Simplify or otherwise redesign work processes to reduce costs, improve effectiveness....
  - Reduce project risk by avoiding or isolating custom designed components....
  - Structure major acquisitions into useful segments with a narrow scope and brief duration, make adequate use of competition and appropriately allocate risk between Government and contractor
  - Institute performance measures and management processes for monitoring and comparing actual performance to planned results.[2]

- *Ethics.* Governance plays an important role in allowing executives to have open debate on the ethics of one idea versus another (for example, the decision to fund one grant over another where each grant may result in real improvements to the human condition).

The governance process is most often used in the IT environment, where IRBs act as the primary mechanism for executing governance functions. At NRC, the governance structure maps to critical touchpoints in the IT decision-making chain (see Figure 11-3).

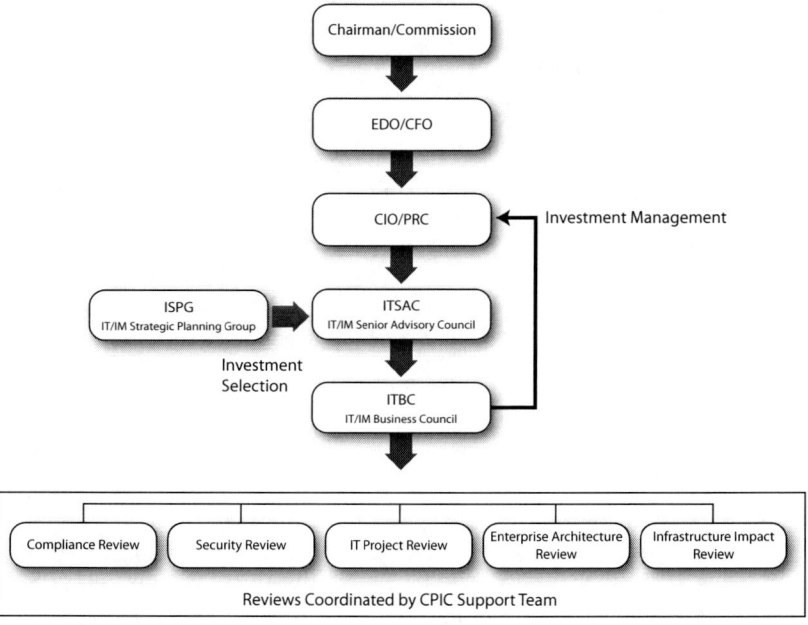

**FIGURE 11-3:** NRC Governance Structure for IT

For example, the enterprise architecture (EA) review is charged with considering all projects that need to address the NRC EA model. The EA model is "a strategic information asset base, which defines the mission; the information necessary to perform the mission; the technologies (hardware and software) necessary to perform the mission; and the transitional processes for implementing new technologies in response to changing mission needs."[3] The objective of the EA review is to ensure compliance with the NRC model and, ultimately, federal requirements.

Moving up the ladder, the IT Business Council (ITBC) fulfills the role of the investment review board. The ITBC is an interactive group of business and IT executives that recommends investments in the agency's IT portfolio. Once an investment is approved, the ITBC reconciles its various aspects with NRC's overarching IT transition plan, which is a multiyear, direction-setting document for the agency. Throughout the investment lifecycle, the ITBC also monitors investments to ensure they are on track and meeting performance goals.

Next in the chain is the IT Senior Advisory Council (ITSAC). Chaired by NRC's CIO, the ITSAC is composed of directors from the major offices within NRC. The ITSAC plays a key role in the creation and maintenance of the agency's IT strategic plan and advises the CIO on agency-level IT initiatives.

One complaint about governance structures is that the internal bureaucracy slows down decision-making. This is a legitimate concern, and governance committees need to be responsive to their stakeholders. One way to do this is to develop expedited procedures for specific types of requests, such as those under a certain dollar threshold.

## PROJECT PORTFOLIO MANAGEMENT

Portfolio management is the integrated coordination and oversight of selected groupings of projects (or investments). Portfolio management is integral to the work that is done in governance, with each providing inputs and outputs to the other. For example, portfolio management produces the critical performance and financial/resource data that executives need to perform the governance function. In governance, executives make decisions that impact the portfolio. These decisions must be integrated back into each project in the portfolio, and the overall portfolio must then be recalibrated.

In the federal government, governance and portfolio management tend to be tightly coupled within agencies. Agencies that have invested in one of these functions typically have a robust process for the other as well.

Particular features differentiate portfolios from a simple grouping of projects. For example, portfolios have:

- *Portfolio manager.* An accountable person is charged with the overall health and well-being of the portfolio.

- *Defined boundaries.* Portfolios are defined by their budgets, scope of investments, and organizational boundaries.

- *Criteria for inclusion.* To be accepted into the portfolio, a project or investment must meet certain criteria, such as a risk score.

- *Integrated reporting.* Portfolios tend to be tallied and examined en masse so that executives and others can view the totality of the portfolio across different dimensions (e.g., resources, budget, demand, performance).

Portfolios often address the full lifecycle of the asset—selection and planning, implementation and control, operations and maintenance, and eventually retirement. Project management informs part of the lifespan of the asset but usually stops at operations and maintenance and retirement. In other words, at some point the asset is no longer a project but a depreciating asset "owned" by a business unit that is part of the unit's annual budget.

Portfolio managers perform much of the nuts-and-bolts work required to enable governance-level decision-making: calculating EVM, producing reports, and interfacing with other systems like HR and accounting. The portfolio manager must endeavor to integrate key management interfaces, such as:

- *Strategic plan:* ensure that the portfolio addresses division, agency, and governmental priorities.
- *Risk:* manage the individual and cumulative exposure of the investment portfolio.
- *Architecture:* verify that projects adhere to the overall architectural guidance, as defined in the federal enterprise architecture (FEA). Each agency maintains a plan that adheres to the FEA.
- *Portfolio management strategy:* ensure that investment prioritization techniques are robust and valid for the organization.
- *Inventory:* incorporate clear boundaries and reconcile with the budgets associated with the portfolio.

A single portfolio comprises multiple projects and programs. Yet the portfolio itself should have an objective. After all, why group these particular items together? Generally, portfolios are created around functional units, such as IT, or around budgetary items, such as funding for a specific purpose. For example, an IT portfolio may have as its objective the efficient use of IT investment dollars. Project portfolios must address the notion of tradeoffs over time, such as how much to invest now versus later. Moreover, portfolios need to incorporate specific processes around performance management, risk management, and investment management.[4]

Figure 11-4 depicts an approach to project portfolio management that supports the governance process. In proposal support, investment ideas are gathered and processed for selection. This function is sometimes referred to as "demand management," and indeed, that is what is happening. In any organization, there is no shortage of good ideas, so the proposal support process allows for these good ideas to be developed iteratively without necessarily requiring a significant commitment from the organization. Following proposal support comes governance support, whereby the portfolio is made ready for governance review via report production, data verification, agenda development, etc. Also, governance committees are often managed as a function of governance support. This means that the committees are scheduled, facilitated, and documented by the portfolio management team. Finally, inventory management occurs, whereby the portfolio is assessed and adjusted to reconcile governance decisions as well as changes in project and program baselines.

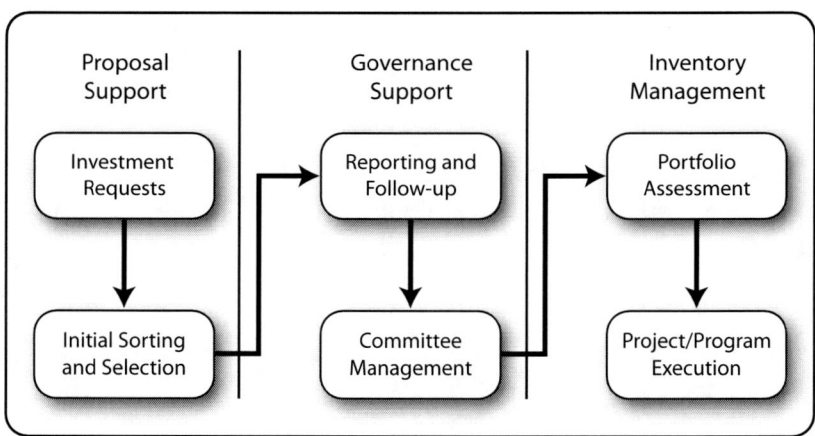

**FIGURE 11-4:** Integration of Project Portfolio Management and Governance

Portfolio management should create efficiencies across projects through macro-level resource management. Inventory management seeks to understand key aspects of the portfolio, including:

- The skills and abilities needed across the portfolio

- Whether the current portfolio of projects addresses the agency's major growth areas adequately
- The major risks across the portfolio
- How individual projects in the portfolio are performing.

Portfolio management often exacerbates the challenges associated with managing large organizations. In the federal environment, agency leadership teams continue to struggle with integrated strategic decision-making on several fronts:

- *Too much information.* Executives faced with strategic decision-making authority must process enormous amounts of information. This can include laws, regulations, performance reports, analyses, projections and estimates, and past decisions. The sheer amount of information makes it hard to differentiate the truly important data from the less important.

- *Not enough input from business stakeholders.* Sometimes, as a result of too much information, stakeholders get locked out of the process. In a sense, the portfolio really belongs to those business stakeholders, yet their input is sometimes sought out too late or too quickly, with poor results.

- *Inadequate processes.* The portfolio management and governance processes need to be bolstered with adequate processes and tools to be able to handle the budget issues, power struggles, and other calamities that befall the portfolio in any given year.

- *Conflicting internal priorities.* Investment management requires tenacity and conviction to see an investment through in the face of tough budget shortfalls and important near-term goals. Yet again, executives must also understand when to cut an investment and redefine priorities.

Despite these challenges, a new generation of project portfolio management tools is emerging. These tools facilitate EVM, resource management, streamlined information (through dashboards), and related portfolio functions. Many federal agencies are recognizing that portfolio management is a data-intensive effort and that robust tools are a key differentiator between mediocrity and a successful portfolio management approach.

> Many federal agencies have adopted the basic practices of governance and project portfolio management within their IT environments. Looking ahead, agencies need to develop more effective methods of integrating these disciplines with project management methodologies. A more coordinated approach to managing investments is critical, especially in these tough economic times. Project management leadership must take the lead in bridging the divide between internal teams and their customers, executives and staff, and agency goals and individual actions.
>
> Successful agencies are proactively pursuing new ways of doing business. To support these innovations, agencies need robust governance and portfolio tools. For example, new portfolio management tools are providing insights into resource constraints and high-risk projects. Agencies that devote resources to improving governance and portfolio management will realize the results of streamlined decision processes and higher-quality investments. The savings realized will enable more efficient operations. The future is bright for agencies that maximize the efficient use of the core processes of governance and portfolio management.

## NOTES

1. Memorandum for the Heads of Executive Departments and Agencies, January 21, 2009, http://www.whitehouse.gov/the_press_office/Transparency_and_Open_Government.
2. OMB Circular No. A-11 Part 7, Planning, Budgeting, Acquisition, and Management of Capital Assets, p. 7.
3. NRC Project Management Methodology, Enterprise Architecture.
4. http://www.army.mil/ArmyBTKC/gov/pfm.htm (accessed November 2, 2009).

## Chapter 12
# Adopting and Applying Methodologies: Choosing the Right Path

*Everything should be made as simple as possible, but not simpler.*

—Albert Einstein

In 2010, the U.S. population is projected to be roughly 309 million people living in 134 million housing units and more than 270,000 group quarters (such as prisons, dormitories, and nursing homes). In that same year, the U.S. Census Bureau will endeavor to count every single one of those people once and only once. Called the "decennial census," this is the largest peacetime activity undertaken by the federal government. To accomplish this task, the Census Bureau will hire 1.4 million temporary workers in nearly 500 local offices to count a population that resides over more than 3.5 million square miles of land mass.

Planning and executing the 2010 decennial census will take more than 14 years and will involve 44 interrelated operations with more than 9,000 tasks. To accomplish this feat, the Census Bureau relies on a robust project management methodology that is built around the following key components:

- *Integrated program plan.* This plan includes the mission, vision, goals, and objectives of the decennial census.
- *Risk management.* The Census Bureau tracks risks at two levels: program and project. Program-level risks involve threats to the overall decennial census. Project-level risks are limited to a specific operation or task. All program risks have mitigation plans and may have contingency plans as well.
- *Schedule management.* The Census Bureau maintains a master schedule and a formal change control process to ensure that changes to any of the 9,000 tasks are handled with care. The "schedule alert report," which contains critical path tasks, is reviewed weekly and acted upon by Census leadership.
- *Lifecycle budget.* The funding stream for the decennial census accounts for activities from the earliest planning to the last data product delivered. The budget includes funding for people, technology, office space, forms and printing, data processing operations, and more.
- *Formal decision-making processes.* Numerous weekly meetings are held, reaching from the decennial census leaders to the overall Census leadership, to its parent the Commerce Department, and onward to the White House and Capitol Hill as needed. Each of

the meetings has defined objectives and outputs, which create an effective cascade of decision points and information flow.

- *Teams.* The decennial census deploys a wide range of team to support getting work done. Each team has a charter and a distinct focus. The central team is the census integration group (CIG). This team reviews the status from operations and systems teams, reviews funding requests, and reports to the decennial leadership team.[1]

The decennial census simply would not work without a systematic, coordinated approach to handling such a large endeavor. It thus provides a great example of how a federal organization can thrive in the face of an enormous challenge through use of an effective project management methodology in conjunction with a product development lifecycle.

## PROJECT MANAGEMENT METHODOLOGIES

At the individual project level, a methodology provides guidance and coordination to the team. A project management methodology defines the structure for moving through the stages of a project. A methodology can provide a set of templates that will aid in the development of a consistent approach to doing the work, a common language, and predictable outputs.

Most federal agencies have adopted or developed a project management methodology in some part of their organization. Yet many organizations within agencies still struggle with the basic tenets of implementing project management.

Project management methodologies are products of their environment. No two are exactly the same, in part because of differences in culture and organizational structure. Agencies must strive to tailor their project management methodology to their business practices in a meaningful way.

Two methodologies commonly used in the federal environment are the waterfall methodology and the agile methodology.

## Waterfall Methodology

Many projects in the federal environment follow a waterfall approach, whereby discovery leads to design, which then informs implementation, validation, and closeout. These phases each tend to be completed once in a project, with little iteration. This is the classic project management methodology—the "the archetypal project cycle model from which all others derived...."[2]

As Figure 12-1 shows, the waterfall methodology relies upon earlier work to be completed for later work to proceed. One strength of this approach is that emphasis is placed on getting the up-front discovery done correctly. Conversely, a weakness is that if a team does a poor job gathering requirements, the resulting system will reflect incomplete or poor-quality requirements.

Because the waterfall approach is sequential, it involves substantial documentation. This reliance on capturing information at a point in time can lead to problems as requirements change. Project management leadership needs to construct processes that allow for review and update of the requirements in later phases of the project, suggesting a modified waterfall approach. In a modified waterfall approach, iterative loops allow for feedback on specific content areas, like requirements, that are typically generated very early in the project.

# CHAPTER 12  Adopting and Applying Methodologies

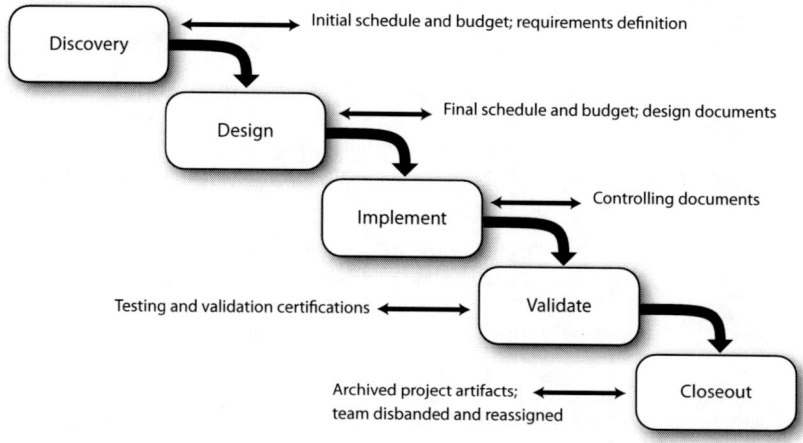

**FIGURE 12-1:** Traditional Waterfall Methodology

The Government Accountability Office (GAO) conducts about 1,000 engagements or evaluations in a typical year, each one its own project. GAO executes projects according to a detailed, five-phase waterfall methodology: acceptance, planning and design, data gathering and analysis, product development, and results. These phases are performed within a quality assurance framework designed to ensure that:

- Work is professional, independent, and objective
- Evidence is complete and reliable
- Conclusions and products are fair
- Recommendations are sound.[3]

The "products" of GAO's projects are analyses, recommendations, and reports; the agency has tailored its methodology accordingly. Table 12-1 highlights the features of each phase.

| Phase | Features |
|---|---|
| Acceptance | At an engagement acceptance meeting, senior GAO management considers:<br>■ Is the request a significant priority (per defined selection criteria)?<br>■ Availability of skills, resources, and data.<br>■ Level of senior management participation (from both GAO and the target department).<br>■ Level of cost, complexity, and controversy.<br>■ GAO authority and access to information.<br>■ Staff allocation. (Most engagements are multidisciplinary and require team members from different GAO units.)<br>■ Which government audit standards apply?<br>■ What is the source of the data/information?<br>■ What is the timeframe? |
| Planning and Design | ■ Design, review, and document project plan with stakeholders.<br>■ Establish timeframe.<br>■ Ensure that audit is objectively designed and customer (primarily Congress) agrees to scope and deliverables; changes are managed against this agreement. |
| Data Gathering and Analysis | This is the longest phase of most engagements and includes a wide variety of GAO staff roles (e.g., project managers, analysts, lawyers, contract specialists, other SMEs).<br>■ Gather data to address questions.<br>■ Develop evidence and analyze.<br>■ Validate that results reflect significant findings.<br>■ Meet with key stakeholders to develop "messages." |
| Product Development | Produce the final deliverables, applying:<br>■ GAO reporting standards<br>■ Core values—fair, objective, balanced, complete<br>■ Quality check—facts go through a quality check by GAO staff who did not participate in the engagement<br>■ Multiple reviews of draft products<br>■ Agency review and comment. |
| Results | GAO tracks implementation of the recommendations included in its reports for internal measurement and to determine their effectiveness. |

**TABLE 12-1:** GAO's Customized Waterfall Methodology

## Agile Project Management

Agile project management, created for software development but generally applicable to all types of projects, is gaining some ground as an alternative to the traditional waterfall approach to projects. Agile project management is a way to "energize, empower, and enable project teams to rapidly and reliably deliver business value by engaging customers and continuously learning and adapting to their changing needs and environments."[4] The founders of this approach promote the following four tenets in their "Manifesto for Agile Software Development":

1. Individuals and interactions over processes and tools
2. Working software over comprehensive documentation
3. Customer collaboration over contract negotiation
4. Responding to change over following a plan.[5]

These founding principles may seem counter to the operation of government enterprises, with their regulated structure and high levels of accountability. However, the flexible nature of agile project management requires the discipline and structure that some more mature project organizations can provide.

Agile project managers have to achieve a balance between emergent order and imposed order. While imposed order is a top-down approach to organizational control, emergent order uses a bottom-up approach. Successful project managers will use a mixture of imposed and emergent order to achieve an ideal work environment. To accomplish this balance, project managers should:

- Collaborate with stakeholders to understand the vision for the project, how it aligns with the goals of the organization, and how it will be used. Information flow is needed at all stages of agile management because any problems will have to be corrected quickly.

- Organize a group discussion with the team to generate a common project vision. This is the first step toward establishing the teamwork needed.

- Identify, communicate, and maintain this guiding vision.

- Establish a planning process that defines the purpose and goals while giving team members autonomy and allowing team innovation.

- Implement a flexible management approach based on observation as well as planning. A project manager who has visionary leadership is continuously observing, learning, and acclimating to the environment.

Agile project management has five phases (see Table 12-2) that were originally developed for IT projects but apply to a broad range of project types.

| | |
|---|---|
| Envision | Define the project vision and scope, and describe what the results will be, the project community, and how the team will work together. |
| Speculate | Develop a feature-based release, milestone, and iteration plan to deliver on the vision. |
| Explore | Deliver tested features in a short timeframe, constantly seeking to reduce the risk and uncertainty of the project. |
| Adapt | Review the delivered results, the current situation, and the team's performance, and adapt as necessary. |
| Close | Conclude the project, pass along key lessons learned, and celebrate. |

**TABLE 12-2:** Agile Five-Phase Methodology[6]

The Bureau of Indian Affairs' PMO supports an array of projects, most of which are IT-related. Allan Roit, former director of the PMO, explains that BIA is applying an agile methodology on its IT projects. In the "speculate" phase, for example, the project scope is developed over time, as the project's complexity is uncovered and understood. The project team then develops "story points," akin to use cases, to promote speed in developing the solution. In concert with the implementation of some agile concepts, a system lifecycle that integrates the development and acquisition lifecycles is used. Roit anticipates continuing to introduce additional agile elements as project teams grow more comfortable and achieve success.[7]

While agile project management adds speed and flexibility to sound project management practices, the "radical" nature of this approach may be too large a leap for some organizations steeped in more traditional project management methodologies. However, applying some of the agile principles, as BIA has done, can fill the gap between the "chaos" of the agile approach and the highly structured waterfall method.

## Other Federal Project Management Methodologies

The traditional waterfall methodology tends to be the most prevalent in the federal environment, with agile increasing in use across the federal environment. Embedded within agencies are a wide variety of "one-off" and truly customized methodologies, may of which are variants of the waterfall model. These include:

- *RAD.* Rapid application development (RAD) is a method used in software development. In this methodology, the emphasis is on iterative development and the rapid rollout of prototypes. RAD allows the development team to evolve the requirements with each development iteration.

- *Spiral.* Like RAD, the spiral methodology relies on an iterative approach to development; it differs from RAD in that it uses four quadrants: objectives, evaluation, develop/test, and planning. The objectives are set for that particular iteration, alternatives are evaluated and one is selected, development and testing occur, and the next phase is identified based on the results. In this methodology, the scope of the effort gradually increases with each turn around the spiral.[8]

The key for federal agencies in selecting and upgrading their project management methodology is to determine its purpose. A methodology is only a tool, a set of steps to be commonly used in getting work done. The power of a project management methodology resides in its ability to bring multiple stakeholders together. Project management leadership would be wise to focus less on selecting the perfect methodology and more on building effective strategies for coordinating the methodology across the agency.

## **PRODUCT DEVELOPMENT LIFECYCLES**

In the federal government, projects create all kinds of outcomes, services, products, and results. From new highways to drug development protocols, jet fighters to websites, the federal government relies on industry standards to shape these products. Projects must adhere to these industry standards and processes, called product lifecycles, to be effective. Product lifecycles determine how the primary deliverables of the project are designed, developed, tested, and implemented. For example, the construction of a new federal building follows a process that addresses design, materials acquisition, foundation, floors, roof, utilities, outer cladding, and landscaping.

Projects must integrate core product development tasks with the project management tasks that enable an effective flow of activities and resource

# CHAPTER 12 Adopting and Applying Methodologies

use. As shown in Figure 12-2, the project management methodology and the product development lifecycle are independent, with the connecting lines showing the concurrent phases. Notice how the "validation" stage in project management begins before the "commissioning" stage in construction is over. At some point in the commissioning lifecycle, the delivery of the product ends and validation of the product begins. These links are often negotiated by the project team during planning processes.

| Project Management Methodology | Discover | Design | Execution | Validation | Closeout |
|---|---|---|---|---|---|
| Product Development Lifecycle | Design | Contract Award | Construction | Commissioning | Operations |

**FIGURE 12-2:** Integration of Project Management and Product Development

This simple graphic does not do justice to the complexities involved in managing a major construction project. Construction project managers must understand all facets of both the project management methodology and the product development lifecycle to ensure that the designs, budgets, permits, materials, labor, and equipment all flow into the stream of tasks and staging involved in a construction project. To be effective, a product lifecycle should be documented via the work breakdown structure and schedule. A WBS integrates both processes into one set of deliverables.

The Treasury Department's Bureau of the Public Debt, Administrative Resource Center (ARC), is a certified shared service provider (SSP) for the federal government.[9] ARC's mission is to aid in improving overall government effectiveness by delivering responsive and cost-effective administrative support to stakeholders within the government, and thereby to improve other government agencies' ability to deliver services to their constituencies. ARC, which is an OMB-approved "Center of Excellence for Financial Management," continually reviews its processes to maintain and improve performance. To accomplish its mission, ARC must effectively use the project management and product lifecycles to ensure that its customers—other federal agencies—are satisfied customers.

Jason Hill and Shaun Willison, project managers, explain that one of ARC's key services is financial system conversions. The ARC PMO led a project team that developed an end-to-end methodology, based in part on PMI's *PMBOK® Guide*, that includes a simplified approach to addressing IT and change management. The customer conversion methodology includes five phases: discovery, initiation and planning, configuration and design, development and testing, and deployment.

One of the key tools employed by the ARC PMO to ensure a tight fit between service development and project management is a strong discovery process that uncovers customer requirements early and provides an effective, risk-reducing customer intake process. This phase is focused on uncovering the government customers' requirements, resulting in proactive program planning. The outcome of this phase helps determine the level of project management required throughout the remainder of the project.

As the project team assesses the client's needs to determine the fit with ARC's products and services, it is completing the first pass at the project schedule, scope, budget, and quality assurance plans. This effort in the discovery phase contributes to effective scope management and increases the potential that the needed products and services will be delivered.

To be effective, agencies need to establish tight linkages between the product and project management lifecycles. Project management is only as good as the end result of the project. However, it is important that project management not overshadow the development of the core deliverable. When the two methodologies are linked correctly, project management builds value into each phase by formalizing the planning and management activities.

## PROJECT MANAGEMENT ENABLERS

The past ten years have seen an explosion of project management methodologies and maturity models. Many are proprietary or embedded into various tools; others are available for use in the public domain. The following is a sampling of these methodologies and maturity models, which can be instrumental in the successful development of project management in a federal environment.

### Organizational Project Management Maturity Model (OPM3®)

PMI has promoted individual competency and certification in project management for many years. The organization has raised the bar on project management across nearly every industry and discipline through the *PMBOK® Guide* and its focused add-ons (e.g., the government extension). Released in 2003, the Organizational Project Management Maturity Model (OPM3®) seeks to increase capabilities at the enterprise level.

Organizational project management focuses on the relationship between an organization's project management capabilities and its effective implementation of strategy. The results of a survey determine a maturity level based on the effectiveness of an organization's project management practices and processes. OPM3®'s five maturity levels are ad hoc, planned, managed, integrated, and sustained. An organization's size, complexity, and initial maturity will determine the path required to improve its project management maturity.[10]

## Capability Maturity Model Integration (CMMI®)

Carnegie Mellon University's Software Engineering Institute (SEI) is known worldwide for its Capability Maturity Model Integration (CMMI®).[11] The CMMI® models represent best practices from a wide variety of industries and are intended, like other models, as a guide for organizations to improve their processes. Given the importance of acquisition in the government arena, the CMMI® model for acquisition (CMMI®-ACQ) is particularly relevant to project management in the federal government.

The CMMI®-ACQ model is based on the foundation CMMI® model, with an additional six acquisition-specific areas: agreement management, acquisition requirements development, acquisition technical management, acquisition validation, acquisition verification, and solicitation and supplier agreement development. Like other models, the CMMI®-ACQ assesses both the capability (six levels) and maturity (five levels) of an organization for a given set of processes.

## Six Sigma

Six Sigma is best known by the acronym DMAIC, denoting the elements of the standard six sigma framework: define, measure, analyze, improve, and control.

Six critical elements that are required to implement six sigma in an organization reinforce project management best practices regardless of the methodology being followed:

1. *Genuine focus on the customer.* The customer is the highest priority in six sigma. Responsiveness to customer needs and full customer participation in the project are considered key successes in the six sigma approach.

2. *Data- and fact-driven management.* Decisions based on fact and information are critical. The data has to be based on specific measures that will reveal the true status of the project.

3. *Process focus, management, and improvement.* Achieving the highest process efficiency is the source of the greatest improvements in time, cost, and satisfaction. As a result, six sigma projects are grounded in process performance measurement and improvements.

4. *Proactive management.* Awareness, insight, and understanding of the three previous items enable project managers and an organization's senior leaders to set clear goals, avoid risks, and act with creativity and innovation.

5. *"Boundaryless" collaboration.* Organizational and project silos are replaced with integrated project teams, cross-project and organizational coordination, and implementation of shared processes and tools.

6. *Drive for perfection, tolerate failure.* Balancing quality and time requires a certain tolerance for errors, mistakes, and possibly outright failure. This does not mean taking unnecessary risks, but taking risks that are well understood and have the potential to yield better results, significant improvements, or breakthrough innovation.[12]

## National Competence Baseline

Another project management organization charged with promoting the discipline is the American Society for the Advancement of Project Management (asapm), www.asapm.org. Asapm is the U.S. member organization of the International Project Management Association (IPMA), www.ipma.ch. This organization emphasizes and provides the USA National Competence Baseline, version 2.0, a four-level competency-based certification for project and program managers. Asapm is also developing an organization-level certification for project management competency called the asapm Performance Rated Organization, or aPro. While asapm and IPMA do not have the same level of prominence in the United States that PMI does, their competence-oriented philosophies provide substantially different paradigms for training and certification.

## Process and Enterprise Maturity Model (PEMM™)

Michael Hammer, the father of process reengineering, finalized the process and enterprise maturity model (PEMM™) in 2006 as an alternative to other maturity models. Whereas models like OPM3® and CMMI® apply to specific processes or practices (project management and software development, respectively), PEMM™ provides organizations with a tool for assessing their overall process maturity and capabilities. PEMM™ is easy to self-administer; an organization applies PEMM™ to its relevant processes to understand and assess five "process enablers" (design, performers, owner, infrastructure, and metrics) and four "enterprise capabilities" (leadership, culture, expertise, and governance).

These enablers and capabilities are consistent with sound project management practices and structures; thus, PEMM™ assessments can indicate project management maturity or capacity. "The PEMM™ framework doesn't make the road to process transformation easy to traverse. However, in process transformations . . . knowing where you stand and having a road map to follow beats stumbling in the dark."[13] This advice, of course, applies to any legitimate maturity model.

# CHAPTER 12  Adopting and Applying Methodologies

Just as governance and portfolio management play a critical role in determining the best use of available resources for investments, project management methodologies and product development lifecycles support the more tactical activities of implementing those investment decisions. Census Bureau leadership would not get very far if they could not rely on a set of repeatable processes that are executed every day by the small army that makes up the decennial census team. The Census methodology goes beyond just doing the right steps in a sequence; it actually creates a sense of unity around the process. Everyone has a job to do and a shared vision of the outcome. The project management methodology brings clarity to an otherwise overwhelming proposition.

To be successful, agencies must go beyond building or buying a project management methodology. Serious investment must be made in adoption of the methodology as well. From sponsors to project managers and team members, the organization needs to understand the value of the methodology for it to thrive.

Adopting a project management methodology requires change at a fundamental level, which should not be underestimated. Consensus must be built around the methodology. Agencies that successfully adopt a project management methodology and the related product development lifecycle will be doing themselves a great service.

## NOTES

1. Daniel H. Weinberg, "Managing the 2010 Decennial Census," presented at PMI® North American Global Congress, Orlando, FL, October 12, 2009.
2. Kathleen B. Hass, *Managing Complex Projects* (Vienna, VA: Management Concepts, 2009), p.84.
3. Personal interview with Steve Backhus, Director, Office of Quality and Continuous Improvement, Government Accountability Office, November 24, 2008.
4. Sanjiv Augustine, *Managing Agile Projects* (Upper Saddle River, NJ: Prentice Hall, 2005), pg. 23.
5. "Manifesto for Agile Software Development," www.agilemanifesto.org (accessed June 9, 2009).
6. Jim Highsmith, *Agile Project Management: Creating Innovative Products* (Upper Saddle River, NJ: Pearson Education, Inc. 2004), p. 81. © 2004 Pearson Education, Inc. Reproduced by permission of Pearson Education, Inc.

7. Personal interviews with Allan Roit, former Director, Project Management Office, Bureau of Indian Affairs, September 15 and October 21, 2008.
8. Hamidreza Monajjemi, "Determining Matchable System Development Model for Low Cost Carriers (LCCs)," p. 5, http://necsi.org/events/iccs7/papers/252MonajjemiEngSys.doc (accessed November 2, 2009).
9. Personal interview with Jason Hill and Shaun Willison, Administrative Resource Center, Bureau of the Public Debt, Department of the Treasury, October 19, 2008.
10. Project Management Institute, "An Executive's Guide to OPM3®," http://opm3online.pmi.org/demo/downloads/PP_OPM3ExecGuide.pdf (accessed November 2, 2009).
11. Software Engineering Institute, "CMMI® for Acquisition, Version 1.2," November 2007, http://www.sei.cmu.edu/library/abstracts/reports/07tr017.cfm (accessed November 2, 2009).
12. Peter S. Pande, Robert P. Neuman, and Roland R. Cavanaugh, *The Six Sigma Way Team Fieldbook: An Implementation Guide for Project Improvement Teams* (New York: McGraw-Hill, 2001), pp. 8–10.
13. Michael Hammer, "The Process Audit," *Harvard Business Review*, April 2007, vol. 9, no. 2.

## Chapter 13

# Aligning Federal and Project Planning Cycles: Untangling the Knot

*The ability to formulate business strategy that is effective and distinct from tactical strategy and to move the organization successfully in a different direction is going to become the trademark of public sector managers and leaders in the 21st century!*

—Thomas G. Kessler and Patricia Kelley
The Business of Government: Strategy, Implementation, and Results

Every federal agency must comply with external planning processes and requirements. Mandated planning and reporting cycles are important considerations for federal agencies as they define their priorities and structure their operations. Many agencies devote considerable resources to maintaining their planning and performance documentation. These efforts inform the project environment and play an important role in creating an environment conducive to project success.

Federal agencies, with few exceptions, maintain many layers of management across multiple separate organizations. This up-and-down and side-to-side complexity permeates the bureaucratic machine that is government, presenting unparalleled planning and operational challenges.

Moving a large federal agency in a coordinated fashion can be a herculean feat, requiring a robust planning effort to steer the ship. Coordinating and implementing plans and projects within federal agencies is an especially challenging endeavor, as appointees and civil servants must maneuver through political priorities, short-term programs, and longer-term objectives, all within an asynchronous budgeting process. (In January 2010, for example, Congress finalized the FY2011 budget and began drafting the FY2012 budget.) The various department-level milestones in place to support this effort affect the planning and execution of any given project.

In most federal agencies a dedicated staff is charged with developing and maintaining agency-level planning and reporting. While agency-level budgeting and planning processes are beyond the scope of most project managers' responsibilities, project managers play an important role in an agency's efforts to improve its services.

Agencies with successful project management practices have established clear links between projects and the organization's goals. Project managers must understand their agencies' planning and budgeting processes and have an appreciation for the overall federal planning process. Project managers and team members must be able to assess the impact of agency-level and external budgeting and planning milestones on project schedules and risks.

## THE FEDERAL PROJECT PLANNING AND REPORTING ENVIRONMENT

Organizational planning is a process whereby scarce resources are prioritized and aligned to the agency's mission and goals. Federal agencies, like private sector organizations, face challenges in aligning project plans with traditional planning cycles because the traditional cycles can conflict with project timelines and priorities. The latest E-300 format, which asks for more detailed project information, is helping tie project investments into the agency budget and thereby create an overall picture of the investment portfolio for the investment stakeholders. Yet a gap between official planning requirements and the work undertaken by projects still remains for many agencies.

This gap is sometimes heightened by the sheer number of federally mandated requirements that occur at the same time. As depicted in Figure 13-1, each "planet" orbiting the center reflects a process or cycle that influences project planning and execution. Project size, complexity, duration, and other characteristics determine the extent of the influence that each process or cycle wields.

To be successful, project management must integrate with the myriad planning and reporting processes. The most successful projects begin by aligning themselves with the highest goals of the agency. Project objectives should also support the strategic goals and objectives set forth in the agency's strategic plan.

**FIGURE 13-1:** The Project Planning and Execution Environment

## GPRA AND PROJECT MANAGEMENT

The Government Performance and Results Act (GPRA) of 1993 is probably the most influential piece of legislation affecting the federal planning lifecycle. The objective of GPRA is good government: efficient and responsive programs and alignment between current operations and longer-term goals. The GPRA framework is the primary structure by which agencies are held accountable for using resources effectively and achieving project results.

GPRA planning requirements have evolved over the years from a somewhat limited emphasis on completing required deliverables toward a stronger emphasis on outcomes and annual performance. Consider the differences between outputs and outcomes. Projects deliver outputs in the form of products, services, and results, such as a shuttle mission or a new e-mail system. Outcomes are the results of those project deliverables, such as a deeper knowledge of space exploration and improved productivity resulting from better e-mail. Agencies must proactively negotiate between delivering project outputs via short-term funding cycles and meeting the longer-term business outcomes in their strategic plans.

GPRA drives agencies toward aligning current actions with long-term business outcomes; however, projects are generally scoped to yield immediate outputs, not the longer-term business benefits. In evolving project management practices, agencies must attempt to link projects and long-term objectives through the GPRA framework.

Under GPRA, agencies must develop a five-year strategic plan, annual performance plan, annual performance budget, and annual performance and accountability report (see Figure 13-2). All projects and programs must be accounted for in the overall planning cycle.

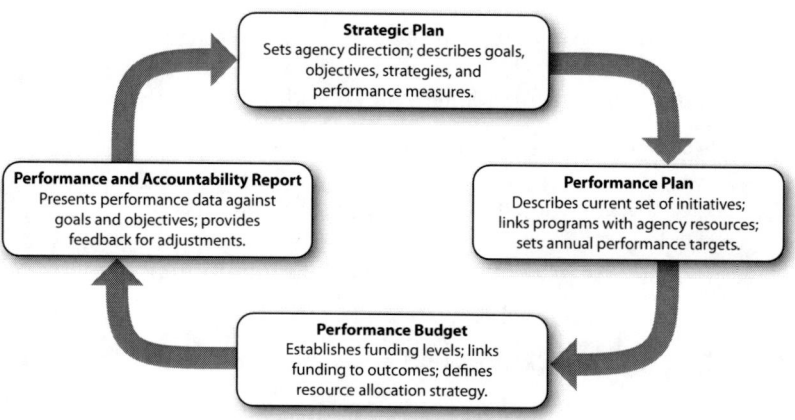

**FIGURE 13-2:** GPRA Planning in the Federal Environment

Projects should strive to create a direct link between their objectives and the agency's goals. To do that, the project team may need to participate in GPRA-related planning tasks, which should be built into the overall project documentation. If the project team takes these proactive steps, the agency's planning unit will recognize the alignment and value of the project, increasing the project's chances for continued funding. Much of the GPRA information is readily available, and the project manager should consider GPRA requirements when developing these documents.

## Strategic Plan

The strategic plan links the agency's mission with long-term goals and objectives. Objectives may contain sub-objectives and performance measures. The plan should describe how the agency intends to achieve its goals throughout the five-year horizon stipulated by GPRA.

The strategic plan is an important link between the overall direction of the organization and specific initiatives within the organization. For example, the Department of Justice (DOJ) strategic plan for 2007–2012[1] laid out three goals:

1. Prevent terrorism and promote the nation's security.

2. Prevent crime, enforce federal laws, and represent the rights and interests of the American people.

3. Ensure the fair and efficient administration of justice.

Strategic goals are broad brush and, in their totality, tend to describe the agency's mission. A level down from goals, strategic objectives define the areas the agency will focus on. For example, objectives for Goal 2 of DOJ's plan include "Reduce the threat, trafficking, use, and related violence of illegal drugs" and "Combat public and corporate corruption,

## CHAPTER 13  Aligning Federal and Project Planning Cycles

fraud, economic crime, and cybercrime." The objectives are important to understanding the agency's real priorities and, more important, what objectives a project must address to get funded.

Successful project management organizations, such as DOJ, create a framework that aligns project objectives with the organization's strategic objectives, goals, and mission. This level of justification is important so that when both internal and external reviewers (like OMB) evaluate the project, the linkage between the project and the agency's goals is apparent. This link should be clearly identified in the project charter and reinforced through the project's scope, schedule, and communication documents.

### Performance Plan

The next deliverable in the GPRA framework presents the agency's annual commitments and initiatives supporting achievement of the goals and objectives set forth in the strategic plan. Technically, this deliverable is part of the agency's budget submission and includes both outcome measures and performance goals. According to GPRA, an outcome measure "means an assessment of the results of a program activity compared to its intended purpose ... [and] the tabulation, calculation, or recording of activity or effort and can be expressed in a quantitative or qualitative manner. ..."[2]

The annual performance plan defines the metrics used to evaluate each program. Metrics should provide a qualitative approach to agency effectiveness with measures and targets. Performance measures define the type of measurement, such as the number of users or dollars saved. The emphasis is on outcomes rather than outputs. Project managers must work with their teams to develop metrics that draw a direct line of sight between the project's outcomes and their contribution to improving the agency's programs and services or achieving its mission and goals.

The annual performance plan is an opportunity to align an agency's project portfolio with its key measures of success. For example, one of the measures related to DOJ's Goal 2 involved the conversion of firearms investigations:

- *Performance Measure:* Percentage of firearms investigations resulting in a referral for criminal prosecution.[3]

This performance measure describes a core process for the FBI—investigating and referring crimes for prosecution. Fulfilling the performance measure is not inherently project-oriented work. However, underlying this performance measure are a host of information technology systems, data collection processes, and other work efforts that were commissioned and run as projects. Projects must be linked with the important areas of measurement in the annual performance plan for the organization to be seen as a priority.

## Performance Budget

The GPRA-mandated performance budget depicts an agency's funding needs from both organizational and program-based perspectives. The performance budget links funding and outcome measures with the organization's strategy to ensure that the required resources are available to carry out the plans.

One important link between a project and the planning process is Exhibit 300. E-300 is a key element in the capital planning process for major projects (see Chapter 3, Regulations and Legislation, and Chapter 6, The Crucial Role of Communication), as it provides the overall framework and specific data fields for reporting project performance to OMB. For example, E-300 requires a description of the project objectives, scope,

CHAPTER 13  Aligning Federal and Project Planning Cycles

partner agency stakeholders, deliverables, project manager's name and qualifications, and work breakdown structure. E-300 is intended to be fully integrated into an agency's overall funding request. In other words, it is a key link between projects and the performance budget. E-300 demonstrates that an agency's project is aligned with agency and overarching goals, is running efficiently (within 10 percent of its baseline), and is on track to meet the deliverable schedule.

## Performance and Accountability Report

The final GPRA requirement is the performance and accountability report (PAR), which evaluates an agency's progress toward achieving performance commitments in specific, predefined, quantifiable measures. The PAR demonstrates accountability, explaining deviances from the intended outputs and the impact on future efforts. This reporting process provides an opportunity to understand and correct problems early in the project lifecycle.

The role of performance reporting is clearly stated by the 2008 DOJ performance and accountability report:

> We recognize that performance information is vital to making resource allocation decisions and should be an integral part of the budget. Our budget and performance integration efforts have included a full budgetary restructuring of all of the Department's accounts to better align strategic goals and objectives with resources. In addition, the Department provides detailed component-specific annual performance plans within individual budget submissions, which also serve as the Department's annual performance plan.[4]

To be successful, project management leadership must recognize the role that projects play in achieving specific targets in the report. Expectations about which goals a particular project supports, and how the project will achieve those goals, should be clear. Sometimes project objectives must be adjusted to support the agency's overall performance. Scope may be increased on one project and the budget decreased on another project to help meet the agency's targets. These are often tactical decisions that have strategic consequences. Nonetheless, project management leadership should proactively engage other agency leaders to understand these tradeoffs and make the best decisions possible.

## PERFORMANCE ASSESSMENT RATING TOOL

In addition to the GPRA-mandated outputs, agencies must meet certain other requirements. For example, agencies must participate in the performance assessment rating tool (PART) process.

Established by OMB in 2002, the PART is intended to monitor and evaluate federal programs in four key areas: purpose and design, strategic planning, program management, and results and accountability. Agencies must also comply with a set of detailed financial reporting requirements and certify that they meet government accounting standards and maintain adequate internal controls. Individual projects and programs generate reports, audits, and evaluations throughout the year. Some agencies also issue annual reports designed for various audiences, such as the public, Congress, special stakeholder groups, and relevant industries.

## LINKING PROJECTS WITH PLANNING OUTPUTS

Project managers in federal agencies should proactively account for required deliverables and seek to link projects with key outcome deliverables. As depicted in Table 13-1, project management deliverables should align with specific planning cycle outputs.

| Planning Cycle Output | Project Management Link to Planning Cycle Output | PM Documentation |
|---|---|---|
| Strategic Plan | The project team should work to align the project with the organization's mission, goals, and specific objectives. | ■ Project charter<br>■ Scope statement<br>■ Communication plan |
| Performance Plan | The project team should define project performance measures that directly support project and agency measures. | ■ Scope statement<br>■ Project schedule<br>■ Benefits realization plan |
| Performance Budget | The project team should develop a time-phased budget that is configured to extract the required planning information. | ■ Project schedule<br>■ Project/program budget<br>■ Resource management plan<br>■ Contractor task orders |
| Performance and Accountability Report | The project team should maintain a set of project performance measures that support the PAR. Project progress can be linked with the PAR through the communication plan. | ■ Status reports<br>■ Benefits realization plan<br>■ Risk management plan<br>■ Communication plan |

**TABLE 13-1:** Aligning Deliverables with Planning Cycle Outputs

Achieving perfect alignment of the various planning cycles is nearly impossible. The Department of Defense uses a program planning and budgeting system (PPBS) to coordinate the process and timeline for developing, submitting, and spending its portion of the federal budget, but the civilian agencies generally do not have a similar, coordinated process across agencies. Many agencies do, however, devote considerable resources and organizational space to developing and maintaining federal planning documents.

It is essential for project leaders and staff to understand the role these planning documents will play in a particular project. Moreover, it is important for the project team to put the project into the larger context of the organization and consider how the project supports the mission of the organization. Project managers must take it upon themselves to apply their understanding of the planning and budgeting cycles to the schedules and risks associated with their projects.

Will Brimberry of the Department of the Interior's program management office (a unit within the chief information officer's organization) and Allan Roit, former director of the PMO in the Department of the Interior's Bureau of Indian Affairs, shared their efforts to document and describe the interrelationships among key cycles and processes in their respective agencies. Existing department policies and practices require negotiation and alignment of scope and cost/budget for each project. The DOI PMO ensures alignment between budget, scope, and strategy as part of the planning phase rather than during design or later phases when it is too late. This approach, which puts business needs analysis before project execution, is codified in the department's OCIO Directive 2008-016.

The DOI PMO provides guidance to agency departments that includes a model depicting the integration and relationships between their core planning cycles: capital planning and investment control, project management (PMI's *PMBOK® Guide*), OMB circular A-11 (including Exhibit E-300), and a "generic" software development lifecycle. Will Brimberry uses the model to show the relationship between the phases within each of these key lifecycles (see Figure 13-3). He explains that Interior employs a "federated" management philosophy; each organization within the agency (e.g., Bureau of Land Management, National Park Service) has unique issues, so a one-size-fits-all management framework will not work. BIA has customized this model to fit its specific environment.

Allan Roit describes BIA's participation in the development of the department-wide model and its relationship with the "local" version (shown in Figure 13-4). This model enables project managers to adjust their projects, if needed, to account for potential impacts from these other

## CHAPTER 13  Aligning Federal and Project Planning Cycles

cycles. According to Roit, the next version of this model will include other key cycles and processes like risk, earned value management, and the agile methodology the BIA PMO is adapting to its environment.

| Life Cycle | Standards<br>Standards Organization | Acquisition (Project) Lifecycle Phases | | | | | | |
|---|---|---|---|---|---|---|---|---|
| SDLC | | Plan | Analyze | Design | Build | Test | Implement | |
| OMB Investment<br>(300 Process) | Circular A-11<br>OMB | Plan (ABC Code: 80) | | Develop (ABC Code: 81) | | | | Operations and<br>Maintenance<br>(O & M) |
| Project<br>Management | PMBOK®<br>ANSI 2000 | Initiate | Plan | | Execute | Control | Close | |
| DOI Investment<br>w/Acquisition | CPIC Guide<br>Interior | Pre-Select | Select | | Control | | Evaluate | |

**FIGURE 13-3:** Relationship Between Lifecycle Phases Across Disciplines at DOI

| Indian Affairs<br>System Lifecycle | Generic<br>Project Lifecycle | OMB A-11<br>Investment Stages | DOI<br>CPIC Cycle |
|---|---|---|---|
| System Concept Development | | Initial Concept | Pre-select |
| Planning | | Planning | Select |
| Requirements Definition | Initiation | Full Acquisition | Control |
| Design | Planning | | |
| Development | Execution & Control | | |
| Test | | | |
| Implementation | Closure | Steady State | Evaluate |
| O&M | | | Steady State |
| | Modernization/<br>Enhancement Project | Modernization/<br>Enhancement<br>(Mixed Lifecycle) | |
| Disposition | | | |

**FIGURE 13-4:** Alignment of Core Planning Cycles at BIA

Project management leadership has a tendency to act at too low a level, especially when individual project budgets are beneath any significant threshold. Project managers should maintain a strategic view of their budgets, keeping aware of the total allocation for particular areas. This information should be shared with agency executives to help them understand the real role of project management in their agency and how the project structure can lead to new efficiencies.

> Project managers in federal agencies must effectively address external planning cycles to ensure continued funding and a place in the agency's portfolio. Agencies need to ensure that they are proactively managing their portfolio of projects against the requirements these external planning processes impose. Portfolio management, effective project reporting, and cross-functional/cross-agency discussions can help align the various planning cycles operating in the federal government.
>
> To ensure a project's success in the federal environment, project managers should:
>
> 1. *Get to know the GPRA team in your agency.* Most agencies have entire offices dedicated to strategic planning. These people can be a terrific asset in helping project managers understand the external planning processes, especially in terms of positioning the project. Establishing an effective rapport with the GPRA staff will help project management leadership be a partner and not an obstacle in working with external agencies.
>
> 2. *Conduct a portfolio review against the agency's strategic plan.* A critical review of the agency portfolio establishes a shared understanding that the portfolio is justified. Moreover, the agency will be able to undercover areas where projects are not in alignment with the external plans. The project portfolio should be reviewed against the agency's various goals and objectives. The portfolio manager and executives should work to identify and fix areas of misalignment.

# CHAPTER 13 Aligning Federal and Project Planning Cycles

3. *Participate in the process.* Project management can be a tool for meeting GPRA requirements. As agencies move toward implementing new data collection and reporting tools, a role should evolve for project management methodology. Active participation will enable the project side of the organization to become familiar with these reporting requirements and be able to respond when the need arises.

The planning and reporting cycles that operate concurrently in the federal environment can complicate the project management environment. Yet, project management leaders in the federal sector need to continue to see these external processes as the lifeline for their projects. Understanding and integrating the various cycles enables project managers to expose potential risks and pitfalls, communicate the project's context within the broader organizational environment to team members and stakeholders, and achieve the greatest alignment possible across these important processes.

## NOTES

1. U.S. Department of Justice, 2007–2012 Strategic Plan, http://www.justice.gov/jmd/mps/strategic2007-2012 (accessed December 4, 2009).
2. Government Performance and Results Act of 1993, section 1115(d), http://www.whitehouse.gov/omb/mgmt-gpra_gplaw2m/#h1 (accessed November 2, 2009).
3. Department of Justice, FY 2008 Performance and Accountability Report, p. II-11, http://www.justice.gov/ag/annualreports/pr2008/TableofContents.htm (accessed October 20, 2009).
4. Department of Justice, FY 2008 Performance and Accountability Report, p. II-1.

## Chapter 14

# Implementing Knowledge Management Practices: Reusing the Wheel

> *Humans are not ideally set up to understand logic; they are ideally set up to understand stories.*
> —ROGER C. SCHANK, COGNITIVE SCIENTIST[1]

Over the decades, the space shuttle program has leveraged repeatable processes while implementing new technologies and materials. Today's shuttle missions are very different from those of the 1980s in terms of technologies and types of missions, yet they still have to obey the laws of physics and gravity while launching and landing a shuttle. To accomplish these miracles of human ingenuity, NASA must mobilize massive amounts of knowledge for each flight—including design documents, operational procedures, safety plans, quality assurance methodologies, scientific research, and experimental mission-based logistics.

Consider the major tasks of the final mission to the Hubble telescope: building replacement and upgraded instrumentation for the telescope; blasting a space shuttle 220 miles into orbit; rendezvousing, retrieving, and fixing the Hubble telescope; relaunching the telescope; and landing the shuttle back on earth. Taken together, these tasks seem an impossible feat of imagination. But the highly competent teams at NASA routinely achieve such incredible feats, thanks in part to effective knowledge management. A shuttle flight itself generates many terabytes of data, added to those generated by the preparation and analysis carried out prior to flight. Such a knowledge-intensive environment provides an interesting example of the challenges associated with knowledge management (KM) in the federal project environment.

Thirteen days after liftoff, the Shuttle Atlantis touched down at Edwards Air Force Base in California, concluding a colossally successful trip to Hubble. The crew was debriefed and the shuttle was stowed for its post-flight maintenance. This important mission was complete, but rest assured, NASA analysts and operational staff were busy understanding the knowledge gained.

The U.S. government is the largest spender of money in history. Federal budget figures (and federal deficit figures) are almost beyond comprehension. But spending money is not really the federal stock in trade. Information is the main federal commodity. The government is involved with virtually immeasurable masses of information flowing in, being used, and flowing out. Any system that can help manage this information, and perhaps use federal funds more efficiently, will benefit project management in particular and government operations in general.

## KNOWLEDGE MANAGEMENT DEFINED

*Knowledge management* can be defined as "the concept under which information is turned into actionable knowledge and made available in a usable form to the people who can apply it."[2] KM is also a system established to capture, store, retrieve, disseminate, and contextualize information throughout the project lifecycle. Both of these definitions are useful in the project management context because they address the two sides of KM: knowledge at the individual level and knowledge as part of a system.

The core of KM is functional and practical reuse of the data, information, and knowledge generated within an organization or project. Consider the food chain of knowledge management: data → information → knowledge. Data are numbers, characters, words, images, or other points of input or output. When combined into a meaningful array, data evolve into information—ideas formed and shaped into larger concepts.

The word *information* has broad applications that include specific technical data. These nuanced definitions of data and information are often lost on the busy project manager, but in the federal environment, it is important to understand the evolution of singular data points into information and knowledge. A standard knowledge management process is depicted in Figure 14-1.

Knowledge is at the top of the food chain. In their textbook on project management, professors John M. Nicholas and Herman Steyn define knowledge as:

> ... information put to use. Everything that happens in projects, intentional or not, is a source of information, but to learn from that information managers and teams must think about what happened, what they did, and the outcome. They must reflect on their experiences

and draw conclusions, otherwise they will not have learned from what happened or will quickly forget whatever they learned.[3]

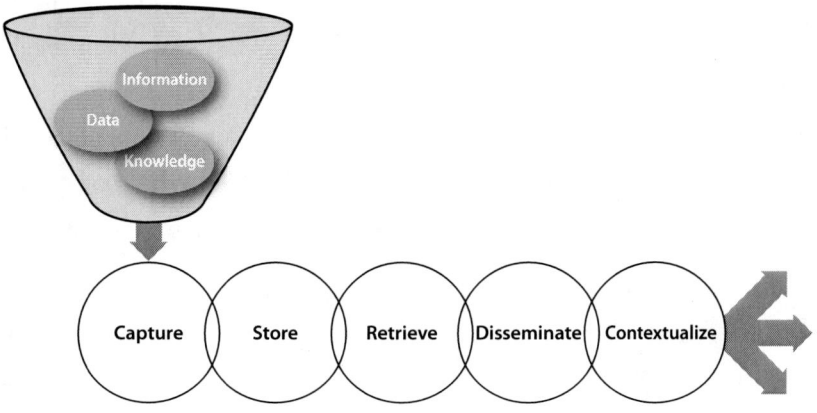

**FIGURE 14-1:** Typical Knowledge Management Process

Knowledge is more than the sum of data or information combined in a system. Judgment or filters must be applied to create the essence of knowledge. The components of knowledge must also be applied through practical experience, scholarly endeavor, or intuition to create what we understand as knowledge (see Figure 14-2). Using the definition of knowledge as data and information in context, linked to the larger world in a meaningful way, what are the implications for projects? How much information can realistically be captured on a project, and how do the data and information transform into knowledge?

# CHAPTER 14 Implementing Knowledge Management Practices

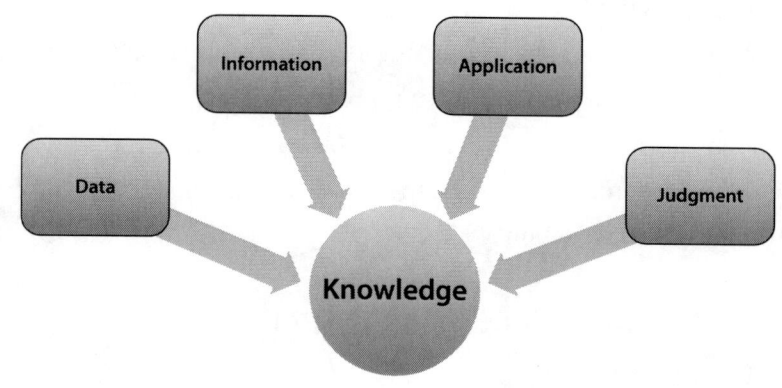

**FIGURE 14-2:** Components of Knowledge

## KNOWLEDGE MANAGEMENT IN THE FEDERAL ENVIRONMENT

Knowledge management is a relatively new discipline in the federal environment, but it is gaining ground. In 2001, a survey conducted at an E-Gov conference found that more than 88 knowledge management programs were underway across a wide range of defense and civilian agencies.[4] Today, the Federal Knowledge Management Initiative (FKMI) offers federal workers and contractors a forum for sharing ideas and developing KM across the federal government. FKMI conducts annual conferences and has developed an agenda for growing knowledge management throughout the federal government, which includes:

- Establishing a federal KM center to provide consulting and services to agencies related to knowledge management

- Recognizing a chief knowledge officer role in the federal government, similar to the chief information officer role

- Building a knowledge-sharing culture across the federal government, which changes the mindset "from 'need to know' to 'need to share.'"[5]

All these efforts bode well for project management because projects tend to generate lots of new knowledge. Projects are often at the leading edge of innovation for agencies. New processes, technologies, and applications of the law are developed and tested in a project setting. The challenge is for projects to transfer the knowledge developed in the project setting to the organization at large.

## THE ROLE OF KNOWLEDGE MANAGEMENT IN PROJECT MANAGEMENT

A project's value lies in part in its ability to take information, transform it, and provide to it back to stakeholders contextually and as needed. Yet, most projects address information capture only, and they do so by providing a repository. The later phases of knowledge management are often underused or totally ignored on projects.

Full use of KM practices offers many benefits to the federal project manager and the organization overall. Specifically, knowledge management:

- Helps individuals carry out their jobs by providing needed information and skill backup
- Builds a sense of teamwork and community within the organization
- Helps team members and other stakeholders keep up-to-date with project information
- Helps team member keep their skills current
- Provides team members opportunities to contribute to project and general operations.

At the team level,[6] knowledge management:

- Develops professional skills by enabling individuals to learn from others outside their immediate organization
- Promotes peer-to-peer mentoring and assistance
- Improves networking and collaboration beyond the project team
- Develops a common means of communicating concepts within the field.

Organizationally, a knowledge management program can play an important part in linking people and project knowledge across disparate entities. For the organization, knowledge management:

- Helps drive strategy
- Solves problems more quickly than if each team has to "reinvent the wheel"
- Increases knowledge of best practices
- Improves the general level of knowledge and the quality of products and services
- Provides expanded and different perspectives on problems
- Helps agencies stay ahead of problems.
- Expands organizational memory and enables more teams to benefit from this memory.

As Figure 14-3 depicts, the knowledge management lifecycle is not limited to simply gathering lessons learned, but is really about transferring that knowledge in a way that has maximum meaning for the receiver of that knowledge.

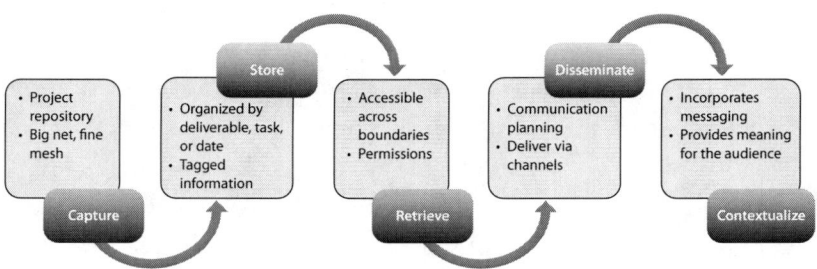

**FIGURE 14-3:** Knowledge Management Lifecycle

Nearly all federal agencies struggle with different aspects of knowledge management. The challenges of KM relate to both technology—having an infrastructure for moving information—and business practice—determining what knowledge to capture and how to transform it into something that can be used.

## CHALLENGES OF KNOWLEDGE MANAGEMENT

Effective project knowledge management is increasingly difficult to achieve on federal projects. Specifically, four challenges must be overcome to advance KM within an organization: volume, complexity, information assurance, and discipline. These four challenges are being addressed at the federal level through FKMI and other agency entities. Project management leaders in agencies should consider their approach to integrating these emerging practices into the project environment.

### Volume

In the federal environment, reams and terabytes of information are generated during projects. Unmanageable masses of information can even be dangerous in the intelligence services, where "actionable intelligence" on threats to the United States can be hidden in the overwhelming bulk of inconsequential material.

Federal project managers can endeavor to collect as much information as possible for future use. For example, the sheer volume of information generated by a space shuttle launch is a powerful tool in the arsenal of future development teams. Myriad connections can be made in that mountain of data. To make these connections, however, the project requires both formal and informal methods for accumulating and organizing information. Federal project managers need a systematic approach that can easily capture information as it flows.

Volume is both an input and an output problem. In other words, an agency needs a robust set of practices and tools to both capture the information and provide a viable path for distribution. Strategies for dealing with volume in a project setting include:

- *Repositories.* Agencies should create project repositories. Well-organized electronic repositories help ensure that the "net" for catching information is readily available. Efforts should be made to ensure that the repositories are not hampered by nonproject business requirements and technology shortcomings.

- *Information portals.* From a project management perspective, a single interface for information is immensely useful. Team members can navigate to the information they need, and the portal becomes a common area of focus for the team. The downside is that portals are expensive and require significant programming resources to maintain.

- *E-learning.* Individuals with knowledge need effective methods for sharing best practices, lessons learned, and other project information. E-Learning helps with the volume of information generated on projects by providing a channel that can be accessed securely and over time to share the knowledge. E-Learning can be used to break up material in a way that provides a deeper context for the receiver.

- *Document management.* Effective document management practices can help minimize outmoded or outdated information. Document management and the project management process of configuration management should work hand-in-hand.

- *Communities of practice.* A team or even a formal community of practice (COP) can define a set of standards. Dozens of knowledge management COPs are currently in place across the U.S. government. These groups serve an important function in instilling a culture and processes for KM to work for an agency.

## Complexity

Complexity of content must be overcome if users are to gain insight into the knowledge base. Complexity increases with more and different inputs, such as documents, images, e-mails, databases, and time-sensitive information. Complexity can also increase via midstream information processing, such as when various points of information are combined or pulled apart to form a new set of knowledge. Business analytics increases the pressures for more complex project information (e.g., computing schedule, estimating cost against risk). On the output side, complexity increases with the number of access points to the knowledge base, the channels used for output, the laws and regulations governing release and use of information, etc.

Project managers can address complex layers of information in multiple ways, including:

- *Collaboration.* To become effective project players, individuals need to devise ways to understand complex issues. Collaboration is a recognized KM practice that can help shorten the uptake of complex information. The collaborators need to define their objectives up front to ensure that the collaboration results in knowledge sharing, and they should consider using a facilitator to ensure that the collaboration is effective.

- *Knowledge fairs.* Another, perhaps more creative approach to dealing with complexity in the project setting is to conduct a "knowledge fair," whereby individuals can visit exhibits and gather the information they need. Knowledge fairs are event-based and can be held in a large room where multiple mini-presentations can occur simultaneously. This approach works well with a large project, especially at the beginning of a phase.

## Information Assurance

A lack of information assurance can undermine the project quickly through the dissemination of poor-quality information. Information assurance is the embodiment of trust: Can the information/knowledge be trusted and used? To determine this, several factors must be evaluated:

- *Authenticity.* The information must come from a trusted source.

- *Confidentiality.* The information should be restricted to those individuals authorized to use it.

- *Integrity.* Information integrity addresses the rules related to authorizing and making changes.

In the project setting, a sound information assurance strategy is essential, and it must address topics like internal stakeholders' need to know. One effective mechanism is the project communication plan. Information assurance rules and knowledge sharing should be embedded into the communication plan to create a single source that defines the project's policies for knowledge management.

## Discipline

An organization needs the discipline to address knowledge management over the long term. Executive sponsorship is critical to ensuring that KM is a priority. Agency-wide practices and policies should be established regarding how knowledge is captured, stored, processed, disseminated, and contextualized. Expertise should be developed internally so that staff members have an internal resource. And finally, the agency KM owners need to define a tool set for knowledge capture and retention.

Discipline is also needed at the project level. Projects can often be frenetic environments, with staff and information in multiple locations. It is incumbent upon both the project sponsor and the project manager to ensure that the project is addressing knowledge management issues so that the project (1) adheres to the law and local policies regarding information management and (2) creates an environment conducive to the transfer of knowledge between team members.

To begin to develop the necessary internal discipline around knowledge management, the project manager must consider the organizational context and act accordingly:

- *Begin with the basics.* Set the objectives, scope, and roles for the effort. Expect resistance, and plan to enlist executive support.

CHAPTER 14  Implementing Knowledge Management Practices

- *Establish a KM leader.* Knowledge management should rely on a system that is based on accountability.

- *Cast a wide net.* Knowledge management practices should not be foreign to project team members. Tools, like standard documentation templates, should be easy to access.

- *Use technology.* Tag information, use web technologies for repositories, and be open to displaying information in new ways.

- *Stop using e-mail for KM.* E-mail is not a good way to ensure that knowledge has been disseminated. E-mails get lost, attachments are never opened, and they can be forwarded without your knowledge. Try instead to leverage standard methods of knowledge management.

## KNOWLEDGE MANAGEMENT IN ACTION

While we don't always know when knowledge management is working, its failures have been in our consciousness for many years. Consider two recent KM failures:

- *September 11, 2001.* The FBI had knowledge of and was investigating foreign students who were learning to fly, but not land, aircraft. This knowledge never made it from the localized investigation team to the larger intelligence network in a way that could have prevented the attacks.

- *Response to Hurricane Katrina.* In the aftermath of this devastating hurricane, mass chaos ensued in part because the various agencies involved did not have the right information or communication tools.

As a result of these events, the public safety sector has embraced knowledge management and begun to put it to use. Most large U.S. cities have developed and implemented plans for integrating all local public safety forces to mobilize in the event of an emergency. In the Washington D.C., area, this has involved building a common response capability across several dozen policing agencies, fire departments, the U.S. Secret Service, and the U.S. armed forces. Different scenarios are considered, each requiring a different response, from chemical attacks in a subway, to a shipping collision, to explosions, etc.

In any scenario, multiple jurisdictions must respond. Ensuring that all jurisdictions are prepared to respond effectively means addressing several challenges:

- *Communication.* In the past eight years, new 800-megahertz digital radio systems have evolved that allow for multijurisdictional communications and host hundreds of channels that enable communications to be parsed quickly into smaller work groups. In addition, all response vehicles have numbered designations that fall within a standard taxonomy so that they can be easily identified. These new tools are enabling large-scale responses to become more efficient.

- *Protocols.* Major incidents require very fast mobilization. Protocols have been developed that define the parameters of different response scenarios, such as roles and responsibilities for primary, secondary, and tertiary jurisdictions; use of shared resources; decision-making; and other key aspects of incident command and execution.

- *Knowledge sharing.* Jurisdictions must know the capabilities and inventories of their counterparts across the region. To accomplish this, regional training events and scenario planning sessions occur regularly. In this face-to-face setting, policy and operational experts can share knowledge and interact in meaningful ways.

# CHAPTER 14 Implementing Knowledge Management Practices

The challenges of knowledge management faced by public safety officials are analogous to the challenges faced by project teams. Like public safety incidents, projects are sporadic, of varying size and levels of urgency. As with public safety, a structure must exist for projects to quickly access the tools and processes needed for effective KM. Some federal agencies have developed structures that are helping projects.

Consider the critical nature of knowledge management at NASA. In a 2003 article, Dr. Ed Hoffman, Director of the NASA Academy of Program and Project Leadership, wrote that:

> Typical of most project managers, our staff doesn't want to hang around at a project's completion to write memoirs; team members want to move on to the next big, exciting project. However, we must stress the importance of taking time for lessons learned. We must continue to ascertain how NASA can become better by reflection and application of our experiences. Such a strategy incorporates lessons-learned database systems, case studies, development assignments and the like. For this purpose, NASA has established an in-depth knowledge sharing program...."[7]

NASA's approach to knowledge management is connected to its project management methodology. A "typical" space shuttle mission uses many KM techniques, including collaboration, mission portals, and document management. Projects are required to link into these processes and must undergo rigorous reviews to ensure that they have met the standards of the organization before they can proceed. Additionally, post-implementation reviews are held to review and assign lessons learned to owners when a project phase is closed out.

The Hubble mission, like so many before it, was fraught with challenges. Would the replacement equipment work? What other damage would the astronauts find once they had retrieved the telescope? To help answer these questions, NASA resources were dedicated to reviewing Hubble logs and previous maintenance missions. In addition, key staff—long-time dedicated personnel who know the telescope inside and out—were key to answering these questions and planning the mission. For a shuttle launch that costs millions of dollars and involves thousands of people, knowledge management is but one of the tools in the NASA tool kit, and it is an important way to ensure that the mission objectives are achieved safely.

> No uniform federal standards currently govern knowledge management. While extensive laws and regulations address the uses and storage of information, the idea of actually transferring knowledge between individuals and teams has not yet matured in the federal government. However, the need for and value of such standards have been recognized by several government groups. In an April 2009 report, the Federal Knowledge Management Working Group stated that:
>
>> ...the purpose of any KM Policy, or KM Standard, for the Federal Government should be to ensure that the knowledge assets under the government's control are managed consistently and effectively throughout their life-cycle.[8]
>
> As a catalyst for change and the generation of new information, project management will be at the forefront of any innovations in knowledge management. To achieve project success in federal agencies, project management leaders will need to understand knowledge management and work with KM experts to integrate a standard set of practices into the project management methodology. In the future, the volume of information will continue to explode upwards and outwards. Concurrently, the tools around content management, Web 2.0, and project management will evolve to provide greater contextualization so that stakeholders, citizens, project executives, and others can get just the information they need.
>
> As the knowledge management study group recognizes, KM will vary depending on the project and the agency. But certain principles apply across the board. Knowledge management in the federal project process starts with project initiation. When the project manager establishes communication procedures, he or she is setting up the project's knowledge management procedures. The project manager will use

# CHAPTER 14  Implementing Knowledge Management Practices

professional judgment in establishing these procedures, but will also consult with upper management and with FOIA and information security experts. The project manager will read relevant "after-action" reports from similar past projects, taking advantage of the lessons learned and the institutional memory they represent.

Knowledge management, through two-way communication, provides the information needed for project evaluation throughout the course of the project. Of course, the KM procedures themselves can be evaluated. At the end of the project, the project managers will prepare their own report on how the project went and what they learned. Their knowledge will be passed on to the next project managers, ideally helping make federal operations both more efficient and more effective.

## NOTES

1. Daniel H. Pink, *A Whole New Mind* (New York: Riverhead Hardcover, 2005), p. 102.
2. Kimiz Dalkir, *Knowledge Management in Theory and Practice* (Amsterdam: Elsevier Butterworth-Heinemann, 2005), p. 5.
3. John M. Nicholas and Herman Steyn, *Project Management for Business, Engineering, and Technology* (Amsterdam: Butterworth-Heinemann, 2008), p. 588.
4. Federal Knowledge Management Working Group, KM Practice Findings and Recommendations, http://wiki.nasa.gov/cm/wiki/?id=6843 (accessed October 28, 2009).
5. Federal Knowledge Management Initiative, Federal Knowledge Management Initiative Backgrounder, http://blogs.nasa.gov/cm/wiki/?id=5984 (accessed November 25, 2009).
6. Dalkir, p. 20.
7. Ed Hoffman, "NASA Reduces Uncertainty and Minimizes Risks with Project Methods," *PM Network*, vol. 17, no. 6, June 2003.
8. *Knowledge Management Policies and Standard (KMP&S) for the Federal Government: A Report from the Federal Knowledge Management Working Group*, KMP&S Action Group, April 10, 2009, p. 1.

## Chapter 15

# Understanding Project Performance Management: Uncovering Success Early

> *In the social sectors, the critical question is not 'how much money do we make per dollar of invested capital?' but 'how effectively do we deliver on our mission and make a distinctive impact, relative to our resources?'*
>
> —JIM COLLINS
> GOOD TO GREAT AND THE SOCIAL SECTORS

Congressman Elijah Cummings (D-MD) is a senior member of the House Committee on Oversight and Government Reform. The main investigative committee in the House of Representatives, Oversight and Government Reform has jurisdiction to investigate any federal program, as well as any matter that has federal policy implications. Congressman Cummings is committed to eliminating waste, fraud, and abuse in government. He works to ensure that government runs effectively and efficiently, using every taxpayer dollar responsibly. Cummings also sits on the House Subcommittees on Domestic Policy, the Federal Workforce, the Post Office, and the District of Columbia. As one who listens to a lot of testimony about federal expenditures, he understands the issues associated with managing project performance.

The Committee on Oversight and Government Reform has a mandate to improve the structures, policies, and leadership for promoting more efficient and effective use of taxpayers' money. Some examples of large, public failures that Congressman Cummings has seen on his watch include:

- *Kaiserslautern "Ktown" community center*, the largest military community outside the continental United States. The project to build a lodging, entertainment, and recreation facility for American troops and their families was marred by significant cost overruns, bungled contracts, and disputes between the U.S. and German governments.

- *Hurricane Katrina*, in particular, the Federal Emergency Management Agency trailer fiasco. The trailer effort was plagued by flawed construction, toxic materials, and lax government oversight, and it is still not resolved more than three years later.

- *Iraq rebuilding*. The U.S. government spent billions of dollars restoring power and other basic services across Iraq. Now, many years into U.S. involvement, more than $2.5 billion cannot be accounted for.

Performance management shortfalls are not limited to ultra large initiatives like these, however. In fiscal year 2009, the federal government obligated more than $ 72.4 billion toward IT expenditures (up from $71 billion in 2008)[1] for thousands of large, medium, and small IT projects. In the 2008–2009 timeframe, more than 472 IT projects with a collective

### CHAPTER 15 Understanding Project Performance Management

budget of $4.8 billion[2] found their way onto the OMB watch list and the GAO high-risk list for poor planning or poor performance.

Tracking investment dollars is a familiar activity in the federal environment. Yet it remains unclear how much value the federal government and American taxpayers receive from the massive investment in projects. The performance management framework that operates in the federal environment can shed some light on this value.

## PERFORMANCE MANAGEMENT IN THE FEDERAL GOVERNMENT

Over the past 20 years, the U.S. government has pursued a strategy of performance-based management that has built upon earlier generations of management concepts and tools. The current configuration of performance management includes the use of E-300s, GAO's high-risk list, OMB's management watch list, IT scorecards, variance reports, corrective action plans, and other tools. Cost, schedule, and performance goals must be established for all major acquisitions, and agencies must achieve, on average, 90 percent of those goals. OMB Circular A-11, Part 7, provides a critical source of guidance in its Capital Programming Guide supplement, which lays out the important acquisition steps and identifies earned value as a method of measuring project progress. In total, these systemic changes to performance management have brought about improvements to the methods agencies use to establish strategic goals, work with contractors, use performance data, and manage projects.

Performance-based management involves establishing, managing, measuring, and evaluating performance data. Project performance must link into the overall performance management program, and the organization must ensure that projects are able to be measured individually and in tandem with other projects in the portfolio. This is a significant challenge for many agencies.

Success in project management in the federal environment includes recognizing the following:

- Performance management is multidimensional, requiring collaboration and coordination between acquisition, finance, operations, policy and planning, human resources, oversight, and other agency divisions.
- Performance management involves all levels of the government, from the single project to agency executives, OMB, and Congress.
- Performance management is predicated on the effective implementation of earned value management.
- At the heart of effective performance management is good data, including information about the reliability of the data.
- EVM and project management systems have evolved to the point where effective project reporting can be accomplished by agencies with limited project management expertise.

The primary focus of the performance-based management strategy has been on major IT systems and the use of earned value management to monitor progress. While EVM and its predecessors have been in use in the federal government since the 1960s, EVM is only now gaining widespread traction across both defense and civilian agencies. The government continues to develop the performance management capability to ensure that capital investments are performing well.

# CHAPTER 15  Understanding Project Performance Management

In the context of the broader federal performance measurement system, project performance management offers opportunities for agencies to improve project performance management across three phases of a project:

- *Establish project performance measures.* Performance systems are developed at the organizational level, and baselines are put into place at the project level.

- *Manage project performance.* Effective performance management strategies help establish a rigor within the project team.

- *Oversee project performance.* An independent oversight board examines the project to verify that performance is on target and that the underlying systems and data are adequate.

Each of these phases lends itself to an overall system of project performance management. Each fits into the larger flow of performance data that flows upward from project to agency to government-wide performance scorecards, and ultimately to congressional hearings.

## Establishing Project Performance Measures

As the old adage goes, "If you can't measure it, you can't move it." Performance measurement systems should enable a project manager to closely monitor the project and enact changes. Establishing performance measures in a project environment involves creating measures at the individual, work team, and project levels, as well as creating policies and the operational framework to ensure that high-quality performance data is generated. To ensure a successful project performance measurement program, the sponsor and key agency leadership need to consider three key areas that will enable a full-fledged performance management system: investment review boards, EVM, and non-EVM performance criteria.

### Investment Review Boards

At the organizational level, the agency must create an environment conducive to high performance. For example, in IT projects, OMB has recommended the use of an IT investment management (ITIM) maturity framework, whereby the agency creates one or more investment review boards, or IRBs, to oversee the development of IT investments.

The IRB is a common mechanism in agencies for bringing together IT and business executives in a process to define and understand the investment. The investment has to be clearly understood in terms of both its costs and its benefits by all stakeholders. Under this framework, IRBs consider new projects and reevaluate prior investments to ensure they are on track. To do this, IRBs must establish new performance baselines and evaluate existing project performance data.

The ITIM framework is not without challenges. IRBs must have the right people involved in the process. To be effective, senior directors from across the organization must participate in the process. Because the IRB is a decision-making body, delegating IRB meetings to lower-level staff is not a good practice. These boards must also have the right technical and nontechnical staff in attendance. The complexity of these investments, and their success, sometimes rests upon arcane technical details that will make or break the investment.

The IRB must also have the right processes in place for considering new investments, reviewing existing investments, and assessing performance. When those processes are not in place, investments can be ignored or left unanalyzed. In addition, when corrective actions are called for, the IRB must be prepared to track the completion of those actions. GAO recommends that agencies "strengthen and expand the board's oversight responsibilities for underperforming projects...."[3] These challenges are

# CHAPTER 15 Understanding Project Performance Management

longstanding, but clearly the ITIM framework, and the IRBs, allow for continuous evaluation of project performance data at the appropriate levels of the agency.

## Earned Value Management

At the heart of performance management in the federal government is earned value. Earned value is a project management concept whereby the value of the work completed in a given period is compared with the planned value of the work and the actual value of the work. Cost and schedule data are used to help understand the true performance of a project. For example, if a project team completed a new $2 million parking lot at an actual cost of $3 million, there would be a −$1 million cost variance.

Schedule data also informs the performance data and uses the earned value of work for a given time period as compared with what was expected to be completed at the end of the time period. For example, if, at the end of the month, the project team has completed $1 million of the work, but was budgeted to have completed $1.1 million, the project would have a −$100,000 schedule variance.

The objective is to understand the planned value of the work at any given point—the earned value. This level of information provides executives and stakeholders across the government a look into the status and overall health of the project.

Defense Department upper management has come out in strong support of EVM. In a July 3, 2007, memo, the Under Secretary Defense for Acquisition, Technology and Logistics began a memo on continued EVM implementation by noting that:

> EVM is considered by many in the project management community to be the best option currently available for holding all parties accountable

for the effective management of large and complex projects. EVM provides a disciplined approach to managing projects successfully through the use of an integrated system to plan and control authorized work to achieve cost, schedule, and performance objectives. The fidelity of the information produced by the EVM System (EVMS) is critical to providing an objective assessment of a program's performance from which well-informed management decisions can be made. Moreover, EMV is not just a cost report; it is a tool to help program managers and their team members operate more effectively in managing their programs."[4]

The DOD 2006 *Earned Value Earned Value Management Implementation Guide* provides more details on what EVM can accomplish.[5] The guide states that EVMS allows for:

- Planning of all work scope for the program to completion
- Assignment of authority and responsibility at the work performance level
- Integration of the cost, schedule, and technical aspects of the work into a detailed baseline plan
- Objective measurement of progress (earned value) at the work performance level
- Accumulation and assignment of actual costs
- Analysis of variances from plans
- Summarization and reporting of performance data to higher levels of management for action
- Forecasting of achievement of milestones and completion of contract events
- Forecasting of final contract costs

- Disciplined baseline maintenance and incorporation of baseline revisions in a timely manner.

On the civilian side of the federal government, only a handful of agencies have vigorously embraced EVM for many years, including NASA and DOE. These agencies have adopted the American National Standards Institute/Electronics Industries Alliance national standard for EVM, called ANSI/EIA-748, which provides the "industry process for the use of EVMS including integration of program scope, schedule and cost objectives, establishment of a baseline plan and accomplishment of program objectives, and use of earned value techniques for performance measurement during the execution of a program."[6]

Federal management and acquisition teams have begun to focus on EVM in recent years. EVM can be used as a stand-alone system or in conjunction with other measurement methods. It can be applied at various levels, from individual projects all the way up to cabinet-level department initiatives.

Earned value relies on extensive data—including direct labor data, materials cost data, schedule data, indirect cost data, and contract data—from a wide variety of sources. The systems that enable earned value are complex, and in the case of contractors, must be certified by the federal government as appropriate for use as an EVM tool. An EVM system must be aligned with the organization and its resources to ensure the proper allocation of work. The organizational breakdown structure (OBS) is essential to linking work with specific organizational units. The resource breakdown structure (RBS) accomplishes a similar objective, but with project resources.

The first step in defining an effective EVM system is to overlay the WBS, OBS, and RBS. In other words, effort should be catalogued by its WBS reference number, the assigned organization, and the actual resources used. The project manager will thereby be able to track performance across those various elements.

Any federal EVM implementation must adhere to ANSI/EIA-748. The standard sets forth 32 guidelines that enable EVM systems implementation. To be compliant, an EVM system must address all 32 guidelines, which cover such items as (1) "Define the authorized work elements for the program," (16) "Record direct costs in a manner consistent with the budgets in a formal system controlled by the general books of account," and (31) "Prevent revisions to the program budget, except for authorized changes."[7]

A fully compliant system is no small feat, as the guidelines address organizational structure; accounting, budgeting, and finance; project management; and human resources. Additionally, OMB has established "key practices" supporting systems acquisition programs, summarized into three areas:

1. Establish a comprehensive EVM system.
2. Ensure that the data resulting from the EVM system are reliable.
3. Ensure that the program management team is using earned value data for decision-making purposes.

While the three areas are interdependent and each area is important, the third is the most critical for the agency. EVM helps ensure that better decisions are made through the integration of performance data.

### *Non-EVM Performance Criteria*

EVM provides essential performance data; however, the project also maintains other performance criteria that are important to evaluating the overall success of the effort. For example, safety performance criteria are not necessarily embedded within the EVM calculation, although injuries and work slowdowns due to unsafe conditions will impact project performance. The team may have a performance criterion that states "This project will incur zero accidents until its completion." This is a goal that is separate and apart from the performance of the project, but should nonetheless be used to evaluate the overall success of the effort.

Another example is training. Ensuring that all project staff receive proper training can be tracked as a separate performance measure even though it will impact overall project performance. Training will probably be built into the schedule, so if it is not completed on time, it will directly impact the EVM calculation. Viewed separately, untrained staff members lead to poor-quality deliverables and rework, so clearly training impacts performance. Moreover, the organization will not be prepared to maintain and operate the final deliverables if staff members have not received the proper training. So tracking training goals as a separate performance measure provides a meaningful way to realize the outcomes of the project.

If a project manager maintains a zero variance for cost and schedule, but does so because the project is hiring lower-quality labor and not providing safety equipment or training, the project's risk profile will increase. Non-EVM performance criteria should drive decisions about tasks, budgets, and timeframes. These are important filters for understanding how projects are faring.

## Managing Project Performance

Performance management goes hand in hand with project management. The project team executes on the plan and generates the performance results. Invariably, problems arise that degrade the performance of the project. For example, resource shortages may occur or the cost of materials may increase. Sometimes these issues were planned for and alternatives can be implemented with minimal disruption. Other times these circumstances occur without foreknowledge and the team must scramble to get back on track. In either case, an effective management strategy must be followed to ensure that project performance is monitored and corrected as necessary.

Performance management is cyclical, with each turn presenting opportunities for improvement (see Figure 15-1).

**FIGURE 15-1:** Project Performance Management Cycle

These opportunities include:

- *Maintain accountability.* An effective project performance strategy begins with accountability. The project manager must know his or her role and responsibilities, as should the rest of the team. Individuals should be accountable for specific outcomes and results. Accountability is the precursor of ownership, which is a critical element in performance. In short, today's knowledge workers must care or performance will likely degrade.

- *Actively monitor.* A performance management strategy also requires an effective monitoring plan. Performance should be monitored and evaluated regularly through performance reports, post-implementation reviews, and on-site reviews. Yet, performance issues do not always come from reports, but often arise from direct observations and interactions with staff. The project team needs to be able to discuss performance issues honestly without defensiveness or fear of retribution.

- *Regularly measure.* Performance measurement is the mechanism for collecting, reporting, analyzing, and evaluating project performance data. The data used in many federal systems has been noted as suspect, due to poor collection processes.

An example of project performance measurement involves the United States Coast Guard (USCG), which is in the midst of a complete overhaul of its fleet of ships and boats, as well as other key operational assets. Dubbed Operation Deepwater, this $25 billion effort will take more than 25 years to repair, build, and procure the entire USCG inventory. As with many programs of this size, problems have arisen in planning and implementation, primarily related to a failure in procurement practices and inappropriate contract provisions. In some cases, contractors were allowed to determine their own bonus schedule and performance measures. In other cases, boats couldn't float, equipment was dangerous to personnel (some radios caused shocks when wet), and the technology often failed to implement basic mission principles (communications were not encoded). According to Congressman Cummings, Deepwater is a prime example of the lack of oversight that promotes a culture of mediocrity.

In a 2007 report, GAO had this to say about Deepwater:

> The Coast Guard's ability to assess [Integrated Product Team] IPT performance continues to be problematic. Former assessments of IPT effectiveness simply focused on measures such as frequency of meetings, attendance, and training. As a result, IPTs received positive assessments while the assets under their realm of responsibility—such as the National Security Cutter—were experiencing problems.[8]

To address these issues, the Coast Guard has implemented sweeping changes to Deepwater. Leadership was changed, as were key personnel. The new team established measurements that included outcome-based metrics such as cost and schedule performance of assets (ships, aircraft, and command, control, communications, computers, intelligence, surveillance, and reconnaissance). GAO, in this and other reports, discussed the types of improvements that a project or program can make to manage performance more effectively. Subsequent GAO reports have shown that the USCG has made significant improvements in the Deepwater program.

- *Take corrective action.* Next, the team needs the ability to respond to performance issues. The team should be empowered to act on the performance data within the parameters of its responsibilities. For

CHAPTER 15  Understanding Project Performance Management

some federal projects, this may mean implementing contingency plans. In other instances, it may require executing scenario-based training. Corrective action should address the core issues related to performance.

While many different strategies will be effective in managing performance, this straightforward set of steps can enable federal managers to positively impact their projects.

## Overseeing Project Performance

The federal government has invested in tracking tools designed to oversee projects and programs that aren't meeting performance goals. Early detection and correction of problems, while the project is underway, is becoming a best practice in federal projects. In recent years, increased emphasis has been placed on measuring projects more consistently. OMB retains much of the responsibility for implementing programs that will result in improvements. For example, OMB now requires that all large projects use an earned value management system. On the congressional side of the measurement spectrum, GAO provides oversight and accountability in its reviews of individual programs and agency results.

OMB's role in project performance has been increasing in recent years, through the use of such tools as the Program Assessment Rating Tool, Exhibit 300, and performance dashboards (see Chapter 12, Aligning Federal and Project Planning Cycles). These tools are evolving into effective instruments for tracking and improving project performance. Further, OMB has the authority to impose consequences if agencies do not deliver. For example, on June 4, 2009, *Federal News Radio* reported the following:

> The Office of Management and Budget has told agencies to get data on their information technology projects ready for public viewing.

In a Chief Information Officer's Council meeting May 27, federal CIO Vivek Kundra introduced the administration's next transparency initiative, an IT project dashboard.

A government source, who attended the meeting, says Kundra told agencies to resubmit their earned value management data from their exhibit 300 business cases in preparation for public posting.[9]

Not only does OMB's scorecard include traditional data elements, but this new version posts photographs of the agency CIOs. The intent of putting a literal face to senior management is to drive accountability throughout the entire agency.

OMB leadership has clearly come to realize that project performance management is an ongoing process. Project evaluation and measurement, both during and after projects, are conducted not just to identify and correct errors but also to determine and evaluate what worked and how successful methods might be replicated.

## THE NEW ROLE OF CHIEF PERFORMANCE OFFICER

At the agency level, various jobs and roles support performance measurement and accountability. For example, most federal agencies now have a chief performance officer (CPO). Establishment of this position in many agencies reflects a growing recognition that performance management is an important component of delivering value. According to a 2007 memo discussing Executive Order 13450, which established the need for performance improvement:

> Performance Improvement Officers are responsible for coordinating the performance management activities of the agency, including:
> - Development and improvement of the agency's strategic plans, annual performance plans, and annual performance reports, as

well as ensuring the use of such information in agency budget justifications;

- Ensuring program goals are aggressive, realistic, and accurately measured;
- Regularly convening agency program management personnel to assess and improve program performance and efficiency; and
- Assisting the head of the agency in the development and use within the agency of performance measures in personnel performance appraisals, particularly those of program managers, to ensure real accountability for greater effectiveness.[10]

Project managers in the federal environment should embrace the establishment of this new role and rely on the CPO for advocacy, performance management resources, and advice on project performance issues.

> Federal project managers and their contractor counterparts are faced with a dilemma of divergence. On the one hand, projects are rapidly increasing in complexity. From legislative and regulatory requirements to technical challenges, the level of project complexity has never been greater. On the other hand, stakeholders are demanding more and more for their tax dollars. Citizens and lawmakers alike understand that projects must deliver value and they have the tools to be heard.
>
> Project performance management starts at the agency level. To be successful in the federal environment, agency leadership would do well to understand how EVM works. Pursuing performance management takes courage and conviction because it will invariably show areas where performance can be improved. Yet, it must be done. As projects take up more time, dollars, and operational space, it is important to build the proper support structure to be able to manage new initiatives as effectively as possible.

## NOTES

1. IT Dashboard, IT All Investments Report, http://it.usaspending. gov/?q=content/current-year-fy2009-enacted (accessed October 30, 2007).
2. U.S. Government Accountability Office, "Management and Oversight of Projects Totaling Billions of Dollars Need Attention," GAO Report 09-624T, April 28, 2007, p. 7.
3. U.S. Government Accountability Office, "Federal Agencies Need to Strengthen Investment Board Oversight of Poorly Planned and Performing Projects," GAO Report 09-566, June 2007, p.7.
4. "Use of Earned Value Management (EVM) in the Department of Defense," July 3, 2007, memo by Kenneth J. Krieg, Undersecretary of Defense for Acquisition, Technology and Logistics, http://www.acq.osd.mil/pm/documents/evm_rolesresponsibilities_signed_3jul07.pdf (downloaded May 11, 2009).
5. U.S. Department of Defense, *Earned Value Management Implementation Guide,* October 2006, p. 3, http://acquisition.navy.mil/rda/home/acquisition_one_source/cevm/evm_policy_regulations_and_requirements/osd_evm_memos_and_policy (downloaded May 10, 2009).
6. Federal CIO Council, "A Framework for Developing Earned Value Management Systems (EVMS) Policy for Information Technology Projects," December 5, 2005.
7. Federal CIO Council.
8. U.S. Government Accountability Office, "Preliminary Observations on Deepwater Program Assets and Management Challenges," GAO Report 07-446T, February 15, 2007, p. 18.
9. Jason Miller, Executive Editor, "CIOs cautiously optimistic about OMB's IT dashboard," *Federal News Radio.* June 29, 2007.
10. Memorandum for the Heads of Departments and Agencies from Clay Johnson, Deputy Director for Management, OMB, "Implementing Executive Order 13450: Improving Government Program Performance," December 7, 2007.

## Chapter 16

# The Promise of Project Management in the Federal Government: Looking Ahead

> *There is no quick road to project management maturity, but with perseverance and a thick skin, much can be done.*
> —ALLAN ROIT, ASSISTANT PMO DIRECTOR, FINANCIAL CRIMES ENFORCEMENT NETWORK, U.S. DEPARTMENT OF THE TREASURY

Among the things Americans expect, today more than ever, is effective government. Regardless of methods or tools, fundamental project management structures and individual skills are the key drivers to project success in the federal government. On a more macro level, the discipline of project management is a primary means of creating more effective government. What lies ahead for project management in the federal government?

The state of project management in the federal government varies from agency to agency. Yet, several trends are evident in the federal project management arena. While these trends do not represent the sum total of the future of project management in the federal government, they do indicate the direction project management is taking. Those on the front lines offer some insights and ideas for improving the discipline of project management across the federal government.

## PERSPECTIVES ON KEY TRENDS AND LESSONS LEARNED

Successful practices are being implemented across a broad range of federal organizations. These success stories provide lessons learned for organizations looking to implement or improve their project management practices, tools, skills, and techniques.

### Organization and Structure

Some of the greatest strides in federal project management are likely to be in the area of organization and structure. The increasing interest and oversight demonstrated by Congress through hearings and legislation, OMB through initiatives such as FAC-P/PM, and GAO through its high-risk list will likely promote the formalization of project management organizations and structures within federal agencies.

Implementation of formal governance processes, establishment of enterprise-level PMOs, increased accountability, and greater centralization of project management across the federal government are current trends emerging in this arena. The massive infusion of funding from the American Recovery and Reinvestment Act of 2009 may accelerate these trends, as requirements for close management, tracking, and reporting on the results are attached to the money. The increased level of visibility

**CHAPTER 16** The Promise of Project Management in the Federal Government

into projects across the entire federal government is readily apparent at www.Recovery.gov.

Those who have been working to implement governance processes, methodologies, or PMOs offer some advice relating to organization and structure:

- "Institute simpler project management processes and allow practitioners the flexibility to tailor the processes to suit their situations, mindful that they do not stray from the intent of the original process." This advice from Siva Sankar, Chair of the PMI Government Special Interest Group, is reinforced by a caution from Allan Roit, Assistant PMO Director at Treasury's Financial Crimes Enforcement Network: "Beware of going overboard with project oversight without the relevant and commensurate project management education and mentoring." Both suggest that success is not measured by the implementation of organizations, structures, or processes, but that these are means to deliver results. Further, establishing these structures without providing personnel with the appropriate tools or training is a recipe for failure.

- "Acquisition and program personnel need to work together at the inception of a project to define the outcomes, agree on the acquisition strategy, and develop a clear performance management plan. Taking time to establish the shared vision at the beginning of a project greatly increases the chances of success." Lesley Field, Deputy Administrator for Federal Procurement Policy at OMB, clearly recognizes the increasing interdependence between acquisition and project management.

## People

While many trends are affecting the "people" component of project management in the federal government, such as the aging workforce and the economy, our interviews and research pointed to two areas that are receiving particular attention: stakeholders and skill and practice development.

### Stakeholders

Project stakeholders are becoming increasingly sophisticated. Greater access to information has piqued their higher levels of interest and engagement. In response, project managers must develop comprehensive communication strategies that employ both traditional techniques and emerging technologies. Beyond increased communication, project managers will find themselves integrating key stakeholders more directly into activities throughout the project lifecycle. Failing to meet stakeholders' expectations for greater involvement can derail a project or distract the project manager from more critical project tasks.

A key stakeholder group, executives and other department leaders, is often cited as the most essential to a project's success. Two executives offer their advice to leaders and project managers:

- "Be transparent. Talk to us early and candidly about challenges and setbacks, but also don't be afraid to ask for assistance," recommends Darren Ash, Deputy Executive Director for Corporate Management at NRC. Mr. Ash's suggestion to project managers to be open, honest, and up-front, avoiding surprises, was echoed by nearly every executive or senior project or program manager we interviewed and in many reports we reviewed. This important advice is, perhaps, some of the easiest to implement.

- NASA's Dr. Ed Hoffman, Director of the Academy for Program/Project and Engineering Leadership, suggests, "Leadership support is key to project success. Set a vision and goals to create alignment from the vision all the way to projects. The result is developing loyalty—project managers are loyal to the project and the organization, leaders are loyal to their projects and programs." In essence, the project manager is a stakeholder in the success of the project, which is ultimately "owned" by the organization's leaders. Leadership support for project management creates loyalty to the organization and, potentially, greater commitment to success.

- Jason Hill, project manager in the Administrative Resource Center at Treasury's Bureau of the Public Debt, described a measure of success in implementing project management practices. "As a bit of barometer of sorts of our growing success, we are finding that our organization's executives are asking PM-related questions more and more, like 'What is the project's top risk?' or 'How can it be mitigated?' or 'What is the expected end date given the scope you have outlined?' These are all good indicators that the executive culture is changing toward project management and certainly one we believe will lead to more successful corporate deliveries." Subsequent efforts to expand or improve project management practices and skills will be easier with this stakeholder group on board.

### *Skill and Practice Development*

The key trends related to project management skills and practices are the formalization of training and certification, expansion of the government-wide project management community to proliferate best practices, and specialization in project management. Increasingly, organizations will support certification of project management personnel initially resulting from new mandates, such as the FAC-P/PM requirements, but ultimately because agency executives and project sponsors will understand that improved professional competency helps the individual, the organization, and the government at large.

Along with the focus on improving skills, organizations are likely to codify the role of the project manager through the establishment of a career path and the inclusion of project management responsibilities as part of personnel performance reviews. This emphasis on project management specialization will lead to increased participation in project management communities of practice or relevant functional areas (e.g., construction, IT, social services). These communities are growing within government agencies and in industry at large.

Advice from the field regarding key skills and practices addresses risk management, discipline, and project planning:

- "Projects succeed when risk assessments are performed and the project manager had made the necessary and appropriate adjustments to the project plan, schedule, WBS, and budget." This advice from a senior program manager at the Department of Commerce reflects the increasing importance of specialized project management skills like risk and schedule management, as well as recent additions to PMI's suite of certifications.

- "Project management is about applying common sense with uncommon discipline. Project management is the language of getting things done." Michael O'Brochta, a former senior program manager at CIA, boiled the project manager's efforts down to three key points: discipline, communication, and most important, common sense. Overcomplicating the practice of project management on a project will create resistance and embolden those who will argue that the overhead required outweighs the benefits.

- Will Brimberry, program manager at the Department of the Interior, provided an interesting analogy to test whether the project has a sound plan. "A measure of the solidness of the project plan is to answer the following question: 'If this were a private sector project, could we take it to a bank and would they approve a loan to execute the project?'" This approach presents a different perspective for project managers and their teams and suggests applying some skills or techniques not typically associated with the public sector.

- In his advice to executives and fellow project managers, Arnold Hill, project manager in GSA's Design and Construction Division, explains that: "project management is more than a process. Project management is delivering value to meet a business need with an expected result." This point provides a good argument for those who question the fundamental role of project management, as well as those who want to implement the tools of the trade just to say they're in place. Without elevating project management from a set of forms to a core business process and without connecting the need to the end product, project managers and project management proponents will be hard-pressed to convey the true value for the required investment.

## Process

Improvements to project management practices are being implemented across the federal government. One area likely to experience continued and significant change is knowledge.

The broad category of knowledge addresses the quality, volume, access, and use of information. The more sophisticated stakeholders become, the greater their demand for better information that is easily and rapidly accessible. Similarly, the increasing complexity of projects—in terms of size, scope, and products—requires that project knowledge be shared across organizational and geographic boundaries. The effort to collect and disseminate lessons learned can no longer be relegated to the end of the project and only if time and resources permit.

A key driver in the improvement in project knowledge is technology. Technology is only a tool, but one that can vastly improve project management, particularly in support of communication and the evaluation of projects. Intranet-based tools such as project management portals, which are becoming more commonplace, will support improved communication efforts. As the technology matures and proliferates, social networking tools will be applied in the management of projects to mirror the way communication is evolving in society. Project tracking and evaluation tools that support functions like EVM will also come into widespread use, driven in part by OMB requirements.

In light of these knowledge-oriented trends, project management practitioners in the federal government offer the following advice:

- Lesley Field, Deputy Director at OFPP, suggests that real measurement is critical to successful federal project management. "The use of EVM tools, the ability to identify and analyze variances to pick up early indications of derailment, and managing a project and reporting on progress in small measurable amounts is key." Project managers should establish clear metrics that feed an early warning system to allow for small corrections early, rather than big corrections later on.

- "Earned value management without fundamental project management skills and capabilities diminishes the effectiveness and quality of EVM outputs. In some cases earned value-related information is reported without evidence or understanding. Sound project management practices are essential to useful EVM." This declaration from James Rispoli, former Assistant Secretary of Energy, highlights that communicating information without the relevant supporting knowledge or understanding can yield unintentional and potentially harmful results. Executives and project managers must ensure that project personnel are equipped not only with the right tools to share knowledge, but also with the commensurate skills to do so effectively.

Again, the web will play an important part in spreading project knowledge. Sites like www.ExpectMore.gov provide unprecedented insight into government project successes and failures. Recovery.gov provides similar information regarding ARRA-funded projects.

## THE MORE THINGS CHANGE . . .

Despite these clear trends in government project management, some things are not likely to change as a result of time, technology, regulations, or other factors:

- *People.* At the end of the day, projects involve people and people are unique. While the methods may evolve (web, messaging, tweeting, etc.), the techniques for managing, motivating, directing, or counseling project participants or stakeholders will likely not change much over time. Project managers must be able to deal with the good, the bad, and the ugly side of human nature, improving on their own skills and capabilities in this area.

- *Managing change.* The one thing guaranteed not to change is that change will always occur. Project management–related processes, structures, and technologies in particular will continue in a state of flux, challenging organizations and project managers to keep pace, adopt, and adapt. The ability to remain flexible and creative will continue to be an essential attribute of the successful project manager. Furthermore, project managers, team members, and key stakeholders will remain the primary catalysts or change agents responsible for preparing their colleagues and their organizations for the changes resulting from projects.

- *Tools of the trade.* Gadgets and gizmos may have their appeal, but flipcharts, sticky notes, pens, and notepads rarely crash and most people are adept at using them all. While meetings may become more virtual as time goes on, gathering a group around a table to get work done will always be an integral part of every project. Thus, the project manager's ability as facilitator and effective meeting leader will remain a key skill. The ability to define a task clearly and work a group through the process to achieve the desired outcome will remain essential.

- *Communicate, communicate, communicate.* Again, the methods may change over time, but the successful project manager must be a skillful communicator. The project manager and key team members must be able to deliver, receive, and process information from a variety of sources and formats.

## THE OUTLOOK FOR PROJECT MANAGEMENT IN THE FEDERAL GOVERNMENT

For some, raising project management to a prominent and critical position within their organizations is a success story; for others it is a work in progress. Clearly, the practice and performance of project management are on the rise throughout the federal government.

The challenge remains to demonstrate the value of project management. While the meaning of "value" may be elusive, the success of projects is not when measured by timely and cost-effective delivery of expected results. Congressman Elijah Cummings, senior member of the House Committee on Oversight and Government Reform, sums it up best: "Mediocrity is expensive! The cost of executing projects poorly is significantly greater than investing in effective project performance."

Project management is increasingly being viewed as a critical skill set in the federal government. A new breed of manager is emerging, one that was raised on the precepts of project management and is comfortable in an environment marked by frequent and rapid change. Federal project management is maturing, evolving from a purely homespun set of practices into a formal discipline within departments and across the government enterprise.

Considering the full scope of project management within the federal environment is overwhelming. But executives, sponsors, and project managers can take to heart one consistent lesson learned: success breeds success. Take manageable steps to build and improve project management in your organization, and you will find that you have contributed to achieving project management success in the federal government.

# Recommended Resources

Abramson, Mark A., Jonathan D. Breul, and John M. Kamensky. *Six Trends Transforming Government.* Washington, DC: IBM Center for the Business of Government, 2006.

Augustine, Sanjiv. *Managing Agile Projects.* Upper Saddle River, NJ: Prentice Hall, 2005.

Bardwick, Judith. *One Foot Out the Door.* New York: AMACOM, 2008.

Benton, D. A. *CEO Material: How to Be a Leader in Any Organization.* New York: McGraw Hill, 2009.

Bidgoli, Hossein. *Intelligent Management Solutions.* Westport, CT: Quorum Books, 1998.

Bossidy, Larry, and Ram Charan. *Execution: The Discipline of Getting Things Done.* New York: Crown Business, 2002.

Budd, Charles I., and Charlene S. Budd. *A Practical Guide to Earned Value Project Management.* Vienna, VA: Management Concepts, 2005.

Citrin, James M., and Thomas J. Neff, with Catherine Fredman. *You're in Charge—Now What?* New York: Crown Business, 2005.

Cleland, David I., and Bopaya Bindanda. *Project Management Circa 2025.* Newtown Square, PA: Project Management Institute, Inc., 2009.

Cleland, David I., and Lewis R. Ireland. *Project Management Handbook: Applying Best Practices Across Global Industries.* New York: McGraw Hill, 2008.

Cleland, David I., and Lewis R. Ireland. *Project Management: Strategic Design and Implementation.* New York: McGraw-Hill, 2008.

Collins, Jim. *Good to Great: Why Some Companies Make the Leap . . . and Others Don't.* New York: HarperBusiness, 2001.

Collins, Jim, and Jerry I. Porras. *Built to Last: Successful Habits of Visionary Companies.* New York: HarperCollins. 2002.

Dalkir, Kimiz. *Knowledge Management in Theory and Practice.* Amsterdam, The Netherlands: Elsevier Butterworth-Heinemann, 2005.

Duarte, Deborah L., and Nancy Tennant Snyder. *Virtual Team Critical Success Factors* (The Portable MBA in Project Management). Hoboken, NJ: John Wiley & Sons, 2003.

Federal Chief Information Officer Council. "A Framework for Developing Earned Value Management Systems (EVMS) Policy for Information Technology Projects," December 5, 2005.

Flannes, Steven W., and Ginger Levin, *Essential People Skills for Project Managers.* Vienna, VA: Management Concepts, 2005.

Frame, J. Davidson. *Project Management Competences.* San Francisco: Jossey-Bass, 1999.

Greengard, Samuel. "Lessons in Leadership," *PM Network*, vol. 22, no. 8, August 2008.

Hammer, Michael. "The Process Audit," *Harvard Business Review,* April 2007.

Hass, Kathleen B., *Managing Complex Projects: A New Model.* Vienna, VA: Management Concepts, 2009.

Haugan, Gregory T. *Project Planning and Scheduling.* Vienna, VA: Management Concepts, 2002.

Haugan, Gregory T. *The Work Breakdown Structure in Government Contracting.* Vienna, VA: Management Concepts, 2003.

Hiatt, Jeffrey M. *ADKAR: A Model for Change in Business, Government, and Our Community.* Loveland, CO: Prosci, 2006.

Highsmith, Jim. *Agile Project Management: Creating Innovative Products.* Upper Saddle River: NJ: Pearson Education, 2004.

Hoffman, Ed. "NASA Reduces Uncertainty and Minimizes Risks with Project Methods," *PM Network*, vol. 17, no. 6, June 2003.

Irwin, Brian. *Managing Politics and Conflicts in Projects.* Vienna, VA: Management Concepts, 2008.

Kerzner, Harold. *Using the Project Management Maturity Model: Strategic Planning for Project Management.* Hoboken, NJ: John Wiley & Sons, 2005.

Kessler, Thomas G., and Patricia Kelley. *The Business of Government: Strategy, Implementation, and Results.* Vienna, VA: Management Concepts, 2000.

Kotter, Jon. *A Force for Change.* New York: The Free Press, 1990.

Kotter, Jon. *A Sense of Urgency.* Boston: Harvard Business School Press, 2008.

Levy, Buddy. *American Legend: The Real-Life Adventures of David Crockett.* New York: G.P. Putnam's Sons, 2005.

Morris, Rick A., *The Everything Project Management Book.* Avon, MA: Avon Media, 2008.

Newcomer, Kathryn E., and Barry White. *Getting Results: A Guide for Federal Leaders and Managers.* Vienna, VA: Management Concepts and Center for Innovation in Public Service, 2005.

Nicholas, John M., and Herman Steyn. *Project Management for Business, Engineering, and Technology.* Amsterdam, The Netherlands: Butterworth-Heinemann, 2008.

O'Brochta, Michael, "Federal Project Manager Momentum," *PM World Today*, vol. 11, no. 4, April 2009.

Pande, Peter S., Robert P. Neuman, and Roland R. Cavanaugh. *The Six Sigma Way Team Fieldbook: An Implementation Guide for Project Improvement Teams*. New York: McGraw-Hill, 2001.

Phillips, Jack J., and Patricia Pulliam Phillips. *Show Me the Money: How to Determine ROI in People, Projects, and Programs*. San Francisco: Berrett-Kohler, 2007.

Project Management Institute. *A Guide to the Project Management Body of Knowledge—Fourth Edition*. Newtown Square, PA: Project Management Institute, Inc., 2008.

Reichheld, Fred. *The Ultimate Question*. Cambridge, MA: Harvard Business School Press, 2005.

Roberts, Paul. *Guide to Project Management*. London: *The Economist* and Profile Books, Ltd., 2007.

Sistare, Hannah S., Myra Howze Shiplett, and Terry F. Buss. *Innovations in Human Resource Management*. Armonk, New York: M.E. Sharpe, 2009.

Software Engineering Institute. "CMMI for Acquisition, version 1.2," November 2007.

Stratton, Ray. *The Earned Value Management Maturity Model®*. Vienna, VA: Management Concepts, 2006.

Tuckman, Bruce W. "Developmental Sequence in Small Groups," *Psychological Bulletin*, 63, 384-399. Reprinted in *Group Facilitation: A Research and Applications Journal*, no. 3, Spring 2001.

U.S. Government Accountability Office. "21st Century Challenges: Reexamining the Base of the Federal Government," GAO-05-352T. Washington, DC: U.S. Government Printing Office, February 2005.

U.S. Government Accountability Office. "As Initial Implementation Unfolds in States and Localities, Continued Attention to Accountability Issues Is Essential," GAO-09-580. Washington, DC: U.S. Government Printing Office, April 2009.

U.S. Government Accountability Office. "Better Performance Information Needed to Support Agency Contract Award Decisions," GAO-09-374. Washington, DC: U.S. Government Printing Office, April 2009.

U.S. Government Accountability Office. "High Risk Series: An Update," GAO-09-271. Washington, DC: U.S. Government Printing Office, January 2009.

Whitten, Neal. *Neal Whitten's No-Nonsense Advice for Successful Projects*. Vienna, VA: Management Concepts, 2005.

Williams, Meri. *The Principles of Project Management*. Collingwood, VIC, Australia: Sitepoint PTY Ltd., 2008.

## WEBSITES

American Society for the Advancement of Project Management, www.asapm.org

Chief Acquisition Officers Council, www.cao.gov

Chief Financial Officers Council, www.cfo.gov

Chief Human Capital Officers Council, www.chcoc.gov

Chief Information Officers Council, www.cio.gov

International Project Management Association, www.ipma.ch

Project Management Institute, www.pmi.org

U.S. Federal Acquisition Institute, www.fai.gov

U.S. Government Accountability Office, www.gao.gov

U.S. Office of Management and Budget, www.omb.gov

# Index

## A

Academy of Program/Project and Engineering Leadership (APPEL), 79–80, 130, 184
ADKAR model, 110–113
Administrative Resource Center (ARC), 21–22
advanced project management, 93
agency policies, 48
agile project management, 213–215
American Recovery and Reinvestment Act of 2009 (ARRA), 90, 132
American Society for the Advancement of Project Management (asapm), 178–179
APPEL. *See* Academy of Program/Project and Engineering Leadership
applied project management, 22–24
ARC. *See* Administrative Resource Center
ARRA. *See* American Recovery and Reinvestment Act of 2009
asapm. *See* American Society for the Advancement of Project Management
assessing project needs, 93–94

## B

basic project management, 92
Budget and Accounting Act of 1921, 45, 49
Budget and Accounting Procedures Act of 1950, 49
Bureau of Indian Affairs PMO (IAPMO), 72, 133

## C

C/SCSC. *See* cost and schedule control system criteria
CAO. *See* chief administrative officer
Capability Maturity Model Integration (CMMI®), 179, 220
Capability Maturity Model Integration for Acquisition (CMMI®-ACQ), 181
CAPM. *See* Certified Associate of Project Management
CCM. *See* Certified Construction Manager
Census Bureau, 66–67, 140, 144–147, 153, 207–209
Census Integration Group (CIG), 66–67

Central Intelligence Agency (CIA), 39, 133
centralization
  confluence of project management authority and practices, 39
  decentralized project management, 40
  definition, 38
  distributed environments, 39
Certified Associate of Project Management (CAPM), 179, 192
Certified Construction Manager (CCM), 180
CFO Act. *See* Chief Financial Officers Act of 1990
change leader, 126–127
Chief Acquisition Officers Council Project Management Working Group, 46
chief administrative officer (CAO), 35
Chief Financial Officers Act of 1990 (CFO Act), 49–50
chief information officer (CIO), 35, 46
chief performance officer (CPO), 274–275
CIA. *See* Central Intelligence Agency
CIG. *See* Census Integration Group
CIO. *See* chief information officer
CIO Act. *See* Information Technology Management Reform Act of 1996
Circular A-11, 55–57
Circular A-109, 55
Clinger-Cohen Act. *See* Information Technology Management Reform Act of 1996
CMMI®. *See* Capability Maturity Model Integration
CMMI®-ACQ. *See* Capability Maturity Model Integration for Acquisition
coaching, 186
communication
  ADKAR model, 110–113
  context, 105–107
  formal external communications, 107
  formal internal communications, 107
  informal external communications, 107
  informal internal communications, 108
  information access and security, 115–116
  key elements, 109
  media, 114–115
  plan, 110
  project manager's role, 104–105
  types, 108
confidence, 128–129
Construction Manager Certification Institute, 178
continuous process improvement/lean six sigma (CPI/LSS), 180
contracting officer's technical representative (COTR), 81, 133
contractor management, 163–164
contractors, 80–83
cost and schedule control system criteria (C/SCSC), 11–12, 55
cost-plus award fee (CPAF), 163–164
cost-plus incentive fee (CPIF), 163–164
COTR. *See* contracting officer's technical representative
CPAF. *See* cost-plus award fee
CPI/LSS. *See* continuous process improvement/lean six sigma
CPIF. *See* cost-plus incentive fee
CPM. *See* critical path methodology
CPO. *See* chief performance officer
critical controls, 17
critical path methodology (CPM), 11
culture, organizational dimension
  attitudes and beliefs, 29
  behaviors, 28
  importance of, 23–26
  language, 29–30
  relationship to project management, 26–28
  rituals, 30–31

# Index

## D

Defense Acquisition University (DAU), 158
Defense Acquisition Workforces Improvement Act (DAWIA), 158
deliverables, 234–238
Department of Defense (DoD)
    continuous process improvement / lean six sigma, 180
    cost and schedule control system criteria, 11
    earned value management, 265–266
    Office of Acquisition, Technology and Logistics, 187
    program planning and budgeting system, 235
Department of Energy (DOE), 23, 64–65, 134, 184
directives and regulations. *See also* laws
    Exhibit 300, 55–57
    Federal Acquisition Regulation, 53–54
    OMB Circular A-11, 55–57
    OMB Circular A-109, 12, 55–57
    program assessment rating tool, 58
DoD. *See* Department of Defense
DOE. *See* Department of Energy

## E

E-300. *See* Exhibit 300
E-Government Act of 2002, 46, 52–53, 56
EA. *See* enterprise architecture
earned value management (EVM), 11, 265–268
earned value management system (EVMS), 55
enterprise architecture (EA), 198
ethics, 197
EVM. *See* earned value management
EVMS. *See* earned value management system (EVMS)
evolution, of project management
    early twentieth century, 8–9
    late twentieth century, 12–13
    mid-twentieth century, 9–11
    pre-twentieth century, 6–8
    twenty-first century, 13–16
executive orders, 48
Exhibit 300 (E-300), 55–57

## F

FAA. *See* Federal Aviation Administration
FAC-P/PM. *See* federal acquisition certification for program and project managers
facilitation, 172
facilitator, 125
FAI. *See* Federal Acquisition Institute
failure, 5, 253
FAR. *See* Federal Acquisition Regulation
FASA. *See* Federal Acquisition Streamlining Act of 1994
FEA. *See* Federal Enterprise Architecture
federal acquisition certification for program and project managers (FAC-P/PM), 15, 182–185
Federal Acquisition Institute (FAI), 47, 182
Federal Acquisition Regulation (FAR), 53–54
Federal Acquisition Streamlining Act of 1994 (FASA), 51–52, 56
Federal Aviation Administration (FAA), 110
Federal Emergency Management Agency (FEMA), 140
Federal Enterprise Architecture (FEA), 110
federal government, complexity of, 1–3
Federal Information Security Management Act (FISMA), 57
Federal Knowledge Management Initiative (FKMI), 245–246

Federal Managers Financial Integrity Act of 1982, 49–50
federal project director (FPD), 184
federal regulations, 48
FEMA. *See* Federal Emergency Management Agency
financial analysis and budgeting, 166–167
FISMA. *See* Federal Information Security Management Act
FKMI. *See* Federal Knowledge Management Initiative
FOIA. *See* Freedom of Information Act
formal external communications, 107
formal internal communications, 107
FPD. *See* federal project director
framing, 170
Freedom of Information Act (FOIA), 107–108, 115
future, of project management, 16–18

## G

Gantt chart, 9
GAO. *See* Government Accountability Office
General Accounting Office. *See* Government Accountability Office
General Services Administration (GSA), 81, 137–138
Government 2.0, 97–98
Government Accountability Office (GAO)
 audits, 17
 cost estimating guidelines, 81
 creation of, 45
 customized waterfall methodology, 212
 Deepwater program, 272
 engagements, 211
 high-risk list, 17, 45, 141–142, 261, 278
 project managers, 173
 stakeholder management, 141–142, 147–148
 successful communication, 167
Government Paperwork Elimination Act, 56
Government Performance and Results Act (GPRA)
 importance of, 51, 228–230
 performance and accountability report, 233–234
 performance budget, 232–233
 performance plan, 231–232
 strategic plan, 230–231
GSA. *See* General Services Administration
*Guide to the Project Management Body of Knowledge* (*PMBOK® Guide*), 160

## H

high-risk list, 17, 45, 141–142, 261, 278
history, of project management
 early twentieth century, 8–9
 late twentieth century, 12–13
 mid-twentieth century, 9–11
 pre-twentieth century, 6–8
 twenty-first century, 13–16
hosted solutions, 99

## I

IAPMO. *See* Bureau of Indian Affairs PMO
IBR. *See* integrated baseline review
informal external communications, 107
informal internal communications, 108
information
 access to, 17
 security, 115–116
 sharing, 167–168
Information Technology Investment Oversight Enhancement and Waste Prevention Act of 2008, 5–6, 56

Index

information technology (IT)
  advanced project management, 93
  assessing project needs, 93–94
  basic project management, 92
  executing, 95
  federal government, 88–91
  Government 2.0, 97–98
  hosted solutions, 99
  importance of, 88
  intermediate project management, 92
  measuring, 96
  on-demand government, 89–90
  planning, 94–95
  predictive project management, 98–99
  process-oriented project management, 99
  reporting, 96–97
Information Technology Management Reform Act of 1996, 52
integrated baseline review (IBR), 81
integrated project team (IPT), 64–67
integrated reporting, 200
integration, 171
integrity, 173
intermediate project management, 92
International Project Management Association (IPMA), 179–180
inventory, 201
investment review board (IRB), 81, 194, 264–265
IPMA. *See* International Project Management Association
IPT. *See* integrated project team
IRB. *See* investment review board
IT. *See* information technology
IT Business Council (ITBC), 199
IT investment management (ITIM), 264–265
IT Senior Advisory Council (ITSAC), 199
ITBC. *See* IT Business Council
ITIM. *See* IT investment management
ITSAC. *See* IT Senior Advisory Council

## J

just-in-time training, 186–187

## K

knowledge management (KM)
  challenges, 248
  complexity, 250–251
  definition, 243–245
  discipline, 252–253
  failures, 253
  Federal Knowledge Management Initiative, 245–246
  implementation, 253–256
  information assurance, 251–252
  role, 246–248
  volume, 248–249
knowledge training, 187

## L

laws. *See also* directives and regulations
  Budget and Accounting Act of 1921, 49
  Budget and Accounting Procedures Act of 1950, 49
  Chief Financial Officers Act of 1990, 49–50
  E-Government Act of 2002, 52–53
  Federal Acquisition Streamlining Act of 1994, 51–52
  Federal Managers Financial Integrity Act of 1982, 49–50
  Government Performance and Results Act, 51
  importance of, 43–44
  Information Technology Management Reform Act of 1996, 52
  overview, 48
leadership, 161
  authority versus responsibility, 127–128

balancing with management, 123–125
change leader, 126–127
characteristics, 127
confidence, 128–129
facilitator, 125
federal government projects, 132–134
management, compared to, 119–121
mentor, 125–126
project context, 121–123
recognizing and facing reality, 129
role of, 129–131
lessons learned, 165–166
line of balance (LOB), 10

## M

management operation system technique (MOST), 10
matrixed teams, 63
media, 114–115
mentoring, 125–126, 169, 186
MOST. *See* management operation system technique

## N

National Aeronautics and Space Administration (NASA), 23, 79–80, 184, 241–242
national competence baseline, 221–222
negotiation, 168–169
non-EVM performance criteria, 269
nongovernmental organization (NGO), 5
Nuclear Regulatory Commission (NRC), 184–185, 191–193, 198

## O

Office of Environmental Management (OEM), 134, 184
Office of Federal Procurement Policy (OFPP), 45
Office of Information Services (OIS), 192

Office of Management and Budget (OMB)
ANSI/EIA 748-A-1998, 13
Circular A-11, 55–57
Circular A-109, 12, 55–57
importance of, 13
role, 45, 49
OFPP. *See* Office of Federal Procurement Policy
OIS. *See* Office of Information Services
OMB. *See* Office of Management and Budget
OMO. *See* outcome management office
on-demand government, 89–90
OPM3®. *See* Organizational Project Management Maturity Model
organic project management, 22–24
organizational governance
definition, 193
ethics, 197
function, 194
improve, 195–196
investment review board, 194
IT Business Council, 199
IT Senior Advisory Council, 199
legal and regulatory requirements, 197
NRC governance structure, 198
operate, 195
performance, 196
risk, 196
structure, 195
transform, 196
transparency, 196–197
Organizational Project Management Maturity Model (OPM3®), 181, 219
origin of project management, 22–24
outcome management office (OMO), 37–38
oversight, legislative attempts to implement, 5–6

## P

PART. *See* program assessment rating tool

# Index

PBBS. *See* program planning and budgeting system
PBS. *See* Public Buildings Service
PD. *See* project director
PDW. *See* project development workshop
PEMM™. *See* Process and Enterprise Maturity Model
performance and accountability report, 233–234
performance assessment rating tool, 234
performance budget, 232–233
performance management
    chief performance officer, 274–275
    earned value management, 265–268
    establishing measures, 263
    importance of, 259–261
    investment review boards, 264–265
    managing project performance, 270–273
    non-EVM performance criteria, 269
    overseeing project performance, 273–274
    overview, 261–263
performance measurement, 17
performance plan, 231–232
PERT. *See* Project Evaluation and Review Technique
PgMO. *See* program management office
PgMP. *See* Program Management Professional
planning. *See also* Government Performance and Results Act
    cycle outputs, 234–238
    importance of, 227–228
    information technology, 94–95
    strategic, 17
PM COP. *See* project management community of practice
*PMBOK® Guide*. *See A Guide to the Project Management Body of Knowledge*
PMCDP. *See* project management career development program
PMI. *See* Project Management Institute
PMIS. *See* project management information systems
PMO. *See* project management office
PMP. *See* Project Management Professional
PMWG. *See* Project Management Working Group
political landscape, 5
portfolio manager, 200
predictive project management, 98–99
Process and Enterprise Maturity Model (PEMM™), 222
process management, 3
process-oriented project management, 99
product development lifecycles, 216–219
professional development
    American Society for the Advancement of Project Management, 178–179
    Capability Maturity Model Integration for Acquisition, 181
    Certified Associate of Project Management, 179, 192
    Certified Construction Manager, 180
    coaching and mentoring, 186
    Construction Manager Certification Institute, 178
    continuous process improvement/lean six sigma, 180
    development methods for project managers, 186
    federal acquisition certification for program and project managers, 182–185
    Federal Acquisition Institute, 182
    federal project director, 184
    importance of, 177–178
    International Project Management Association, 179–180
    just-in-time training, 186–187
    knowledge training, 187
    Organizational Project Management Maturity Model, 181
    Program Management Professional, 179

project management career
  development program, 184
project management community of
  practice, 187
Project Management Institute, 178
Project Management Professional,
  179, 182
Software Engineering Institute, 179
training, 186
USA National Competence Baseline,
  180
program, definition, 3
program assessment rating tool (PART),
  58
program management office (PgMO), 37
Program Management Professional
  (PgMP), 179
program planning and budgeting system
  (PPBS), 235
project, definition, 3, 7
project analysis and requirements
  definition, 163
project development workshop (PDW),
  72
project director (PD), 65
Project Evaluation and Review
  Technique (PERT), 10
project management, importance of, 3–4
project management career development
  program (PMCDP), 184
project management community of
  practice (PM COP), 187
project management information
  systems (PMIS), 93
Project Management Institute (PMI), 4,
  47, 178
project management methodologies
  agile project management, 213–215
  importance of, 48, 209–210
  national competence baseline,
    221–222
  Organizational Project Management
    Maturity Model, 219

Process and Enterprise Maturity
  Model, 222
product development lifecycles,
  216–219
rapid application development, 215
six sigma, 220–221
spiral, 215–216
waterfall methodology, 210–212
project management office (PMO), 22
Project Management Professional
  (PMP), 179
Project Management Working Group
  (PMWG), 46
project outcomes, 4–5, 37–38
project portfolio management
  architecture, 201
  criteria for inclusion, 200
  defined boundaries, 200
  importance of, 199–200
  integrated reporting, 200
  integration with governance, 202
  inventory, 201
  portfolio manager, 200
  risk, 201
  strategic decision-making, 203–204
  strategic plan, 201
  strategy, 201
Public Buildings Service (PBS), 81,
  137–138
public sector project management, 4–5

# R

rapid application development (RAM),
  215
recognizing and facing reality, 129
request for proposals (RFP), 81
risk, 196, 201
risk assessment/management, 162–163,
  282
risk management plan, 235
risk mitigation, 281
risk profile, 269

## S

schedule, scope, and change management, 164–165
SEI. *See* Software Engineering Institute
six sigma, 220–221
skills, project management
  communicating with clarity, 169
  comparison of traditional and new project management skills, 160
  contractor management, 163–164
  coordination, 161–162
  curiosity and imagination, 173
  Defense Acquisition University, 158
  Defense Acquisition Workforces Improvement Act, 158
  engaging executives, 168
  facilitation, 172
  financial analysis and budgeting, 166–167
  framing, 170
  *A Guide to the Project Management Body of Knowledge*, 160
  importance of, 157–159
  information sharing, 167–168
  integration, 171
  integrity, 173
  leadership, 161
  lessons learned, 165–166
  messaging and context, 170–171
  negotiation, 168–169
  overview, 159–160
  project analysis and requirements definition, 163
  risk assessment/management, 162–163
  schedule, scope, and change management, 164–165
  stakeholder management, 164
  subject matter expertise, 174–175
  supervision, 162
  teaching and mentoring, 169
  workflow management, 171–172
SME. *See* subject matter expert
Software Engineering Institute (SEI), 179
spiral development, 215–216
stakeholder management
  agency leaders, 141
  assessments, 149–154
  Census Bureau, 144–147
  communication, 148
  complex environments, 147–148
  Congress, 139–140
  customer involvement, 154
  department stakeholders, 142
  expectations, 155
  expertise, 148
  federal project stakeholders, 140
  future generations, 143
  General Services Administration, 144–147
  Government Accountability Office, 141–142, 147–148
  industry, 143
  interagency stakeholders, 142
  media, 143
  objectivity, 148
  Office of Management and Budget, 141
  overview, 138–139
  positive relationships, 154
  President of the United States, 141
  public, 142
  sample power/influence matrix, 153
  sample stakeholder engagement matrix, 147
  skills, 164
  stakeholder assessment worksheet, 150
  stakeholder influence-interest relationship, 151
  suppliers, 143
  vendors, 143
  virtual alliances, 154–155
  wide array of, 4
strategic decision-making, 203–204

strategic plan, 17, 201, 230–231
structure, organizational dimension
    center of excellence, 36
    controlling project management
        office, 36
    definition, 34
    functional project management office,
        36
    importance of, 23–26
    outcome management office, 37–38
    program management office, 37
    project management office, 36
    relationship to project management,
        35–36
subject matter expert (SME), 77,
    174–175
systems, organizational dimension
    configuration of authority, 34
    definition, 31
    degree of formality, 33–34
    importance of, 23–26
    intersection of projects and functions,
        32

# T

teaching, 169
teams
    business expert, 76
    co-responsibility, 69–70
    contract specialist, 77
    customer-focused, 69–70
    developing, 77–79
    effectiveness, 80
    establishing, 71–73
    executive sponsor, 75
    financial/budget expert, 76
    importance of, 61
    integrated project team, 64–67
    IT expert, 76
    managing, 79–80
    matrixed, 63

    project director, 75
    project manager, 75
    projectized, 69–70
    roles and responsibilities, 74–75
    rules, 73–74
    self-managed, 69–70
    structures, 62–63
    subject matter experts, 77
    surgical, 69–70
    virtual, 67–69
    workshop, 80
teamwork, 71
training, 186
transparency, 196–197
trends, identification of, 80
trends, in project management
    communication, 286
    managing change, 286
    organization and structure, 278–279
    outlook, 287
    overview, 277–278
    people, 280, 285
    process, 283–285
    skill and practice development,
        281–283
    stakeholders, 280–281
    tools, 286

# U

USA National Competence Baseline, 180

# V

VUE-IT, 96

# W

waterfall methodology, 210–212
Web 2.0, 97–98
work breakdown structure (WBS), 10
workflow management, 171–172

# Complement Your Project Management Library with These Additional Resources from
## MANAGEMENTCONCEPTS

## Project Management Fundamentals: Key Concepts and Methodologies
### Gregory T. Haugan, Ph.D., PMP

**Project Management Fundaments: Key Concepts and Methodologies** takes the mystery out of project management through a step-by-step, detailed approach. Filled with practical examples of project management methodologies, tools, and techniques, this book will help you manage projects successfully, no matter the size or complexity. You'll further enhance your knowledge and skills with special sections about risk and procurement management, maturity models, virtual teams, and IT projects. **Project Management Fundamentals** is your all-inclusive guidebook to implementing project management and achieving project success!

ISBN 978-1-56726-171-4 ■ Product Code B71X ■ 292 pages

## Managing Complex Projects: A New Model
### Kathleen B. Hass, PMP

For organizations to thrive, indeed to survive, in today's global economy, we must find ways to dramatically improve the performance of large-scale projects. **Managing Complex Projects: A New Model** offers an innovative way of looking at projects and treating them as complex adaptive systems. Applying the principles of complexity thinking will enable project managers and leadership teams to manage large-scale initiatives successfully.
\*\*\*Winner of the 2009 Project Management Institute David I. Cleland Project Management Literature Award.\*\*\*

ISBN 978-1-56726-233-9 ■ Product Code B339 ■ 298 pages

## Delivering Project Excellence with the Statement of Work, Second Edition
### Michael G. Martin, PMP

This second edition builds on the foundation of the first edition with a comprehensive yet succinct description of how to develop and apply the statement of work (SOW) to manage projects effectively. With updates throughout and an entirely new chapter on the use and application of the statement of objectives, this book continues to serve as a practical guide for project managers and team members. The new edition includes coverage of project management issues related to the federal government, such as updated FAR guidance on drafting a quality SOW and a discussion of legal considerations related to the SOW. New examples of SOWs from a variety of types of projects and business environments add to the second edition's usefulness.

ISBN 978-1-56726-257-5 ■ Product Code B575 ■ 300 pages

## The 77 Deadly Sins of Project Management
### Management Concepts

Projects can be negatively impacted by common "sins" that hinder, stall, or throw the project off track. **The 77 Sins of Project Management** helps you better understand how to execute projects by providing anecdotes and case studies of the project management sins described by experts in the field.

ISBN 978-1-56726-246-9 ■ Product Code B777 ■ 357 pages

## The Project Management Essential Library

The **Project Management Essential Library** is a series of eleven books, each of which covers a separate and distinct area of project management. The series provides project managers with new skills, clear explanations, and innovative approaches to the fundamentals of managing projects effectively. Whether further developing the skills you already have or adding tools to your repertoire, you will find insights in **The Project Management Essential Library** that you can implement immediately.

### Project Management Essential Library
*Choose individual volumes ... or the complete library ...*
*And give your projects the best chance of success!*

**Six Sigma for Project Managers**
Steve Neuendorf
ISBN 1-56726-146-9 ■ Product Code B469

**Project Estimating and Cost Management**
Parviz F. Rad, Ph.D., PMP
ISBN 1-56726-144-2 ■ Product Code B442

**The Triple Constraints in Project Management**
Michael S. Dobson, PMP
ISBN 1-56726-152-3 ■ Product Code B523

**Effective Work Breakdown Structures**
Gregory T. Haugan, Ph.D., PMP
ISBN 1-56726-1353 ■ Product Code B353

**Project Leadership**
Timothy J. Kloppenborg, Ph.D., PMP, Arthur Shriberg, EdD, and Jayashree Venkatraman
ISBN 1-56726-145-0 ■ Product Code B450

**Project Planning and Scheduling**
Gregory T. Haugan, Ph.D., PMP
ISBN 1-56726-136-1 ■ Product Code B361

**Managing Projects for Value**
John C. Goodpasture, PMP
ISBN 1-56726-138-8 ■ Product Code B388

**Managing Project Quality**
Timothy J. Kloppenborg, Ph.D., PMP, and Joseph A. Petrick, Ph.D.
ISBN 1-56726-141-8 ■ Product Code B418

**Project Risk Management: A Proactive Approach**
Paul S. Royer, PMP
ISBN 1-56726-138-8 ■ Product Code B396

**Managing Project Integration**
Denis F. Cioffi, Ph.D.
ISBN 1-56726-134-5 ■ Product Code B345

**Project Measurement**
Steve Neuendorf
ISBN 1-56726-140-X ■ Product Code B40X

**Full Set**
Product Code B54X

**Order today for a 30-day risk-free trial!**
Visit **www.managementconcepts.com/pubs** or call **703-790-9595**

**MANAGEMENT**CONCEPTS